# TREE
## NURSERIES

For E. F. Luchsinger

# TREE NURSERIES
## CULTIVATING THE URBAN JUNGLE

**Dominique Ghiggi**

**Chair of Günther Vogt**
**Department of Architecture**
**ETH Zurich**

**Lars Müller Publishers**

# A TREE IS A TREE IS A TREE

Foreword by Günther Vogt

"HELIOS" ON THE AUTOBAHN
In 2005 and 2006 the tree artist and tree-instrument inventor Oliver Lüttin realized his dream of "Helios & Helix." He saved the two specimens of *Sequoiadendron giganteum* from destruction and had them transported on October 4, 2005, from Rorschach and March 21, 2006, from the "Drei Weieren" bathing area above the city of Saint Gall in Switzerland to Degersheim, where they were installed on his property. The two trees now "live" on the property in the form of an accessible artwork together with twenty-one young giant redwoods planted in a neighboring private forest on International Forest Day 2007. Tree relocation by Heinrich Roth Forstwart Parkholzhauerei in Stein/Toggenburg, Switzerland.

"Helix" being loaded onto a tractor-trailer above Saint Gall
Photos: Copyright © by H9/Hans Ulrich Gantenbein

Electricity does not come from an outlet or pineapple from a supermarket. That much is clear. Yet for most passers-by, the tree on the roadside or in the park is, well, a tree, which they assume has grown and spent its entire life on the spot where it now stands. Trees belong to the inventory of the city and the landscape and are inseparably interwoven with our culture in manifold ways. They are seen as an immobile part of nature, even though both immobility and naturalness are concepts that need to be qualified when applied to trees in the urban context. Nowadays roadside trees are commonly versions of an extremely mobile product that has been cloned hundreds of times and formed to comply with EU norms.

Yet the tree is such an established embodiment of stability, longevity and a specific morphology that it has become a semantic reference for a whole range of things we talk about in our everyday lives, from family trees to tree diagrams.

The fact that today the production of trees for our forests, cities and gardens has little to do with nature and a great deal to do with a highly efficient branch of industry should hardly come as a surprise. Nevertheless, outside the professions involved in the study, production and use of trees, there is very little awareness of the role played by tree nurseries as producers of our urban greenery, in spite of their economic, ecological, social and cultural significance.

This book sheds light on tree production and its scientific, technological, historical and cultural background from different perspectives while at the same time maintaining a focus on a specialization that also has only a minor place in public consciousness. Landscape architecture's interest in tree nurseries is not based solely on the fact that they provide its most important design element. Of course the range of the available assortment plays a major role in defining the possibilities open to landscape design—and the wishes of designers also leave their mark on this assortment, with the natural delay conditioned by growth. Yet tree nurseries also exercise an influence on our open spaces and our perception as a landscaping and design element. The city impacts the landscape not only in the form of residential, infrastructural and industrial buildings but also in the form of tree nurseries. Large areas of greenery for our cities now grow where apples, wheat, rice or olives were once cultivated. With its aesthetic of ordered, pragmatic, almost urban structures, the grid of plants made up of different species, sizes, habits and densities that gradually dissolves and reforms when trees are sold and transferred to their new habitats not only introduces a new formal element into the landscape. At least since the introduction in landscape architecture of a process-orientation, the tree nursery has also had the potential to return, as a principle of sustainable design, to the open urban spaces from which it has disappeared in recent decades. The projects featured in this book point to various possibilities in this regard.

Since the sixteenth century the overused forests of Central Europe have been replanted with the help of forest nurseries. Wide-assortment tree nurseries—originally created to provide plants for the parks of the nobility—are today, along with forest and specialized nurseries, supplying plants of highly diverse origins to all parts of the world. And as a result, in apparently natural forests and in cities we are now finding an international plant community that has been brought together by people. It is a plant community that has been cultivated and nurtured in tree nurseries and thus one made up of plants that have undergone a process of "socialization" and have been adapted to human needs—whether we are talking about trees pruned for a role as roadside sentinels, columned forms suited to cramped spaces, miniature fruit trees for balconies, or bonsais for window sills. This has also changed our understanding of the concepts of forest and tree.

To paraphrase Gertrude Stein's famous line, a tree is a tree is a tree. Forests and trees are part of our cultural history and, as such, are emotionally laden concepts. They evoke images in our minds that are not necessarily based on our everyday experience. The world of our imagination is composed of a diverse range of influences, images and metaphors originating from centuries during which people and trees lived together—and the image of the tree that is anchored in our minds is one that extends far beyond the plant itself, just as the rose in Gertrude Stein's poem stands for more than a mere flower. The tree nursery represents a formative and yet often forgotten chapter in the history of this coexistence.

50
60
70
80
90
100
120

# FASTWOOD

Introduction by Dominique Ghiggi

Ever since the first attempts to cultivate plants, man has been trying to counter the effects of climatic variations and environmental changes. Today we can produce trees in abundance. Highly specialized production centers are furthering the rapid transformation of landscapes and are an expression of our achievement- and product-oriented society. Tree nurseries as commercial cultivation enterprises have existed in Europe for some five hundred years.

This book is informed by a perception of landscape as an inherently changeable phenomenon and thus as one that constantly needs to be reexamined. This approach opens up a wide cultural-historical field. The production of plants—particularly that of trees—in all parts of the world says a great deal about the relationship between man and nature over time. The desire to produce and the capacity to transform and to be creative has characterized human existence and its surroundings from the very beginning. In this process the landscape emerges as a palimpsest which, like the parchments of antiquity, can be overwritten without completely losing the traces of past natural events and the process of history. Regarding the cultivation and production of trees, we can observe their impact on the landscape, always related to the respective zeitgeist, through the different ages.

As an important ecological and cultural element of our once richly forested landscape, trees are ascribed different kinds of significance. Depending on the vantage point, they simultaneously represent wilderness, beings, resources and products. Their productive character and their capacity to adapt date back to their origins in the Devonian period, 410 to 360 million years ago. Humans realized these qualities could be useful early on and appropriated them by beginning to control the growth of trees and thereby gradually changing them to serve human purposes. Lining out and transplanting trees—processes characteristic of tree nurseries—have turned the tree into an object with which streets, boulevards, parks, squares and entire cities are cultivated and deserts are reconquered. At the same time some eighty percent of the world's original forests have been radically changed by human intervention and climatic changes.

In Europe only a few isolated forest stands have been preserved in their original state. Analyses of floodplain sediments and pollens have provided evidence of large-scale land clearances dating back to the late Neolithic period and suggested that slash-and-burn was the primary means used to clear forest. Over the centuries, technological advances and higher population densities rapidly increased the pace of forest destruction. And the amount of forest covering the world's land mass is still decreasing. Today

Templates. The fourteen birchwood rings correspond to the trunk thicknesses used as a standard in tree nurseries (20–140 centimeter circumference). The rings allow for calculation on a 1:1 scale of required distances between trees and potential compositions of different tree sizes. The rings also serve as a reference for trunk circumferences in the determination of tree quality.
Photo and project: Sophia Carstensen

1

2

3

4

land clearing in Europe is usually associated with infrastructure building projects and with the corresponding obligation to replant specific areas. In the nineteenth century the negative consequences of such clearings gave rise to the first large tree nurseries, which provided trees for the planting of forests. Today, afforested areas throughout the world constitute an integral part of what we consider our most natural landscapes.

This book traces a broad arc from the primeval forest via agrarian forest use and the conquest of the plant world to the industrial production of trees, ending with the examination of two current phenomena, namely, ongoing desertification and urbanization. The tree nursery plays a central role in this context, in both an ecological and an experimental sense. The contributions to this volume take the form of reportages and essays and were written by contemporary experts in the course of their journeys, research and projects. The images and photos accompanying these texts all relate to the theme of forests and tree nurseries around the world and help to illuminate their context, the historical background of their development and their influence on town and landscape planning. The following provides a brief overview of the book's different chapters.

## FOREST CARTOGRAPHY: WILDERNESS AND CULTURE

The forest plays a particularly important role in Central European culture. Since their proliferation following the last Ice Age, forests have shaped our understanding of nature and have remained an enduring part of our landscapes. The quality of our perception—whether methodological or intuitive, intellectual or physiological—determines the way we interact with our environment. And the transformation of what we perceive constitutes an important element of the research process through which we expand our intellectual horizon. Analyses by different disciplines using different media provide distinct ways of looking at forests. Maps present a visualization of the origins and dynamics of tree migrations; images provide insight into the history of our forests; sketches and reliefs document immersive investigations of forest morphology.

## HUNTERS AND COLLECTORS: CURIOSITY AND AMBITION

The development of the European tree nursery is closely linked to the great voyages of discovery and the history of colonialism. Adventurous journeys around the globe and conquests of land resulted in the discovery of numerous plants that significantly enriched Europe's flora, which had been particularly impoverished by the continent's glacial periods. Moreover, exotic plants were regarded as a new, previously unknown manifestation of divine power and were coveted not only by physicians and botanists. These plants were passionately collected and displayed in nature cabinets, arboretums, greenhouses and gardens. Seeds, fruits and even living plants were imported from abroad and cultivated in the greenhouses of botanical gardens and small tree nurseries. The nineteenth century was a time of intensive acquisition of and trade in new plants. Apart from propagation, the cultivation of new varieties by constantly improving techniques became a central activity of ornamental tree nurseries.

## TREE FACTORY: PRODUCTION AND AESTHETICS

Trees, including fruit trees, ornamental plants and forest plants are cultivated on open land or in greenhouses, where they are either lined out in nursery rows in the earth or grown in containers and transplanted as required until they have reached a certain size (tree quality), when they are passed on for resale or sold to end users. The rapid growth of cities has resulted in a high demand for a wide range of trees of differing qualities that can be produced in a short time and at a low price. This development has had a profound effect on the tree industry and its established traditions. Production centers have grown significantly and many have specialized

Transformed landscapes in different regions across the world from Western Africa to Northern Europe
1 Bunso Arboretum, Ghana
2 Bush savanna near Toubab Dialaw, Senegal
3 Durance River landscape near Ganagobie, France
4 Replanted cedar forest in Bonnieux, France
5 Vannucci Piante Tree Nursery in Pistoia, Italy
6 Reforestation near Cripiano in Ticino, Switzerland
7 Arboretum Tervuren near Brussels, Belgium
8 Arboretum Wespelaar in Haacht, Belgium
9 Hillier Nurseries near Romsey, England
Photos: Dominique Ghiggi

5

6

7

8

9

in order to meet the demands of a particular market sector. In addition, production has been rationalized through the introduction of automated and systematized processes and it has—to some extent—become independent of the prevailing climate. Nevertheless, the great passion that numerous family businesses have for cultivation and the handicraft associated with it remains evident and visible to the naked eye.

## SAHEL VERT: MIGRATION AND REFUGIA

Trees in the Sahel have long been part of what is today called "farming." In Africa, the cultivation and tending of trees represents a traditional form of organic farming in which people, plants and trees complement and support one another. Particularly in light of the ongoing desertification, trees here provide a vital resource for countering soil erosion and the overuse of the vegetation cover that is being indirectly aggravated year by year due to migration and the rural exodus to the cities. Agriculture is vital to Africa's future. Reforestation with local, mostly endangered tree species can help promote natural regeneration and thus the preservation of biodiversity. As part of a dynamic system that coordinates the collection and storage of seeds and the production and planting of trees tree nurseries offer enormous potential for both small- and large-scale revitalization projects.

## BETTER CITY: URBAN DEVELOPMENT AND THE FUTURE

In the modern city, life in the urban jungle is accompanied by significant planting programs—for example in Shanghai, where tens of thousands of trees were planted on the site of Expo 2010 prior to the opening of the World Exhibition. Ongoing urbanization in the twenty-first century means that ecological questions will continue to decisively influence economic and social development in the context of urban planning. Old concepts such as the green belt and the garden city remain relevant and are supplemented by new forms of urban agriculture and the integration of green areas into cities. On the basis of studies and projects the question is raised of whether future urban planning should move the production of plants into the cities—a measure that would allow for the expedient temporary use of areas earmarked for large-scale urban development projects.

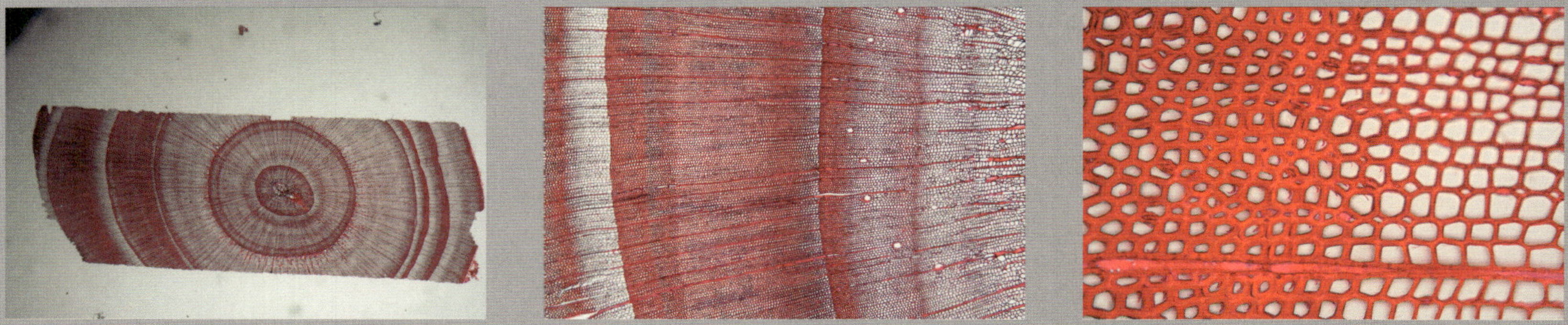

1

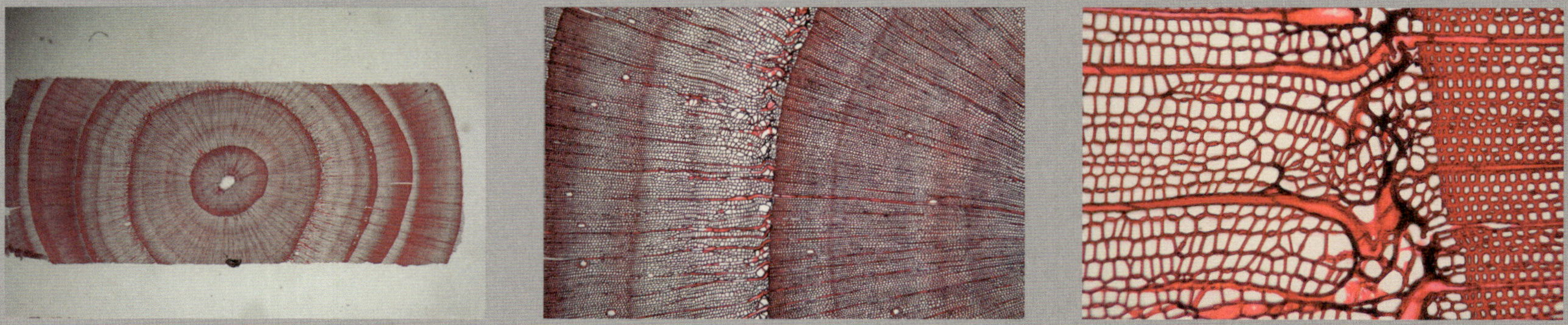

2

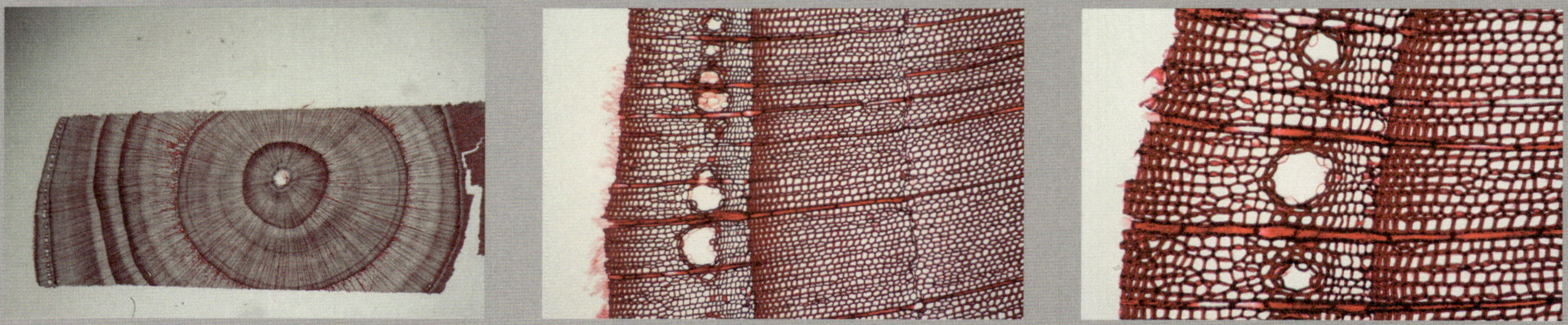

3

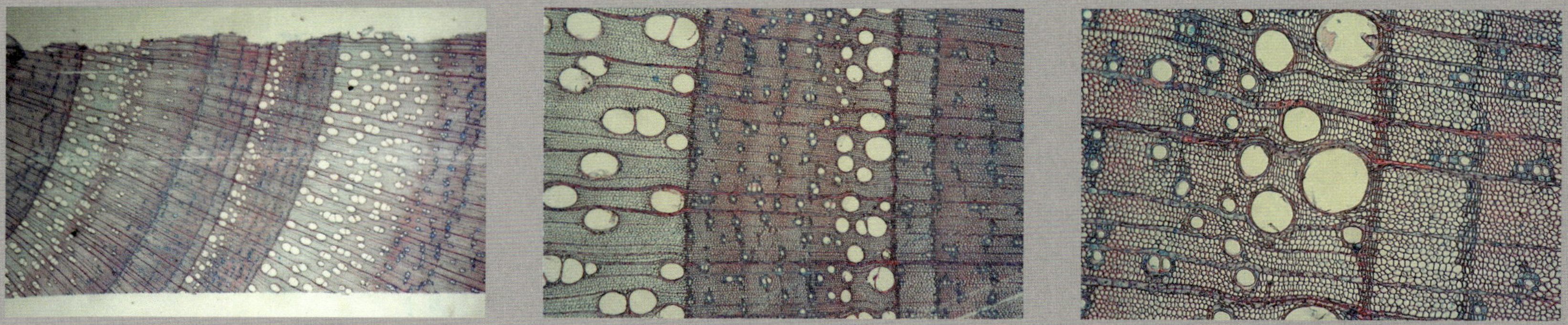

4

5

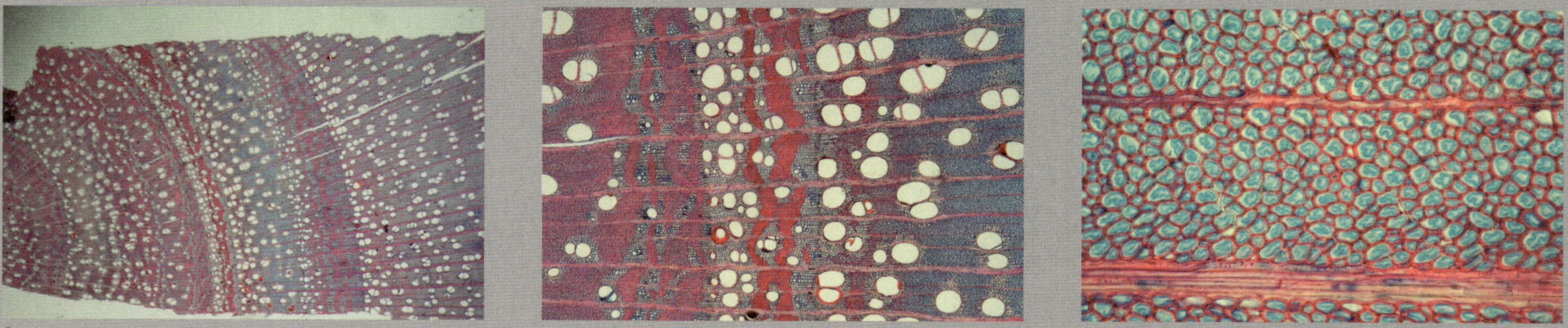

6

# TRANSPLANTED

## MICRO-CROSS-SECTIONS OF NURSERY TREES

**A microtome, a sectioning instrument that allows cutting of extremely thin sections of wood, was used to produce micro-cross-sections with a thickness of 0.02 millimeters from transplanted nursery trees. The cell walls were dyed with red and blue stains. The nonligneous cell walls react to the blue, the ligneous to the red stain. This is necessary to create contrast, since the natural cells are colorless. The microphotos were taken using a normal digital camera.**

Text and microphotos by Fritz Schweingruber
Material: tree cuttings by Georges Lesnino

1 Spruce *(Picea abies)*
The seedling was transplanted into a pot in its second year and set at an angle at the beginning of its fourth year. The plant responded to this manipulation by forming reactive wood. In the case of coniferous woods, this produces compression wood that forms on the stressed side of the trunk. The thick cell walls in this zone stabilize the equilibrium position of the plant. The images are enlarged seven, forty and four hundred times.

2 Spruce *(Picea abies)*
A seedling transplanted in the second winter after germination. As a result of transplantation the root network became slightly dried out, which restricted the water supply to the needles. The result of this water stress was the formation of callus tissue. However, the structure normalized after only a few weeks. The images are enlarged ten, forty and four hundred times.

3 Spruce *(Picea abies)*
A seedling transplanted into a pot in the second winter after germination and poorly irrigated in the sixth year. Careless transplantation in the second winter led to the formation of callus tissue. The plant survived for another four years before suffering water stress, which resulted in the formation of traumatic resin canals. Already in the fifth year poor irrigation resulted in a collapse of the fiber cells. The images are enlarged ten, one hundred and four hundred times.

4 Ash *(Fraxinus excelsior)*
A seedling carefully transplanted at the end of the vegetation period. Disturbances to the root network were expressed in the formation of thin-walled cells in autumn and a narrow but structurally normal annual ring. The images are enlarged ten, forty and one hundred times.

5 Pin oak *(Quercus palustris)*
A seedling carefully transplanted at the end of the vegetation period. Disturbances to the root network were expressed in the formation of thin-walled cells in autumn and a narrow but structurally normal annual ring. The plant reacted to the change of location by generating reaction wood. In the case of broadleaf woody plants, this takes the form of tension wood, which developed on the tension side of the trunk or stem. Gelatinous fibers (blue) have formed inside the cells in order to absorb the tensile forces. The images are enlarged ten, forty and two hundred times.

6 Black Locust/Common Acacia
A seedling planted in the winter following germination. Damage to the root network was expressed in the formation of smaller vessels and a narrow annual ring. As a consequence of being set at an angle, thick-walled, lignified fiber cells formed in the third year and tension wood cells in the following year. The images are enlarged ten, forty and four hundred times.

7 Spruce *(Picea abies)*
A seedling transplanted after its first year. Following transplantation wood growth was weak. However, the damage to the root network triggered a defense mechanism entailing the formation of traumatic resin canals that produced resin to combat potentially damaging organisms. The image is enlarged forty times.

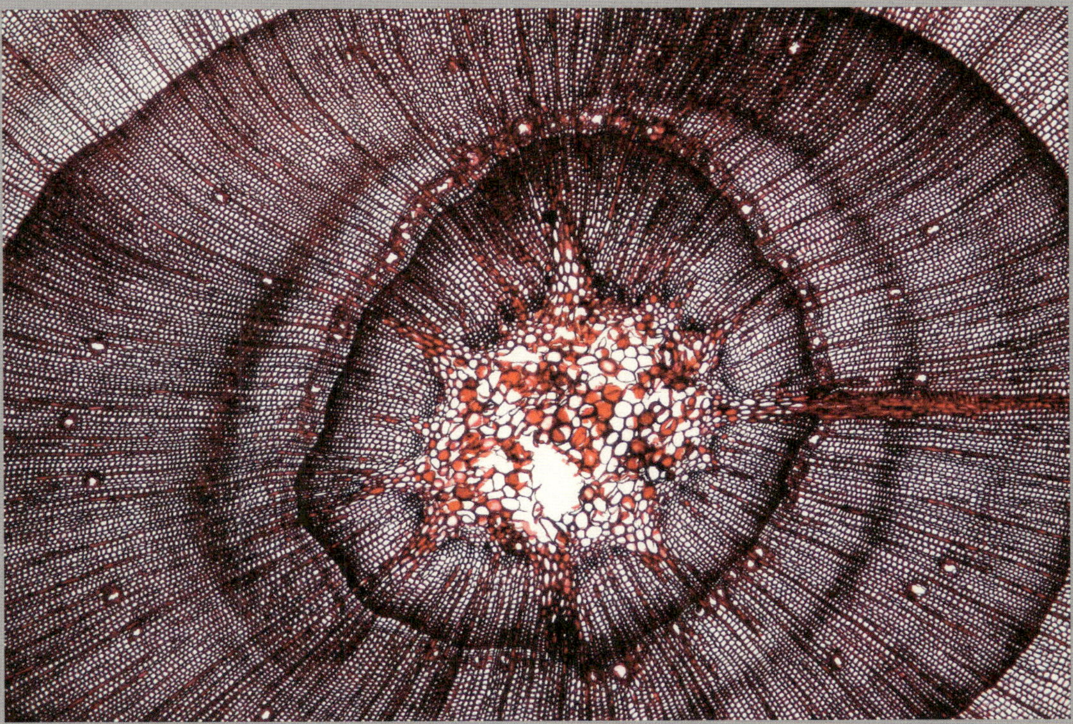

7

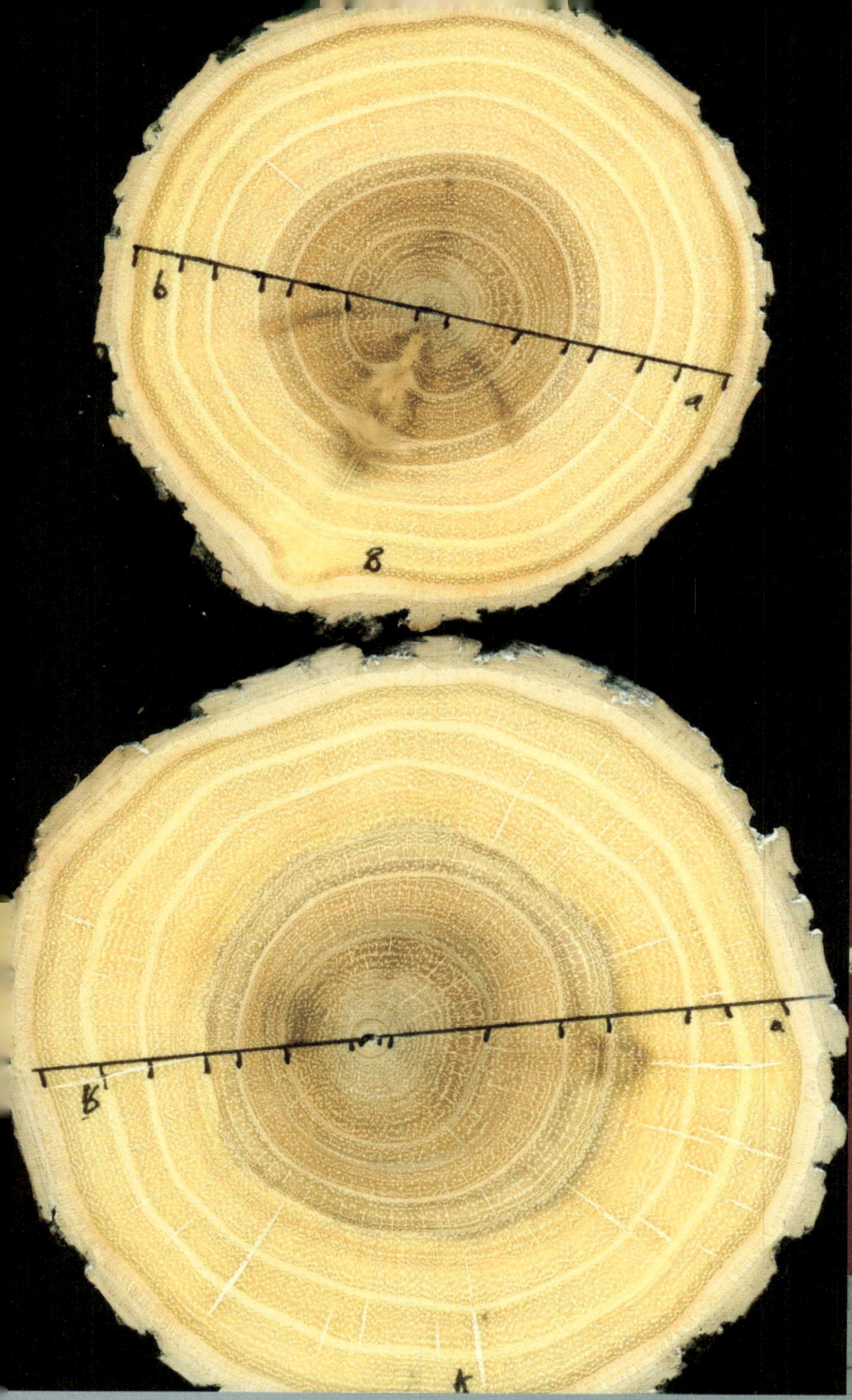

2 3 4 5 6 7 8 9 10 11 12

Tree discs:
Black locust *(Robinia pseudoacacia)*
Pin oak *(Quercus palustris)*
Honey locust *(Gleditsia triacanthos)*
Ash *(Fraxinus excelsior)*
Photos: Georges Lesnino

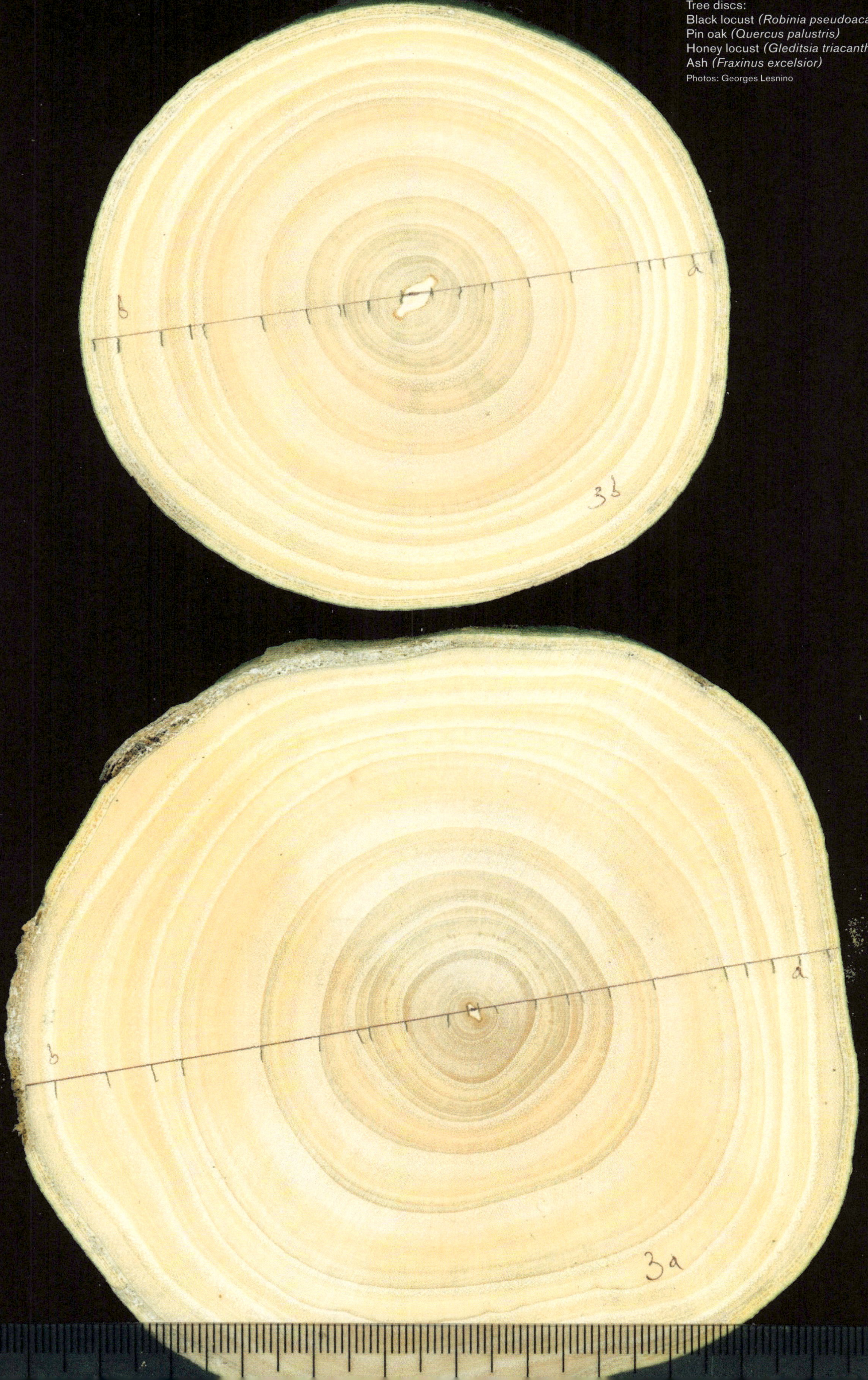

In fact, were I not, with my task well-nigh done, about to furl my sails and making haste to turn my prow to land, perchance I might sing what careful tendance clothes rich gardens in flower, and might sing of Paestum whose rose beds bloom twice yearly, how the endive rejoices in drinking streams, the verdant banks in celery; how the cucumber, coiling through the grass, swells into a paunch. Nor should I have passed in silence the late-flowering narcissus, the twining tendril of the acanthus, pale ivy sprays, or the shore-loving myrtle. For I call to mind how once under the towers of the Oebalian citadel,[6] where dark Galaesus waters the yellowing corn, I saw an old Cilician, who occupied a few acres of unclaimed land, not rich enough for ploughing, nor fit for pasturage, nor suited to the vine. Even so, planting cabbages here and there among the brambles, and white lilies and vervain and fine-seeded poppies, in happiness he equalled the wealth of kings, and returning home late at night he used to load his table with an unbought banquet. First he was in the spring to gather roses, and apples in the fall; and when grim winter was still bursting rocks with her frost and braking the current of rivers with ice, already he was cutting soft-haired hyacinths and chiding laggard summer and the loitering zephyrs. Thus it was that he was still the first to be enriched with teeming bees and a plenteous swarm, and first to gather from the squeezed comb the frothing honey; his limes and laurestines were ever luxuriant, and all the fruits which clothed his fertile trees in their early blossoming, so many they kept in the ripeness of autumn. He would also plant out elms in rows, though late in season, pears when quite hard, blackthorns already hung with sloes, and planes already offering to drinkers the service of their shade. But all this I must pass by, constrained by narrow bounds, and leave to others after me to record.

6 Tarentum, founded by colonists from Sparta, of which Oebalus was king.

Vergilius, Georgica IV, 116–148
In Fairclough H. R. *Virgil: Eclogues Georgics Aeneid 1–6*,
Harvard University Press, 1999, Cambridge Massachusetts, pp. 227–229

# VIRGIL: THE WISE MAN'S MIRACULOUS GARDEN

Text selection by Renzo Petraglio

In the *Georgics* we find not only the "Augustan" celebration of epic and collective work but also the celebration of the countryside as a place for individual realization. In Book IV, which is dedicated to the care of bees, Virgil includes a brief description of the garden belonging to *senex Corycius*. The old man, a former pirate it seems, has managed to create an idyllic space out of a small and apparently infertile and neglected farm outside Taranto. Through his own serene yet untiring activities its fertility is now reminiscent of ideal descriptions of nature's Golden Age.

Although Virgil relates the figure of this old man and his garden to his own first-hand experience *(memini me… vidisse)*, almost as if to emphasize the feasibility and worth of this model, both seem essentially symbolic in value. The wise gardener–whose age is itself a symbol of wisdom and who embodies many of the typical traits of the Stoic-Pythagorean figure of the *sapiens*, or wise man–tends a garden that resembles a new Eden, now in a rustic setting, not the spontaneous product of Nature but created by man's own knowledge.

The georgic space is reinterpreted in the form of a "garden," a personal and private *angulus* (corner or niche). It therefore becomes the place where the wise individual can find his own material and moral self-sufficiency *(autárkeia)* through serene activity that does not rule out *labor* but rewards hard work, and is characterized not by bucolic pastimes but the civil collaboration between man and nature.

from: Elena Sada (ed.): *Paesaggi ideali. La natura nelle Bucoliche e nelle Georgiche di Virgilio*, Carlo Signorelli Editore, Milan, 2000

Tree Factory:
## PRODUCTION AND AESTHETICS



Sahel Vert:
## MIGRATION AND REFUGIA



Better City:
## URBAN DEVELOPMENT AND THE FUTURE

## Forest Cartography:

# WILDERNESS AND CULTURE

**The forest plays a particularly important role in Central European culture. Since their proliferation following the last Ice Age, forests have shaped our understanding of nature and have figured as an enduring element of our landscapes. The quality of our perception—whether methodological or intuitive, intellectual or physiological—determines the way we interact with our environment. And the transformation of what we perceive constitutes an important element of the research process through which we expand our intellectual horizon. Analyses by different disciplines using different media provide distinct ways of looking at forests. Maps provide a visualization of the origins and dynamics of tree migrations; images provide insight into the history of our forests; sketches and reliefs document immersive investigations of forest morphology.**

Wild cherries in Wildegg, Switzerland
Photo: Stefanie Jacomet

# TREE MIGRATIONS

**It may be difficult to believe that trees, as organisms rooted firmly in the earth, can migrate. But it is all a matter of time. It might take them several centuries or millennia, but oak, beech, and fir trees can move from one corner of Europe to another.**

Essay by Brigitta Ammann

Detail of "Lausanne zur Miozenen Zeit" (Lausanne in the Miocene) from Oswald Heer's *Die Urwelt der Schweiz* (1865). Reconstruction based on fossil finds near Vevey and featuring sabal palms, camphor trees, laurel, crocodiles, tapirs, rhinoceroses, etc.
Illustration: Bibliothek ETH Zürich, Alte Drucke

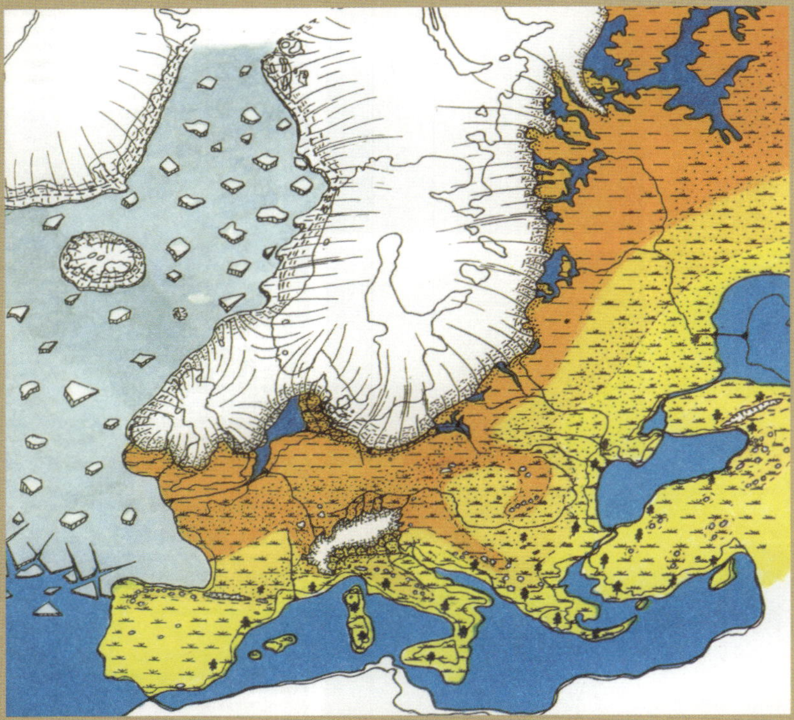

1

2

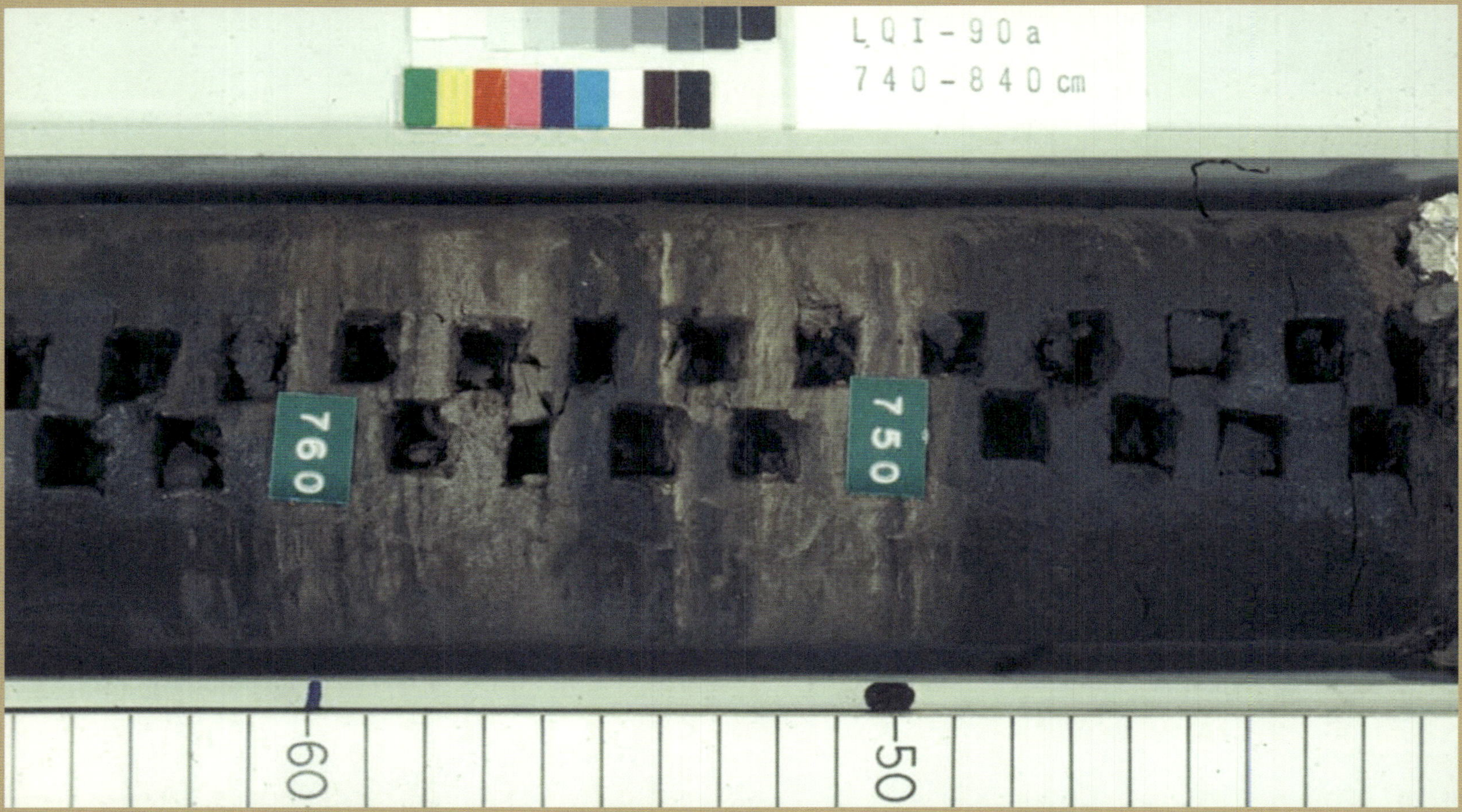


3

| Species | Age at first flowering (years) | Migration speed (m/year) | Dispersal distances (km) | Dispersal vectors |
|---|---|---|---|---|
| **Pioneers** | | | | |
| Birch | 10 | 250 ≤ 2000 | 2.5 ≤ 20 | Wind, water, animals |
| Scots Pine | 10–20 | 1500 | 15–60 | Wind, water, animals |
| **Intermediary species in warm periods** | | | | |
| Hazel | 10 | 500–1500 | 5–15 | Water, animals |
| Oak (deciduous) | 30–60 | 5–500 | 2.2–15 | Animals |
| Linden | 10–30 | 50–500 | 0.5–5 | Wind, water |
| Elm | 30–40 | 100–1000 | 3–30 | Wind |
| **Late-comers** | | | | |
| Silver fir | 30 | 40–300 | 1.2–9 | Wind |
| Spruce | 30 | 60–500 | 1.8–15 | Wind |
| Beech | 40–50 | 175–350 | 7–14 | Animals |

4

5

1 Map of Europe at the time of the Last Glacial Maximum. A continental ice sheet lies over Fennoscandia, and mountain glaciers are present in the Pyrenees, Alps and Carpathians. Sea ice in the north Atlantic stretches to the Bay of Biscay.
Illustration: Bjørn G. Andersen; based on Andersen and Borns 1994

2 Even today dry regions may feature forest belts with a distinctive upper (cold) and lower (dry) forest boundary. The photograph showing an example from South of Barnaul in Russia's Altai region provides an impression of how tree refugia in the mountains of Southern European might have looked during the Ice Ages.
Photo: Brigitta Ammann

3 Sediments from lakes and peat from mires provide documents of the past illustrating changes in flora and fauna over long periods of time. The photograph shows a sediment core from a small lake on the Swiss Plateau. The alternating layers of lake marl (light gray) and organic material (black-brown) indicate changes in the proportions of nutrients and fluctuations in the water level. The samples were used to analyze the pollen content (see fig. 6).
Photo: Brigitta Ammann

4 Migration speeds of several important woody species. Late flowering age and/or short dispersal distances slow the potential migration speed.
Table: based on Lang 1994; Bonn and Poschlod 1998

5 "Lausanne zur Miozenen Zeit" (Lausanne in the Miocene) from Oswald Heer's *Die Urwelt der Schweiz* (1865). Reconstruction based on fossil finds near Vevey and featuring sabal palms, camphor trees, laurel, crocodiles, tapirs, rhinoceroses, etc.
Illustration: Bibliothek ETH Zürich, Alte Drucke

Climate plays the primary role in the migration of trees. Among other things, it determines the borders between the occurrences of different species, meaning the edges of their biogeographic territory. We know today that butterflies and birds have increasingly been observed in northern latitudes since the late sixties, which must be seen as one consequence of the effects of global warming. In the case of highly mobile and agile animals, we intuitively accept the concept of biogeographic adaptation to climate change—but trees that migrate?

Two engravings from Oswald Heer's *Die Urwelt der Schweiz* (The Primeval World of Switzerland, fig. 5 and fig. 11), visualize the climate, flora and fauna differences between the tropical and semitropical Tertiary period and the arctic Ice Ages during the Quaternary. In the Tertiary, which lasted from 65 to around 2.6 million years ago, a variety of warmth-loving tree species flourished in Europe but they were displaced by the numerous Ice Ages in the Quaternary. Interestingly enough, as a glance at our parks shows, it is once again possible to cultivate a number of these species outdoors, including the American sweetgum (Liquidambar styraciflua) and the tulip tree (Liriodendron tulipifera), for which our Central European winters are not too severe.

During the Ice Ages, the trees species that form today's forests in Central Europe withdrew to refugia in Southern Europe. In the last glaciation phase (fig. 1), cold and dry conditions prevailed in the ice-free corridor between the Fennoscandian continental glaciation and the ice masses of the Alpine arc. This is why the vegetation in Central Europe consisted of a steppe that was devoid of trees, also known as steppe tundra.

Even in Southern Europe, there were much colder temperatures and less rainfall during the ice ages than there is today. One main reason for the reduced rainfall was that the atmosphere could not extract as much moisture as earlier from the cold North Atlantic Ocean. However, the mountains on the Iberian, Italian and the Balkan peninsulas in Southern Europe provided tree species with two major advantages: orographic rainfall and a variety of habitats—two fundamental criteria for refugia during the Ice Age. Even today we find landscapes that have forest belts at intermediate elevations, much like the Mediterranean mountains at that time (fig. 2). Another type of Ice Age refugium existed on the plains of Southern Europe, one in which water requirements were met locally. Strips of forest were able to grow along rivers and resembled the gallery forests that run along rivers in dry regions today.

The general ability of plants to migrate is vividly illustrated by the modern problem of invasive, i.e., nonnative botanical species. Several species-specific characteristics play a role in the potential migration speed of present-day invasions, as they did for return migrations following the Ice Age. On the one hand, these characteristics include seed dispersal—i.e., the usual or maximum distance a seed can be disseminated. Most seeds end up rather close to the mother plant, regardless of whether they are spread by wind, water or animals. However, depending on the species, some may also cover astonishingly long distances.[1] The longer the distance a species can be dispersed, the greater its migration speed. Human beings have heavily influenced this aspect of seed dispersal for today's invasive species, e.g., blacklisted species such as giant hogweed and Canadian goldenrod. The increase in land, air and ship traffic has greatly facilitated and promoted their distribution.

Another important characteristic influencing migration speed is the seed-bearing age of a tree species, that is, the age at which that species reaches maturity. This is surprisingly high for a number of trees. If a newly germinated oak must first reach an age of between thirty and sixty before it can blossom, it cannot spread quickly. In other words, the higher the seed-bearing age, the lower the potential migration speed (fig. 4).

Of course the climatic and soil conditions must also satisfy the species' needs in the area that it is colonizing. It did not do birch and poplar seeds much good to be blown across the Alps from Italy just after the melting of the Alpine glaciers around 20,000 years ago. These seeds could not germinate and grow in the new terrain because the climate in Central Europe was too dry and cold and the permafrost froze the crushed rock and stone in the glacier foreland.

This leads us to a second important ecological condition for plant migration. In addition to climate, soils play a large role. Glaciation replenished soils with fine minerogenic material—with loam outside the ice formations and with ground moraines on the inside. Soils containing organic material gradually developed on these moraines.

By contrast, soils in the tropics today are extremely leached out and the nutrients are contained almost exclusively in the living biomass.

In order to find out whether, when and how trees migrate, we can turn to the field of paleoecology. This branch of ecology uses a long geological timeframe and draws on natural archives. For the recent Quaternary period, these archives consist mainly of lakes and moors whose sediments and peats contain the embedded biotic and abiotic remains of past ecosystems (fig. 3). In such low-oxygen environments, tree pollen in particular is preserved, along with seeds, fruit, bud scales and wood. It is possible to identify these biological remains—mostly by genus, sometimes even by species—because of their great diversity of forms (fig. 7). By counting and comparing the cores of older samples from deeper levels and younger samples from higher layers, scientists can develop a history of vegetation (fig. 6).[2]

During the last ten years biologists have built an interesting bridge between the previously separate fields of vegetation history and population genetics. It has become evident that the history of refugia and migrations is to some extent stored in genetic patterns. The work has focused on two important tree species. The first is the beech (Fagus sylvatica; common beech) with its sub-Atlantic and montane to subalpine distribution range; the second is the spruce (Picea abies; Norway spruce) with Nordic-continental and subalpine distribution. Both had numerous Ice Age refugia, which is why their genetic diversity is still especially high today.

A team from the European Union's FOSSILVA project created a remarkable synthesis for the beech (fig. 10).[3] Surprisingly enough, the populations on the peninsulas in Southern Europe hardly migrated at all—that is, they were confined to northern Spain, southern and central Italy, and the Balkans. The colonization of Central Europe, up to the southernmost part of Scandinavia, proceeded from the refugia on the eastern edge of the Alps, from Slovenia and Istria, and perhaps also from southern Moravia (latitude forty-five to forty-nine degrees north). For a montane species such as the beech, low mountains act not as a barrier but as a corridor. By contrast, high mountains and dry lowlands such as the Pannonian Plain, or wide floodplains such as those found along the Danube (fig. 8), are obstacles. The genetic diversity is especially high on all three Southern European peninsulas (the Iberian, Italian and Balkan), and the current goal is to preserve this diversity through nature reserves and sustainable forestry practices.

In the case of the spruce, there is a clear distinction between the genetically uniform refugium in the northeast and the several genetically heterogeneous refugia in the southeast (the southeastern Alps, the Dinarides, as well as the western and eastern Carpathian Mountains). Starting in the refugium on the plains of western Russia, the spruce migrated to Finland, Sweden and parts of Norway. The Alps and the low mountain ranges in Europe were colonized from the southeastern refugia (fig. 9).

Why do we dig so deeply into the past when we face such acute problems in the present and the future? Our understanding of the

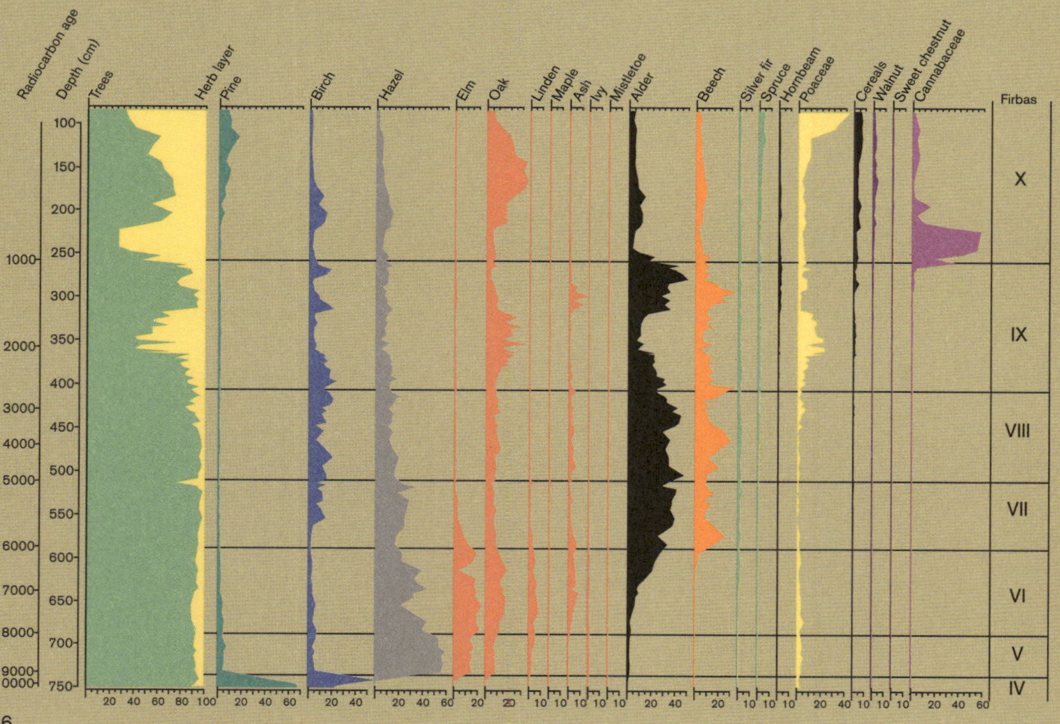


6 The analysis of pollen in a core (see fig. 3) reveals the history of the vegetation at a locality. The proportions of the different tree pollen and several selected herb pollen are represented here on the vertical scale (in percentages of the sum of pollen grains counted per sample) Early-pioneer birch and Scots pine were followed by hazel and a mixed oak forest with elm and linden as well as the latecomer beech, silver fir, and spruce. Walnut was first brought north of the Alps by the Romans. The dominance of hemp in the Middle Ages may give the reader some pause for thought—it is probable that the small lake was used to soak and soften the hemp strands.
Illustration: Brigitta Ammann

7 The forms exhibited by pollen involve their type of opening (pores or furrows), surface sculptures and inner-wall structures (the latter are not visible here in images produced by scanning electron microscope but can be discerned by light microscope).
Photos: Institute of Plant Sciences, University of Bern

a European silver fir (*Abies alba*)
b Montpellier maple (*Acer monspessulanum*)
c Black alder (*Alnus glutinosa*)
d Rock buckthorn (*Rhamnus saxatilis*)
e Dandelion (*Taraxacum alpinum*)
f Common dogwood (*Cornus sanguinea*)
g Sycamore maple (*Acer pseudoplatanus*)
h Green alder (*Alnus viridis*)
i Norway spruce (*Picea abies*)
j Mountain pine (*Pinus montana*)
k Sessile oak (*Quercus petraea*)
l Ash (*Fraxinus excelsior*)
m Common hawthorn (*Crataegus monogyna*)
n Downy oak (*Quercus pubescens*)
o Common hawthorn (*Crataegus monogyna*)
p European beech (*Fagus sylvatica*)
q Kermes oak (*Quercus coccifera*)
r Common buckthorn (*Rhamnus cathartica*)
s White mulberry (*Morus albe*)
t Field elm (*Ulmus campestris*)
u Small-leaved linden (*Tilia cordata*)
v Dandelion (*Taraxacum alpinum*)
w Small-leaved linden (*Tilia cordata*)
x Scots pine (*Pinus sylvestris*)
y Snowball tree (*Viburnum opulus*)
z Sessile oak (*Quercus petraea*)
A Downy birch (*Betula pubescens*)
B Rock buckthorn (*Rhamnus saxatilis*)
C Caucasian wingnut (*Pterocarya fraxinifolia*)
D Rowan (*Sorbus aucuparia*)

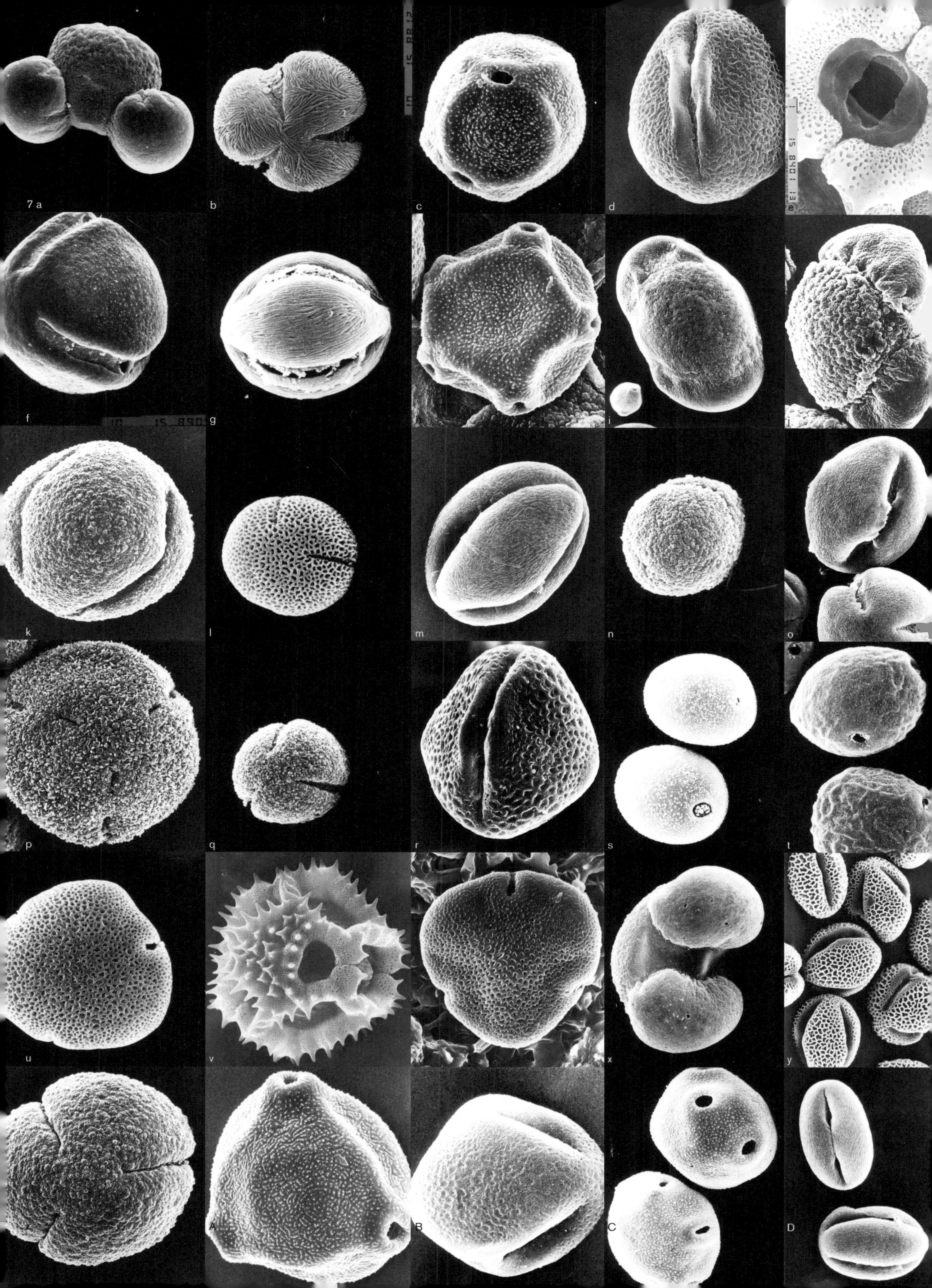
7 a
b
c
d
e
f
g
h
i
j
k
l
m
n
o
p
q
r
s
t
u
v
w
x
y
A
B
C
D

ecological processes that took place in long past periods such as the post-Glacial Age is of enormous relevance today since these ages enable us to study environmental changes whose magnitude and speed are greater than what we find documented for the last one hundred to 150 years in fields such as meteorology. From the past we can learn how ecosystems responded to quick changes such as rapid warming. This improved understanding of processes is important because climate change is expected to be more intense and rapid than it was in the past. Agriculture, forestry, hydrology and risk evaluation in numerous economically and ecologically relevant areas will have to engage with this topic.

1 Bonn and Poschlod (1998).
2 Lang (1994).
3 Magri et al. (2006).

**References:**

Andersen, Bjørn G. and Harold W. Borns. *The Ice Age World. An Introduction to Quaternary History and Research with Emphasis on North America and Northern Europe During the Last 2.5 Million Years.* Oslo: Scandinavian University Press, 1994.

Bonn, Susanne and Peter Poschlod. *Ausbreitungsbiologie der Pflanzen Mitteleuropas: Grundlagen und kulturhistorische Aspekte.* Wiesbaden: Quelle und Meyer, 1998.

Lang, Gerhard. *Quartäre Vegetationsgeschichte Europas. Methoden und Ergebnisse.* Jena: Fischer, 1994.

Latalowa, Malgorzata and W.O. van der Knaap. "Late Quaternary Expansion of Norway Spruce *Picea abies* (L.) Karst. in Europe According to Pollen Data." *Quaternary Science Reviews* 25 (2006): 2780–2805.

Magri, Donatella et al. "A New Scenario for the Quaternary History of European Beech Populations: Palaeobotanical Evidence and Genetic Consequences." *New Phytologist* 171 (2006): 199–221.

Parmesan, Camille and Gary Yohe. "A globally coherent fingerprint of climate change impacts across natural systems." *Nature* 421 (2003): 37–42.

Tollefsrud, Marie M. et al. "Genetic Consequences of Glacial Survival and Postglacial Colonization in Norway Spruce: Combined Analysis of Mitochondrial DNA and Fossil Pollen." *Molecular Ecology* 17 (2008): 4134–4150.

Walther, Gian-Reto et al. "Ecological Responses to Recent Climate Change." *Nature* 416 (2002): 389–395.

8 On the basis of the results in fig. 10 and parallel results for chloroplast DNA, it is possible to determine the glacial refugia (circles and ovals) and migration routes (arrows) of beech.
Illustration: based on Magri et al. 2006

9 The map of Europe combines the migratory history of spruce indicated by pollen analyses (dark-gray areas show regions settled early, light-gray for areas settled late, in millennia before present) with the population-genetic "footprint" of these migrations. The colors indicate genetically similar groups, and the diameter of the circles show the genetic diversity within populations.
Illustration: Christoph Sperisen; based on Latalowa, van der Knaap 2006; Tollefsrud et al. 2008

10 The migratory history of beech is indicated spatially by pollen finds classified by millennia (so-called kilo years, kyr) and by population genetics. Here seven chloroplast haplotypes are represented by colored symbols corresponding to their present locations. Current population genetics thus provides a "footprint," as it were, of postglacial migration.
Illustration: based on Magri et al. 2006

Following double page:
11 "Zürich zur Gletscherzeit" (Zurich During the Glacial Period) from Oswald Heer's *Die Urwelt der Schweiz* (1865). Reindeer, mammoth and marmots graze in the tundra of the glacier foreland.
Illustration: Library ETH Zurich, Alte Drucke

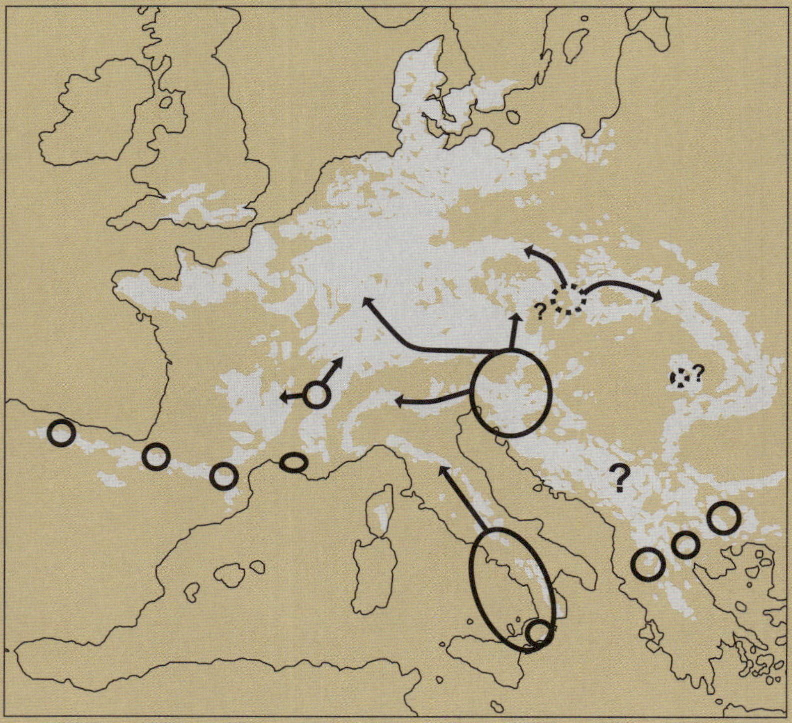
8

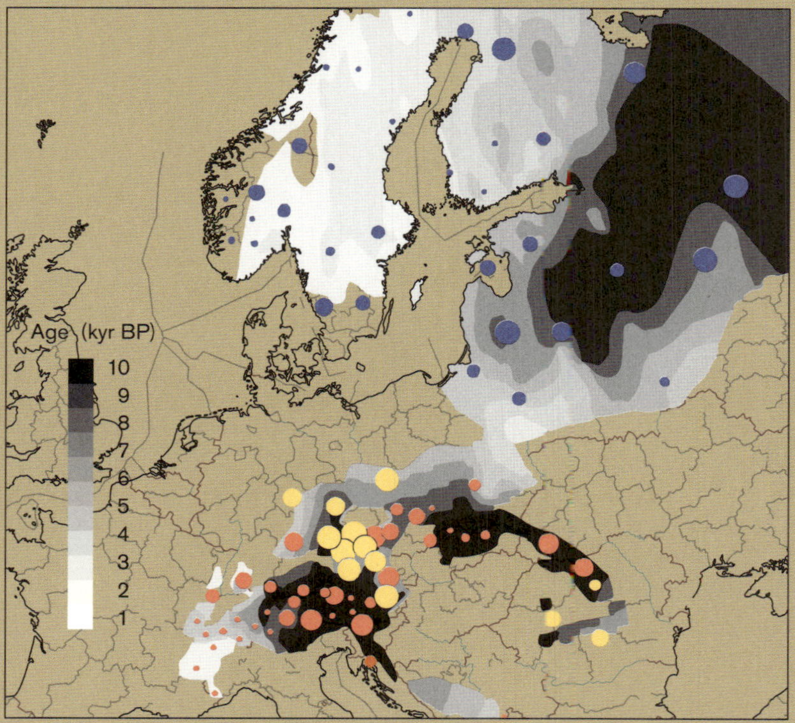

9

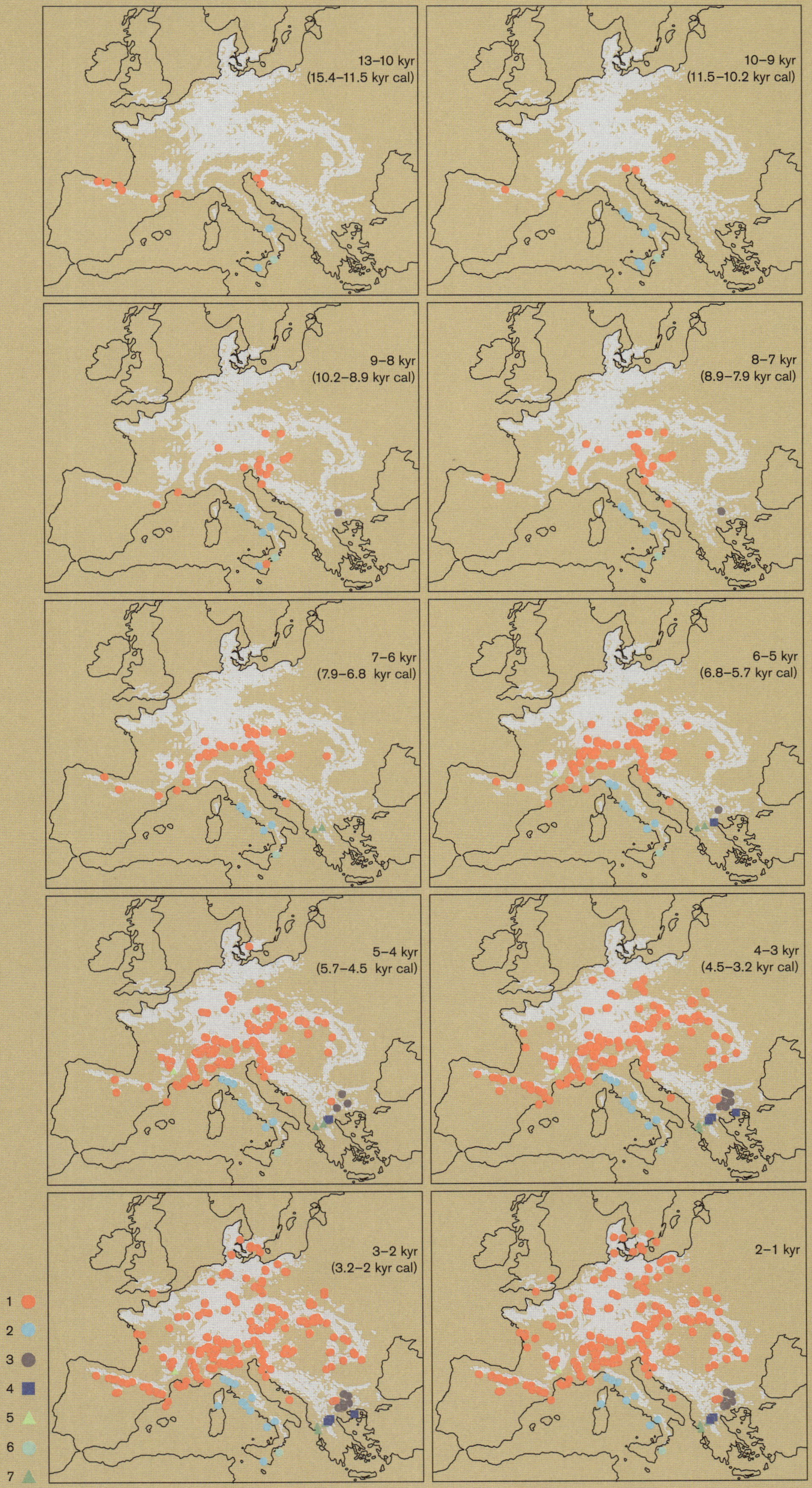
13–10 kyr
(15.4–11.5 kyr cal)
10–9 kyr
(11.5–10.2 kyr cal)
9–8 kyr
(10.2–8.9 kyr cal)
8–7 kyr
(8.9–7.9 kyr cal)
7–6 kyr
(7.9–6.8 kyr cal)
6–5 kyr
(6.8–5.7 kyr cal)
5–4 kyr
(5.7–4.5 kyr cal)
4–3 kyr
(4.5–3.2 kyr cal)
3–2 kyr
(3.2–2 kyr cal)
2–1 kyr
1
2
3
4
5
6
7

10

11

# CONSERVED FOREST

## REICHWALDE MINE

**The Reichwalde mine is a large open-cast mine in east Saxony in Germany and the site of extensive archeological excavations that were started in 1993. These revealed the remains of a large pine and beech forest dating back to the last Ice Age between 12,400 and 11,500 years ago.**

Impressions and photographs of the dig by Britta Pollmann

Reichwalde opencast lignite mine, Saxony, Germany, summer 2002

The excavations uncovered upright tree stumps half a meter high, logs of up to eighteen meters in length with branches of up to 1.5 meters that had fallen over one another to form several layers, and scattered pine cones. What happened? Why was the forest destroyed, and how could the trees and even the forest litter have been preserved without becoming fossilized?

These and other questions have been taken up by a number of different scholars. From 1998 to 2002 a team of archeologists and biologists from the Saxony State Office of Archeology and the University of Hohenheim carefully uncovered the aggregation of fallen trees. They also took wood and soil samples in order to learn more about the history of the forest and its destruction. These revealed pollen, seeds, fruits, needles and other plant remains, which have provided clues regarding the environment and climate of the time.

During the excavations all wood found over an area of 4000 square meters was drawn in detail, photographed and described using a data-recording model specially developed by the Saxony State Office of Archeology. Distinctive features such as traces of fire, the formation of additional roots, direction of detruncation and the degree of preservation were carefully documented for subsequent laboratory evaluation. The growth rings of the trees were measured precisely at the Botanical Institute at the University of Hohenheim in Stuttgart and the Leipzig Center for Environmental Research.

It already became evident during the excavations that the forest must have been subject to fires that at least some of the trees had survived. Burn scars are still visible on the tree stumps. The cause of the fires is unknown. The trees had also been stressed due to waterlogging. Where soil is too wet, roots do not receive enough oxygen and plants react with epitrophic root growth, i.e., the formation of new roots above the first root generation. In the case of the Reichwalde forest, the water came from below and, through the formation of these secondary roots, the plants were able to gain more life-sustaining oxygen. However, the ongoing rise in the water table ultimately caused the trees to die.

The preservation of wood, bark, cones and needles is due to the constant wetness of the soil. The lack of oxygen has meant that microorganism have not been able to break down the organic material or to do so only very slowly. For this reason the high degree of preservation of the forest remains did not require fossilization. This has allowed scientists to gain new insights into the appearance of the forest some 12,000 years ago, at a time in Europe when Stone Age people still lived from hunting and gathering.

The range of information yielded by the excavations in Reichwalde has enabled scholars to reconstruct the history of the local landscape. During the climate fluctuations of the Late Glacial, the landscape in Reichwalde underwent a process of extremely dynamic development. Periods in which the ground water rose significantly saw the formation of shallow lakes and these facilitated the preservation of large areas of pine and beech forest that grew during dry periods. The sand in which the preserved pines and beeches were rooted has also revealed traces of human habitation.

Tree stump from the Late Glacial forest. In front of it is a drafting board with a hand drawing of the wood found on the excavation site, Reichwalde dig RW-06.

**References:**

Jürgen Vollbrecht, *Reichwalde. Spätpaläolithische Besiedlungsspuren aus Reichwalde,* Landesamt für Archäologie mit Landesmuseum für Vorgeschichte, vol. 46 (Dresden 2005).

M. Friedrich, M. Knipping, S. Schmidt et. al., "Ein Wald am Ende der letzten Eiszeit. Untersuchungen zur Besiedlungs-, Landschafts-, und Vegetationsentwicklung an einem verlandeten See im Tagebau Reichwalde, Niederschlesischer Oberlausitzkreis," *Arbeits- und Forschungsberichte zur Sächsischen Bodendenkmalpflege,* vol. 43, 2001, pp. 21–94.

1 Interplay of sun and rain on the dampened remains of the forest dating back to the Allerød oscillation, section 78 of the Reichwalde dig RW-06.
2 Upright tree stump, approx. 60 cm, with epitrophic root growth.
3 Clearly discernible formation of a second generation of roots above the first: epitrophic root growth as reaction by the tree to water logging.
4 The tree stumps stand in the same position they occupied 12,000 years ago. Their extensive root network is still visible.
5 Part of the root network extends deep into the ground, and the existing roots were dug up in order to discern the precise course of their growth.
6 A fallen tree revealing its root plate from below. Comparison with the trowel gives an idea of its size. Section 79 of the Reichwalde dig RW-06.
7 Some trunks, like this birch, still exhibit clearly visible bark. The typical white-black pattern is immediately discernible.
8 Everything is sampled. The tree stump is wrapped in plastic film and the soil in front of the stump is packed in plastic bags. Everything is clearly labeled before the samples are taken to the laboratory for further examination.

9 View over section 78 of the Reichwalde dig RW-06. Work goes on in all weather.
10 The many dark pieces of wood are clearly discernable against the lighter sandy soil.
11 The pace of work in the section 79 of the Reichwalde dig RW-06 is brisk. When the sun is shining samples of the wood have to be taken quickly before they dry out.
12 Drafting board with hand drawing. Since 1993 over 4000 square meters of excavated wood has been drawn. Along with photos, drawings continue to be an important form of documentation.
13 Sampling the tree trunks. The two biologists have sawed a piece out of the trunk. The wood is still hard.
14 The wrapped wood sample is precisely measured and mapped. It is important to document from which part of the trunk the wood has been taken.
15 Earth samples are taken from the profile wall for subsequent pollen analysis in the laboratory.
16 Bleached remains of the Ice Age forest on the excavation site, which is half covered with drift sand. The area is about to be cleared by an excavator.
17 Modern reforested pine forest near the lignite mine and the excavation site. As was the case long ago, fallen trees now lie among cones and other forest litter.
18 Wood sampling in section 79 of the Reichwalde dig RW-06.

1

2

3

4

5

6

7

8

9

10

11

12

13

14

15

16

17

18

After the last Ice Age, which ended around 15,000 years ago, woodlands had largely disappeared from Central Europe, giving way to a mostly treeless steppe tundra and in extreme cases to a polar desert. The areas covered by our tree species today resulted from tree migration and dissemination in the late Ice Age and the Holocene period. Over the course of millennia, the trees returned to Central Europe from their sanctuaries in Eastern, Southeastern and Southern Europe. In several development steps they then formed our primeval forests (also known as old-growth, primal, primary or virgin forest). Although mankind began using and transforming these forests more intensively in the Neolithic Age in the sixth millennium B.C.E., a few small areas have come down to us. However, to anyone who lacks a trained eye and the necessary knowledge to recognize the traces of forest use, our forests may still appear primal. In fact, they exhibit both natural and anthropogenic features. There is no place in Central Europe where we can still see what the primeval forests that existed on the plains or in low-lying mountain areas looked like back then. Although some relics still exist in eastern Central Europe, they are not very large and—as can be shown—they were also used by mankind.

The first solid evidence of agriculture, cattle breeding and forest management in Central Europe dates to the mid-sixth millennium B.C.E. It was then that human beings began actively transforming the environment into a cultural landscape. For 15,000 years the increased use of natural resources has had an ongoing impact on the development of the natural realm—first during the hunter-gatherer phases and then in an economy increasingly geared toward production. Today human influence is omnipresent, but the role it played in early periods of history should not be underestimated.

This essay will provide a glimpse of the history of forest use based on a selection of woods visited and photo-documented over the last twenty years by Stefanie Jacomet, a professor of archeobiology at the Institute of Prehistoric and Archeological Science at Basel University.

**NATURAL FORESTS**
If woodland is not disturbed by mankind, it regenerates and evolves back into primeval forests. The only places where forests cannot develop naturally are those where the soil has been irreversibly destroyed. This is hardly the case in Central Europe. The transformation of commercial timberland into natural forests is a widespread phenomenon across all of Europe since today most forests are no longer managed in traditional fashion but have been allowed to grow into high forests. Or, less frequently, they have been left entirely to themselves.

**NATURAL FOREST: THE SIHLWALD IN ZURICH**
The Sihlwald, or Sihl Forest, is located in the center of the Zurich metropolitan area. Covering Mount Zimmerberg, Reppisch Valley and the entire Albis chain, it forms the largest continuous mixed beech forest in Switzerland. There is evidence that human beings began using it as early as the Neolithic Age (probably in the fourth millennium B.C.E.). Its special characteristics include the yews that frequently grow on its steep slopes. As shown by an analysis of historical sources undertaken by the Winterthur-based historian Margrit Irniger, by 1300 the clearing process had progressed to such an degree that the present-day borders of the Sihlwald had basically been established. From the fourteenth century on, large areas were used as a high forest to acquire timber. In the area of the Schnabel estates, which eventually fell into the possession of the city of Zurich, the forest was expanded by reforestation programs in the nineteenth century. For a long time it was a perpetual forest *(Dauerwald)* in the sense of modern forest management, and it was not until 2000 that it began to evolve into a natural forest undisturbed by human intervention. An important component is the dead wood, which provides nourishment and a habitat for many plants and animals.

# HERMA-PHRODITES

**In many places in the Middle East and Europe there are forests that have developed over 15,000 years and cultural landscapes with a 10,000-year history. They form constellations of tree crowns and trunks in depleted soils and on stony precipices that have been shaped by mankind for millennia.**

Photo essay by Stefanie Jacomet and Dominique Ghiggi
Photographs by Stefanie Jacomet

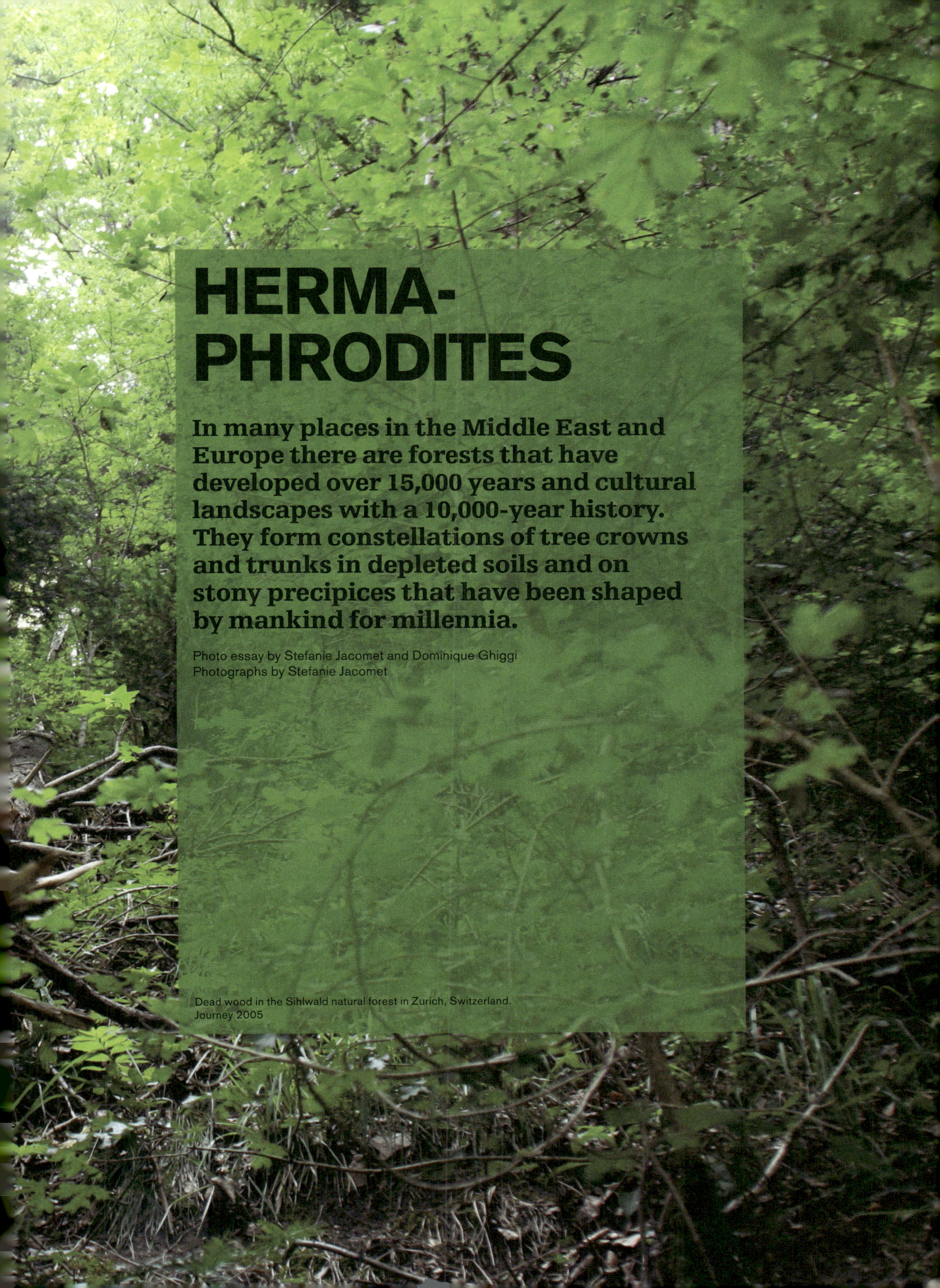

Dead wood in the Sihlwald natural forest in Zurich, Switzerland.
Journey 2005

Abisko, Sweden. Journeys 1990–2003

**THE PLANT-GATHERING ECONOMY**

In the Late Glacial period around 15,000 to 11,500 years ago and well into the Holocene, Central Europe was home to groups of hunters and gatherers. As early as the Paleolithic Age, these groups not only hunted animals, but used wild plants and most probably tended and actively spread them, too. The open forests were changed only slightly by the gathering of berries, nuts, mushrooms and mosses, and the original forest communities remained intact. Wood from shrubs and trees served as a source of energy, and their charred remains provide us with clues as to the way not only wood but also roots, bulbs, seeds and fruits were used. Well-preserved camp sites have been excavated on Lake Neuchâtel and other places in Switzerland, and charcoal analyses of the hearths found there, have shown that dwarf willows were used to make fires. Forests did not yet exist there at that time.

However, as can be deduced from ethnographic sources, the foragers who inhabited closed forests substantially changed their natural environments. Members of early expeditions to North America reported that the Indians burned down forests in order to improve hunting grounds, create clearings for greater mobility in forests, increase yields of the gathered fruits, and harvest shoots from coppiced woods for better building and weaving material.

**THE SAMI IN ABISKO, NORTHERN SWEDEN**

The Sami are hunters and gatherers from Lapland, and some still live a nomadic life today. They provide a good example of a people who practice sustainable forest management methods. It is unclear how long the Sami have inhabited northern Europe within its modern borders, but it is certain that hunter and gatherer groups lived there before them and managed the forest in a similar fashion.

The glaciers melted in Abisko at the end of the Boreal around 10,000 years ago. In the period afterward, various shrub- and tree-shaped birch species—among them the downy birch *(Betula pubescens)* and the dwarf birch *(Betula nana)*—returned from their sanctuaries and spread. The natural tundra landscape has remained largely intact to the present day. Given the open forest structures and the low population density, the Sami have hardly changed their natural surroundings.

**FARMING AND ANIMAL HUSBANDRY**

The Neolithic Age began in Central Europe during the Atlantic period around 8000 to 6000 years ago. It marked the beginnings of farming and animal husbandry. Human beings began planting fields to produce crops and keeping domestic animals that required feed. The first signs that mankind was permanently shaping the landscape appeared some 12,000 years ago in various centers of domestication throughout the world, such as the Middle East, Africa, China, and Central and South America.

During the Atlantic period, temperate deciduous trees formed forests on the plains of Europe. A forest vegetation rich in oaks predominated, including oaks *(Quercus)*, elms *(Ulmus)*, lindens *(Tilia)*, ashes *(Fraxinus)* and maples *(Acer)*. This is why this period is also referred to as the age of mixed oak forests.

Woods were burned down or cleared in order to gain open land for settlements, farming and pastures. The combination of various agrarian uses of the land gave rise to a great diversity of landscapes and species at the local and regional levels. A well-articulated landscape gradually emerged near the settlements featuring clearings, forest boundaries, bushes, hedges, meadowland and ruderal species. But vast primeval forests still existed in the hinterland.

Animal husbandry and, above all, the need for fodder heavily influenced the use of the forests. Until modern times the grazing of livestock in forests was a common phenomenon whose most prevalent side-effects included the selective alteration of undergrowth, the prevention of young stands, ground compaction and erosion. It resulted in a parklike thinning out of the forests and the emergence of permanent open areas.

The use of deciduous and coniferous leaves and hay as fodder for cattle goes back to prehistoric times and can be seen as a relic of the old hunting and gathering economy. It continued to be a highly vital relic in the high mountain regions of Switzerland during the nineteenth century.

**TURKISH FARMING VILLAGE IN COMMAGENE**

Various small farming villages in Commagene in the southeast Taurus Mountains present us today with an impressive pasture landscape that has resulted from the clearing of woodland and the production of feed going back to the Neolithic Age. One highly visible element is the pollarded oaks, whose new growth is used for cow fodder.

Pollarded oaks in Commagene, Taurus Mountains, Turkey. Journey 2009

**POLLARDING IN THE ALPINE REGION**
**Pollarding—cutting back branches to produce fodder—was carried out in the Alpine region to secure feed for goats and cows in winter. In the nineteenth century, the production of fodder by means of green pruning increasingly moved to the edge of the forests. In the twentieth century it hardly took place in Switzerland's forests.**

**The only place where pollarding continued for a long time was in Val di Campo in Ticino and in the Lötschen Valley in Oberwallis. In the early nineties ash trees continued to be pollarded in the Lötschen Valley at altitudes of 700 to 1500 meters. Most were planted expressly for this purpose and stood in meadows, along both ditches and property boundaries, or were combined in entire groves. For practical reasons such fodder trees were kept rather small.**

**The importance of pollarding for the ecology and appearance of the landscape is attributable to the selective planting of suitable trees in open country, which causes a change in the local composition of tree species.**

A POLLARDED OAK IN SOUTH TYROL
A Mitterhof farmer visits his meadow trees in Windlahn in the Sarn Valley in South Tyrol in order to harvest green leaves for fodder. He is carrying a large pack, a billhook and a pickax.

Photographs by Giancarlo Gambino, 1985. Taken from Michael Machatschek, *Laubgeschichten: Gebrauchswissen einer alten Baumwirtschaft, Speise- und Futterlaubkultur* (Böhlau, Vienna, Cologne, Weimar, 2002), 122f.

**ALPINE FORESTS**
The Bronze Age began in the Sub-Boreal, the late warm period 4000 years ago. At this time, the woods on the plains and in the low-lying mountain regions were dominated by beeches. The Alpine areas more than one thousand meters above sea level were also intensely colonized by spruces. Beginning in this period, the changes in forest composition were increasingly of anthropogenic origin. In the Metal Ages—the Bronze Age was followed by the Iron Age around 800 B.C.E.—humans exerted an even greater influence on the landscape through the use of metals. Large amounts of wood were necessary for mining, particularly for ore smelting, and the introduction of metal tools in agriculture led to a more intensive use of the land.

For a long time, the economic value of the forests in Switzerland's mountainous regions was based primarily on their role as pasture land and less on the use of their timber. The public woods where animals were grazed were located on the better, more level sections of the southern slopes. By contrast, the steeper areas with shallower soil were largely covered by closed forests—as were the northern slopes. The decline of animal grazing in forests in the Alps continued well into the twentieth century, but the first large wave took place in the late nineteenth century.

**THE SWISS STONE PINE GARDEN IN GRINDELWALD**
The stand of Swiss stone pines in Grindelwald, located 1851 meters above sea level in the Bernese Oberland, is a relic from the early Holocene period. After the sheets of ice retreated, Swiss stone pines (also called Arolla pines) and larches were the first trees to colonize the higher regions of the Alps. Spruce trees migrated there later on and crowded out these trees in the subalpine levels of the northern Alps. The stocks of Swiss stone pine remained intact only at special locations that were unsuitable for the growth of spruce trees, such as the Grindelwald under the Eiger's northern face, where temperatures were considerably colder than in the surrounding area. It is probable that the Swiss stone pine garden was originally much denser. Its thinned-out parklike structure is the result of logging and possibly of animal grazing in the forest.

Swiss stone pine in Grindelwald, Switzerland. Journey 2000

**HORTICULTURE**
Central Europe was long a marginal region in human history—a region to which "civilization" first had to be imported by the Romans. In this regard it contrasted sharply with the Middle East, Egypt and ancient Greece, where so-called advanced civilizations were established during the Bronze Age. Urban centers emerged in Central Europe in Roman times, together with road systems for international trade. The use of raw materials, particularly for energy production, expanded in tandem, which led to widespread deforestation.

Around Roman times, hornbeams also began spreading in the forests dominated by beeches and silver firs. They were joined by the tree species introduced by the Romans, such as walnuts, plane trees and the sweet chestnuts, which originated in the regions around the southeast Mediterranean and the Black Sea. The local boxwood was actively planted and spread. The origins of modern horticulture in Central Europe also extend to Roman times. Even though it is probable that the Celts maintained some gardens, the cultivation of vegetables, spices, grapes, and fruit and nut trees began on a large scale in this period. Nevertheless, there are only isolated reports of the domestication of trees. Many varieties probably disappeared in the past because it was difficult to propagate them. We know from written sources that domestic cherry trees existed as early as classical antiquity. These sources contain the first mention of the technique of grafting, which is the only method that can be used to create new varieties of cherries (and stone and pomaceous fruit in general). It is not entirely clear where these trees and the technique of grafting came from—presumably from China or Central Asia. Trees that are propagated by means of cuttings—such as olive, fig and grape trees—were probably domesticated much earlier in the Middle East.

**WILD CHERRY TREES IN THE FOREST**
It is unclear whether the modern wild cherry *(Prunus avium)* is really a "wild" tree in our region or whether it is a domestic cherry that at some point returned to the wild. In contrast to the wild forms of apples and pears, there are no remains of wild cherry from prehistoric times, or the finds are of doubtful origin. What is certain is that cherries were first planted in our latitudes in Roman times. We now also know that our local wild apples are not the ancestors of domestic apples, which descend from *Malus sieversii*, a native of Central Asia.

Wild cherry trees (*Prunus avium*) and apricot trees (*Prunus armeniaca*) in Wildegg, Switzerland. Journey 1990

**THE MEDIEVAL CULTURAL LANDSCAPE**
Use of the landscape declined sharply during the Migration period. The relatively open woods of Roman times, rich in oaks, disappeared and were largely replaced by beech forests. However, there is evidence of considerable human intervention in the landscape beginning again in the seventh and eighth centuries. The Abbey of Saint Gall, which was founded in 720 and produced many valuable written documents, is mentioned as proof of the development of the land.

Pollen diagrams show that forested areas began shrinking in the seventh and eighth centuries. Beech stocks decreased but oak stocks increased significantly. Walnut trees were often planted and there is clear evidence of extensive plantations of sweet chestnuts and their resulting natural dissemination. A typical landscape in the early Middle Ages can be described as follows: fields and fruit tree groves were located close to a human settlement; farther away were open pastures; then came large areas that were extensively used for forest grazing, sometimes interspersed with brushland and coppiced forests. Human beings used the forest in a relatively wide perimeter around the settlement, and it was an integral part of the agricultural space for living and production.

**THE OAK GROVE AT WILDENSTEIN**
Wildenstein Castle, which stands on the Jura plateau in the canton of Basel-Landschaft, dates to the thirteenth century and is a typical *Rodungsburg*—a castle built in a forest clearing. In 1792 possession of the entire estate passed to the Vischer family from Basel, who remained owners until 1990. Thanks to their knowledge and sensitivity, the medieval cultural landscape has been preserved to the present, including the unique Wytwald, a forest of oaks with trees more than five hundred years old. In earlier times a three-field system was used to farm the fertile land. The oak woods served as pastureland for cattle, and the oak trees themselves were a popular source of fodder for the animals, mainly pigs, in autumn. At the time pastures dotted with common and sessile oaks were widespread in the area. In fact, in the region of the Ergolz River, these oaks covered more than ten square kilometers. However, Wildenstein is the only place where a section of the oaken Wytwald is still intact. In 1995 the competent Swiss federal authorities declared Wildenstein a site of national importance. Young oaks are planted regularly to ensure that the population of trees does not become too old and lead to the death of the forest.

Oak grove at Wildenstein with trees more than five hundred years old, Switzerland. Journey 1985

**WOOD PRODUCTION**
As early as the Neolithic Age, human beings realized that they could acquire "standardized" timber for building and a higher yield of firewood by using certain woodland management methods. One such method, which was particularly widespread in the Middle Ages, is *Niederwaldwirtschaft,* or coppicing. In a coppiced forest, trees are cut down to their trunks and allowed to rejuvenate and send out sprouts, which leads to an intense thinning out of the forest. The multitrunked trees found in today's forests are attributable to this practice. Rapidly growing hornbeams and hazel trees, in particular, were coppiced for firewood, and the bark of oaks was used for tanning. In the *Mittelwaldwirtschaft,* another coppicing method, some of the trees, particularly oaks, were retained as standards and used mainly for timber and hog feed.

Basically, the sustainable timber production associated with the scientifically based forestry management methods of early modern times emerged between 1800 and 1900. One of the conditions leading to its birth was the decline of agrarian forest use as a result of modernization processes in farming, which emancipated many areas of agriculture from the woods. Earlier, timber production clashed fundamentally with the practice of grazing animals in forests.

**THE ALSATIAN HARDTWALD**
The Hardtwald in southeast Alsace has had an eventful history. In the Middle Ages, it not only provided wood for energy production, but served as common grazing land, not least because its acorns were popular hog fodder. Traces of these uses are still visible in the forest structure today. The Hardtwald is a so-called *Mittelwald,* a coppiced forest with standards. A remarkable number of old oaks can be found in the upper tree layer, and hornbeams are characteristic of the lower tree layer. The increased use of timber was beneficial to the hornbeams because their trunks reshoot and rejuvenate well. When Alsace fell to France in 1648 after the Thirty Years' War, the Hardtwald was declared a state woodland and forest management was regulated. Starting in the nineteenth century, it was managed as a coppiced forest with standards, which ideally preserved the structure of the oaks and hornbeam woods. Today it is not extensively used and, as a result, the diversity of its species is endangered over the long term.

Coppiced forest in the Alsatian Hardtwald, Switzerland. Journey 1987

## SEMI-NATURAL FOREST FORMATIONS

Anthropogenic influences caused new plant communities to emerge from the former woodlands. Due to human intervention the occurrence of various plants increased and the plants were able to colonize new areas. The proportion of plants that signal a human influence on the development of flora is about twenty-five percent of the total flora population on the Central European mainland and up to fifty percent of that on the British Isles.

Prior to industrialization, human intervention led to a significant enrichment of the vegetation in Central Europe. A large number of plant species that had previously led a modest marginal existence were able to spread.

## THE FORESTS OF THE SCOTTISH HIGHLANDS

The Scottish Highlands are characterized by impressive geologic formations, fjord-like bays known as sea lochs, and vast high moors covered with heath. The hardscrabble landscape formed during the last Ice Age and continued to develop under the influence of the oceanic climate. Sheep and Scottish highland cattle graze on the open land everywhere. The northern and western Highlands, far to the north of Great Glen, are among the most geologically diverse regions in Scotland. The native plant formations include extensive areas of heath, savannah-like stocks of trees consisting of hazels *(Corylus avellana)*, birches *(Betula pendula, Betula pubescens)* pines *(Pinus sylvestris)*, as well as temperate rain forests of oaks *(Quercus petraea, Quercus pubescens)*, mountain ashes *(Sorbus aucuparia)*, birches and hollies *(Ilex aquifolium)*.

As part of the Highland culture that existed for centuries, large areas were reforested with foreign tree species for the agrarian use of the forest and for timber production. This went on until around 1750 but was still practiced in the twentieth century. During the Second World War, extensive forested areas were cut down to produce ammunition boxes, which is why only a few remnants of the foreign tree stocks remain today.

The remains of a beech forest planted in the late nineteenth century can be found at the base of a huge gneiss formation in the village of Scourie in northwest Sutherland. The beech tree is not native to Scotland. Professor Oliver Rackham, a scholar of historical ecology, explains that they were introduced primarily in the north of the country for firewood and building timber. The wind that blows over the flat moor landscape from the coast shapes the bent silhouette of the remaining tree stocks.

The bay of Loch nan Uamh is located in the southern Highlands, north of Ardnish Peninsula. Although the forest of oaks that can be found there has the appearance of a native stock, it is a semi-natural old forest that the rural population used in a variety of ways over the course of centuries.[1] The size of the forested area has hardly changed since 1750. Like hundreds of other woods in Scotland's western bays, the original temperate rain forest that was once located there was modified by man in order to increase the number of oak trees. The oak forest that resulted from this process is lushly intermingled with mosses and lichens and continues to play an important ecological role.

By contrast, in the region around Loch Assynt, one encounters the characteristic forms of limestone weathering, including extensive cave systems that are considered the largest in Scotland, but have yet to be explored in detail. Very old limestone can be seen on the surface in many places. An islandlike limestone formation in Loch Assynt is covered by a stand of pines. In 1959, while studying Scotland's native pine woods, the British forest scientists Henry M. Steven and Alan Carlisle concluded that this site must have been planted by humans since the trees were less than one hundred years old and stood in the middle of an area dominated by birches. The nearest natural pine forest—the Caledonian Pinewoods—is around fifteen miles to the south. A plausible interpretation is that the inhabitants wanted to create a more picturesque island by planting the pines.

1 *T. Christopher Smout, A History of the Native Woodlands of Scotland, 1500–1920* (Edinburgh: Edinburgh University Press, 2005).

Planting beeches in Scourie, north Scotland. Journey 2002

Planting pines at Loch Assynt, north Scotland. Journey 2002

Semi-natural oak forest, Loch nan Uamh, north Scotland. Journey 2002

# RESEARCH IN FOREST CARTOGRAPHY

## TREES AND FORESTS IN FRANZ LUDWIG PFYFFER'S RELIEF DER URSCHWEIZ

**With his "Relief der Urschweiz" (Relief of Central Switzerland), the Lucerne-based topographer Franz Ludwig Pfyffer created the first true-to-scale model of the landscape of Central Switzerland; his model also illustrated details of settlements, transportation infrastructure as well as phenomena such as the spread of glaciers, the snow and tree line as well as zones of deciduous and coniferous forests.**

Essay by Andreas Bürgi

Section of the relief by Pfyffer, 3D reconstruction

Illustration: Jana Niederöst, *Das Relief der Urschweiz von Franz Ludwig Pfyffer (1716–1802): 3D-Rekonstruktion, Analyse und Interpretation*, Dissertation ETH Zurich 2005

1 Franz Ludwig Pfyffer, as Lucerne patrician, councilor and Commander of the Order of Saint Louis, this last honor indicated by his "cordon rouge," or red sash. Oil painting by Josef Reinhard, around 1776
Illustration: Archiv Gletschergarten, Lucerne

Franz Ludwig Pfyffer von Wyher was born on May 18, 1716, a descendant of the widely ramified Pfyffer dynasty, which derived its wealth, social standing and political power in Lucerne and the Swiss Confederation from mercenary service. As was the custom for the first-born son, Franz Ludwig, when he was ten years old, traveled to Paris to become a cadet in the family company, commanded by his father, in the regiment of the Swiss Guard. The Pfyffers had served continuously under the French Crown for two hundred years. Franz Ludwig would be the last in the family to earn his living as a mercenary; after the French Revolution of 1789, the business, which had by then already ceased to be very profitable, practically came to a standstill.

The Pfyffer Company, like the other companies of the Swiss Guard, was stationed in Paris and its environs. This regiment, whose responsibility was the protection of the French royal family, was considered to be an elite unit, which meant that its members enjoyed appropriate privileges. The proximity to the court, in particular, allowed some Swiss officers to attain considerable influence and standing in Versailles, and to receive prestigious and lucrative positions; such was the case with Pfyffer. His remarkable career in France was built less upon his military prowess than his superb connections. In 1764, having achieved the rank of lieutenant general and secured considerable retirement income, he ended his military career. This did not, however, mean that his service to the king had ended. Back in Lucerne, he was asked by the then omnipotent minister of Louis XV, Étienne de Choiseul-Stainville, to become the leader of the French Party in Central Switzerland. In modern terms, this means he engaged in lobbying work in the service of France, a position that also brought with it considerable income.

Pfyffer was particularly well suited for this job, not only because he was one of the most powerful citizens of Lucerne, but also because, as a representative of the most important canton of Central Switzerland, he could in addition exercise considerable influence in the small cantons of Central Switzerland. As a member first of the Grand Council and, as of 1752, of the Small Council of Lucerne, Pfyffer played a decisive role in the affairs of Lucerne until the end of the old Confederation. As the head of the French Party he could count on the support of the Court of Versailles; in exchange, he saw to it that the influential councils in Central Switzerland helped advance the interests of France in their respective cantons. These interests primarily entailed guaranteeing the recruitment of sufficient numbers of soldiers for France. In return, the cantons received the precious commodity salt, as well as ample retirement funds.

With the invasion of the revolutionary army in 1789, the Ancien Régime in Switzerland collapsed. The events also removed the representatives of the old elite, including Pfyffer, who for many years had participated in governing Lucerne with a firm and uncompromising hand. During the ensuing Helvetic Republic, he had no influence whatsoever; furthermore, he lost all of his income from France. Franz Ludwig Pfyffer died on February 7, 1802.

In addition to Pfyffer the politician, nobleman and determined defender of the Ancien Régime, there was Pfyffer the scientist and enlightened thinker. This Janus-faced quality of his life, if you will, is expressed in two images: One shows the nobleman wearing the prestigious French medal of the Order of Saint Louis on a red sash; the other gives us the naturalist at work (figs. 1 and 2).

Already during his time in France, Pfyffer had become interested in surveying, cartography and engineering. Since France played a pioneering role in these disciplines, Pfyffer managed to gain considerable knowledge. Under Louis XIV, the Cassini family had begun to survey the country and draw up a map; throughout the eighteenth century, these efforts were continued and refined, both in specialized schools and in the army. Interested officers like Pfyffer were able to profit from these endeavors. In addition France boasted the world's first school of engineering, the École Nationale des Ponts et Chaussées. It was only natural, therefore, that the government of Lucerne commissioned Pfyffer in 1759 to oversee the construction of the new road to Basel, a segment of the significant Gotthard route. A few years later, he also played a key role in the straightening of the Rengg, a stream which repeatedly flooded the outskirts of Lucerne.

His main interest, however, lay in surveying and cartography, which he is known to have already taken up during his time in the army, most likely in contact with the *ingénieurs géographes,* the geographer-engineers who, starting in 1731, were deployed with the troops and required to supply necessary topographical information

2 Franz Ludwig Pfyffer surveying on Mount Pilatus.
Aquatint by Christian von Mechel, 1786
Illustration: Archiv Gletschergarten, Lucerne

for military campaigns. Also in Paris, at the Louvre, he had the chance to visit the well-maintained and steadily expanding collection of French fortress models that were shown to officers for training purposes. This collection must have been the inspiration for what we can rightly call his life's work, the *Relief der Urschweiz*.

The *Relief der Urschweiz* is the first topographical model ever to use triangulation and barometric altitude measurements to depict an area of approximately 3500 square kilometers. Never before had any one managed to represent to scale such a large and above all topographically challenging landscape. And therein lay the true fascination of the relief for his eighteenth-century contemporaries.

The focal point of the relief is Lake Lucerne, Lucerne, Unterwalden, Zug and neighboring regions of the cantons Uri, Schwyz and Bern (fig. 3). It was created over an extended period of time which probably began in the mid-eighteenth century. While the precise date is not certain, it was in these years that Pfyffer began surveying the area around Lucerne and Mount Pilatus. The work was completed in 1786 with the publication of a copperplate engraving by Mechel (fig. 11) and a map by the Zug engraver Jakob Josef Clausner.

Pfyffer obtained the topographical data for constructing his relief using a measuring method that was based on triangulation and contained multiple safeguards. He compiled his measurements during the summer months, spending time on the highest peaks in the Uri and Unterwald regions. Using equipment he obtained from Paris, London and Germany, he took measurements that were first applied to a map; only later did he begin the construction of the relief. He also came back from his tours with drawings containing topographical data.

The large scale of the relief, approximately 1:11,500, was deliberately chosen to allow him to show or at least indicate aspects of the landscape and settlements that included such details as individual farmhouses dispersed across the terrain, or mountainside chapels. The barren mountain peaks are gray, the high cliffs and glaciers covered with snow and ice are colored white. He used twisted silver wire to depict rivers and streams, thus lending them the aspect of a flowing movement. He depicted transportation routes by using string which he stretched between needles across the surface; smaller paths and mountain trails are painted with white paint. For the houses and buildings of towns and cities, he used small metal plates the size of a fingernail, the top edge painted red to indicate the roofs. Church steeples are nails attached to the surface point up, with the points also colored red.

Such a construction is unique in the history of reliefs. And equally unique is the model's inner construction: 136 individual sections, each mounted on a foundation of lath. On some of them Pfyffer drew a grid which served as a directional framework for transferring significant landmarks. He marked the highest points with wooden posts driven into the base. For the raw construction he used pieces of wood and brick, plaster, and charcoal, while he modeled the surface with a mass of sand and plaster, which he then covered with beeswax and painted. Each of the 136 pieces is framed in cardboard and numbered, making it possible to transport the relief. This unusual construction method had never been used before, nor would it ever be used again; the material of choice after Pfyffer was plaster. The relief was exhibited in a room of its own inside Pfyffer's summer residence, which today is the casino at the Löwengraben in Lucerne; it is surrounded by copperplate engravings of Swiss landscapes. It was protected from dust with a large cloth which, by means of an ingenious rotating apparatus and given the appropriate lighting, could be suspended in such a way that a whole day, from sunrise to sunset, could transpire before the eyes of visitors. At the south side of the model there was a staircase which allowed visitors to look down on the Alps from a steeper angle.

The *Relief der Urschweiz* tapped into the spirit of the times. Starting in 1766, when the Zurich pastor and historian Johann Conrad Fäsi became the first to report from Pfyffer's workshop on the yet unfinished model, the stream of visitors increased steadily until it reached its peak in the late 1780s. Pfyffer's relief became one of Switzerland's biggest attractions. Visitors from all over Europe came to marvel at it, traveling from England and Russia, Sweden and Italy, even from as far afield as America. Pfyffer's relief attracted people from all walks of life, classes and occupations: scientists, scholars, writers, musicians, painters, politicians, soldiers, civil servants, princes and counts, as well as poor wretches. It is as if the

3 The *Relief der Urschweiz*, overall view from above. The partly discernable rectangular pattern is formed by the seams between the 136 individual segments.
Illustration: Archiv Gletschergarten Lucerne

4 *Bresteneg entre le sapin et le petit noyer. No 26*; the location is the Hohwald near Wyher Castle. The numbering suggests that the sheet is part of a series of drawings made at this location. Watercolored drawing in pencil and India ink, ink inscription (21 × 34 cm)
Image: Zentral- und Hochschulbibliothek, Lucerne

unanimous enthusiasm for this topographical masterpiece was a manifestation of the equality recognized as the century's overriding principle of reason. For here was an unprecedented scientific effort that revealed, clearly and for all to see, interconnections that until then had been concealed.

The early researcher of the Bernese Alps Gottlieb Sigmund Gruner wrote in 1778, "Do not look at this artwork as something that merely serves to pass the time or amuse the connoisseur, but rather as a work which sheds infinitely more light on the natural history of Switzerland than all the travels that one can undertake, where one is always faced with mountains concealing the distance and the coherence. Here, in contrast, you can view the whole, laid out before you as if in a bird's flight; in this way you can gain an incommensurately clearer notion of the formation of our globe and all the coincidences which affected it." This was the crux of the matter: Finally, it was possible to look down upon the Alps rather than being surrounded by them and seeing them loom threateningly over you. It is no coincidence that at the same time in France, the first experiments with balloon flight were taking place. The mountains, which at the start of the century were still seen as a chaotic accumulation of rock, were now much easier to comprehend. Here someone had demonstrated how it could be done. And while it was only a part of the Alps, it was a start; the principle had been found, the necessary tools were available, and the technology—which until then had only been tested in hilly or flat terrain—had proven itself in the most complicated topography imaginable. With diligence and endurance, the rest would also be mastered. Didn't Pfyffer himself intend to expand his relief southwards towards the Bernese Oberland? The sense of a momentous breakthrough showed itself in visitors' reactions.

These visitors repeatedly mentioned in particular Pfyffer's representation of forests, not only every house, but "even the difference between black and living wood is shown," wrote the awestruck German Baron von Friesen in 1778. By this he meant that the viewer could differentiate between coniferous and deciduous forests. Indeed, the relief not only showed for the first time the elevation of the tree line, but Pfyffer also tried to represent the transition between deciduous and mixed forests to pure coniferous forests by coloring the latter with a darker green. From the very start, he had attached great importance to capturing these and many other details in his depiction of the landscape, even though it was clear to him how much work he was taking on. As early as 1761, at the start of his endeavor, he had written to the Genevan geodesist and engineer Jacques-Barthélemy Micheli du Crest, who at the time was being held prisoner at the Aarburg fortress on charges of conspiracy, "I show the shape of the houses, every little brook, the hedges, the cliffs, the meadows and fields, the canyons. I differentiate between oak, beech and pine forest… You must admit, Sir, that this means much work." But as was the case for his illustration of the permanent snow line, which earned Pfyffer great praise from the famous Genevan naturalist Horace-Bénédict de Saussure in the fourth volume of his epoch-making treatise *Voyage dans les Alpes* (1780), in the eighteenth century there was hardly any systematic knowledge of the structure of forests. For the first time the *Relief der Urschweiz* made an overview possible. Pfyffer not only wanted to show the structure of the mountains from a geological, tectonic and climactic aspect, he was also very interested in the question from the standpoint of vegetation. How meticulous his observations were is evident in a small anecdote related by the German traveler Sophie von La Roche in 1787. In his studio Pfyffer was showing visitors a juniper tree that he had brought back from the zone of the tree line, where, as he explained, juniper trees were not normally found. Today we know how versatile this tree is in reality, and that it is not uncommon to find specimens at such altitudes. But the anecdote does illustrate how little was known about the vegetation zones at the time, and also how important it was to Pfyffer to shed some light on the matter.

Many visitors spoke of the materials Pfyffer used for the forests on his relief. When Fritz Stolberg visited the general in 1794 on his way to Italy and asked him whether he made the pine forests from ash, "he smiled, went to his cabinet and returned with a fuzzy cotton nightcap turned inside-out. 'I take the fuzz,' he said, 'coat it with mastic gum and use it to make the pine forests you see here.'" The story about the nightcap must have made a great impression, for it was told over and over. An analysis of the relief in the year 2000 did in fact reveal that pieces of cotton had been dipped in a pasty mass and

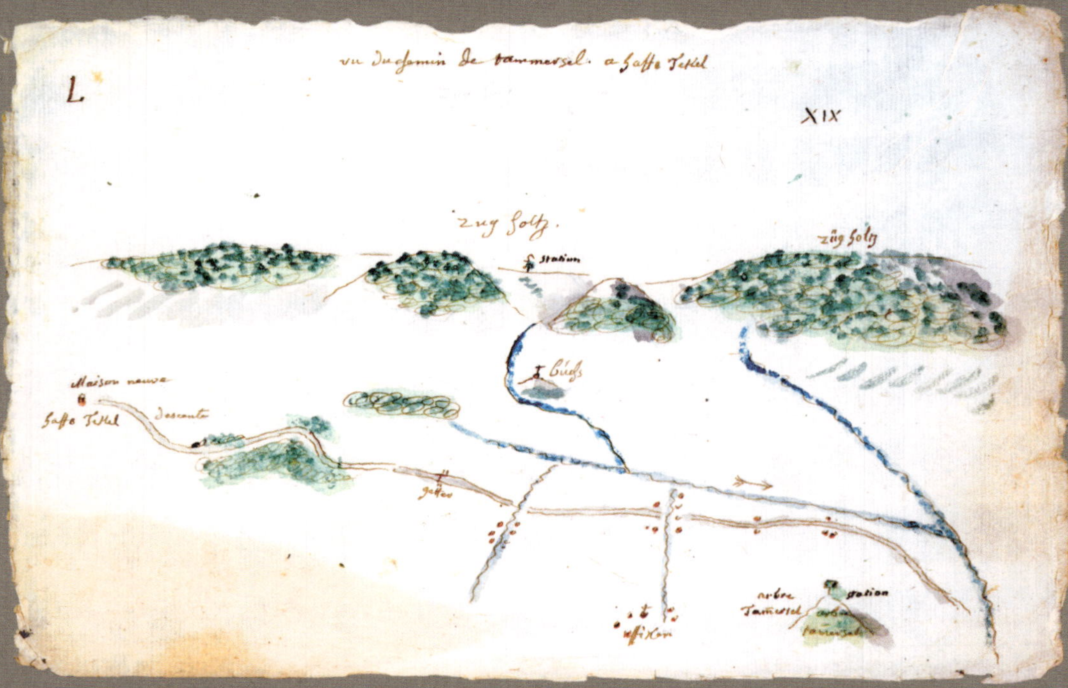


5 *vu du chemin de tammersel. a haffe Tekel*; the "L" in the upper left corner stands for the canton of Lucerne. Watercolored drawing in pencil and India ink, ink inscription (22 × 35 cm)
Illustration: Zentral- und Hochschulbibliothek, Lucerne

colored green. Today, however, the forest zones on the relief can no longer be clearly differentiated; too many years of exposure to dust and light, too many different cleaning agents and, not least from today's standpoint, improper restoration techniques have had the effect that the original coloring can no longer be clearly discerned.

To get an idea of how Pfyffer gathered his knowledge of the forests of Central Switzerland, it is necessary to refer to another source, namely, his topographical drawings. On these he captured the vast array of details which constitute the appearance of the landscape, i.e., all those houses, meadows, canyons, brooks, hedges, etc., that he wrote Micheli about, including, notably, the contours of the forests and their transition from deciduous to coniferous to vegetation-free zones. Pfyffer painted an unknown number of watercolors; the ninety-one which are still in existence are most likely only a fraction of the total. They are approximately 34 × 22 centimeters in size, and they almost exclusively show landscapes depicted on the relief itself, namely, perspectives ranging from a few hundred square meters in area to expansive panoramas. One can assume that Pfyffer sketched these perspectives with pencil in the field and then colored them at home using a particular color key with which he determined certain landscape characteristics.

The drawings also show the surveying positions and the points of focus he used for his measurements. Conspicuously he often used prominent trees in the terrain as focal points. A particularly nice example of this is a drawing he made while on the Hohwald in the region close to his ancestral pile, Wyher Castle, near Ettiswil: *Bresteneg entre le sapin et le petit noyer* (fig. 4). The drawing most likely documents a triangulation on the Brestenegg, namely, between the fir tree discernable in the background, and the walnut tree drawn to the right of Pfyffer's *station;* on the lower edge of the picture, there is the inscription *wacht für,* i.e., a *Hochwacht* or vantage tower, which Pfyffer often used as an outlook or vantage point. Solitary trees in the middle of the landscape, visible from a distance, were important reference points for him, and they can be found in different forms in his landscape sketches, for example, on a sketch depicting the road between Dagmersellen and the region of Hafendeckel near Sursee that features two surveying points, both marked by a tree (fig. 5).

More importantly for Pfyffer, these drawings gave him insight into the structure of the forests. This is also evident in figure 5, in which Pfyffer obviously wanted to establish that the hills of Zügholz near Dagmersellen were forested, or to be precise, judging from the light green coloring interrupted only sporadically by a few scattered darker green tones, that they were mainly covered with deciduous trees.

The collection contains further illustrative examples of this theme. A drawing that Pfyffer made in the vicinity of Wyher Castle near Ettiswil shows Zügholz again, this time from the opposite side, from the south (fig. 6). Here too, there is a precisely contoured forest on the hill, marked with a series of numbers. We can assume that these numbers are surveying points, which again include prominent trees, for example, at points 3, 5 and 11. Furthermore, the hillside in the foreground near Ettiswil bears the inscription *Eich vald,* or oak forest, evidence of Pfyffer's efforts to distinguish between different kinds of forest. This particular sketch also shows another kind of surveying marker that was of importance to Pfyffer, namely, church steeples, in this case that of Ettiswil's church.

Just how interested he was in the structure of the sweeping forests is evident in a perspective of the Rigi, which he made from the standpoint of Lauerz (fig. 7). Here, the forest of one whole flank of the Hochflue is done in a rather dark green tone, an indication of the predominant pine forests.

Pfyffer also uses light and dark coloration to show proximity and distance, as illustrated in a perspective made from Gersau looking eastwards onto the Mythen, with the Glarn Alps in the background and the Fronalpstock, here referred to as "uryberg" (fig. 8). The drawing shows how the higher up or farther away your gaze wanders, the more the forest behind the village of Schwyz blends into the cliff and rocky zones. By contrast, the western flank of the Fronalpstock, which is only half the distance from Gersau, is shown as a colorful mixed forest. A similar view presents itself from the opposite shore of Lake Lucerne, from Ridli near Beckenried. Here, too, the zone of deciduous vegetation in the lower regions is clearly distinguishable (fig. 9). In this drawing Pfyffer was certainly more interested in precisely capturing the contours of the mountains than

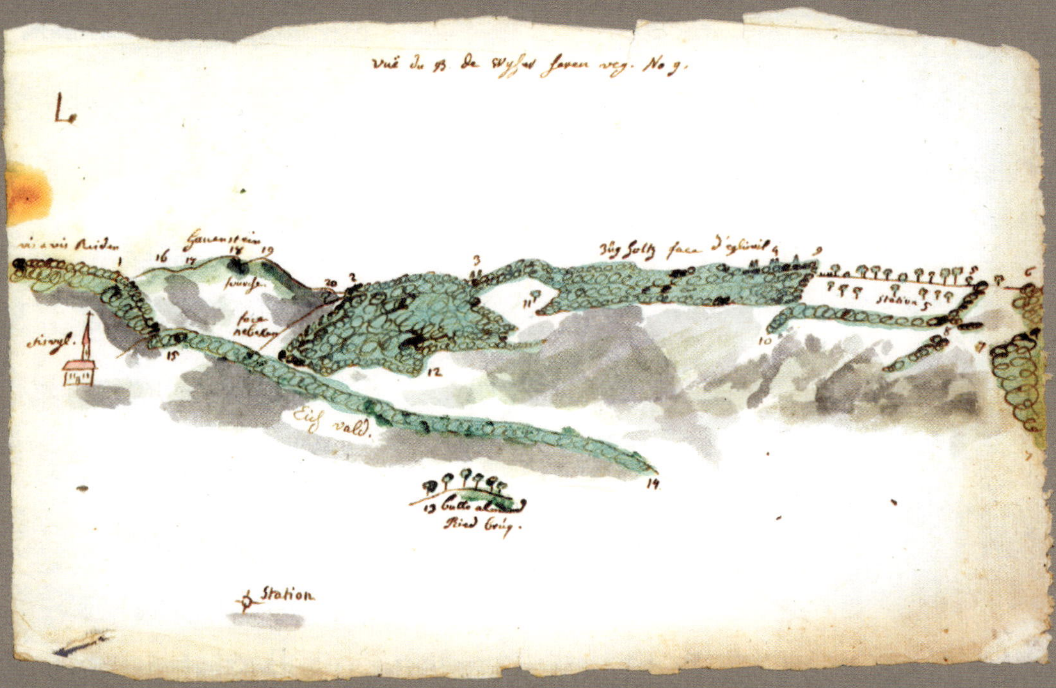


6 *vuë du B. de Wyher heren veg. No 9.* Watercolored drawing in pencil and India ink, ink inscription (21.5 × 33.5 cm)
Illustration: Zentral- und Hochschulbibliothek, Lucerne

the vegetation. A panorama perspective of Ingenbohl looking eastwards, again showing the two Mythen on the right and the village of Sattel on the left (fig. 10), combines both of these functions. Here there is a clear differentiation between forest parcels, very light grassy vegetation, and in the case of the Mythen peaks, the transition to the zone above the tree line.

The work which Pfyffer gathered and compiled year after year, piece by piece, found its rightful expression not only in the relief itself, but also in the colored outline etching *Vue perspective de la partie la plus élevée du centre de la Suisse,* published in 1786 by Christian von Mechel following the completion of work on *Relief der Urschweiz* (fig. 11). The perspective is from the northern periphery and shows the Lucerne hinterland in the foreground, with lakes Hallwil, Baldegg and Sempach, and in the background the high Alps of the Uri and Unterwald regions. The midlands and foothills of the Alps show a forest structure which corresponds to that of Pfyffer's perspectives, as is evident looking at the slopes of the Rigi. It is quite certain then that Mechel was under clear instructions from Pfyffer when it came to his depiction of not only mountains, lakes, rivers and transportation routes but also forests. Thus, thanks to Mechel's work, the results of Pfyffer's efforts in depicting the forests are still visible in utmost detail, despite the fact that now the once highly regarded differentiation of vegetation zones on the *Relief der Urschweiz* is no longer recognizable.

7 *Station 2 art. proche Lawis*; the title suggests that Pfyffer used several locations around Arth; the “S” stands for the canton of Schwyz. Watercolored drawing in pencil and India ink, ink inscription (21.5 × 34 cm)
Illustration: Zentral- und Hochschulbibliothek, Lucerne

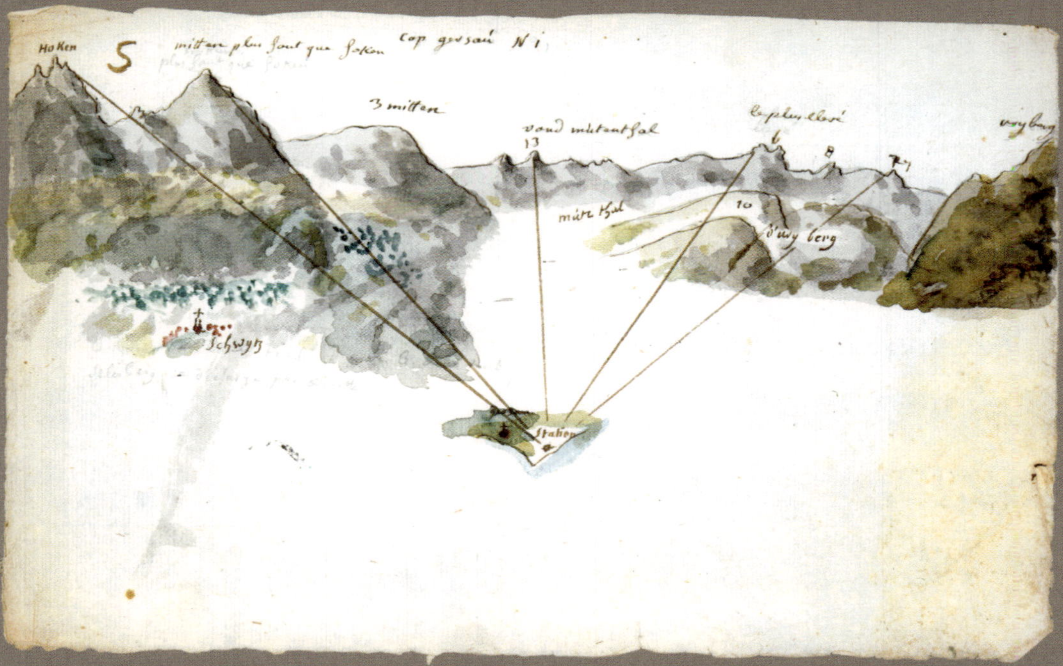


8 *cap gersau N i*; the location of Schwyz is incorrect. Watercolored drawing in pencil and India ink, ink inscription (21 × 34 cm)
Illustration: Zentral- und Hochschulbibliothek, Lucerne

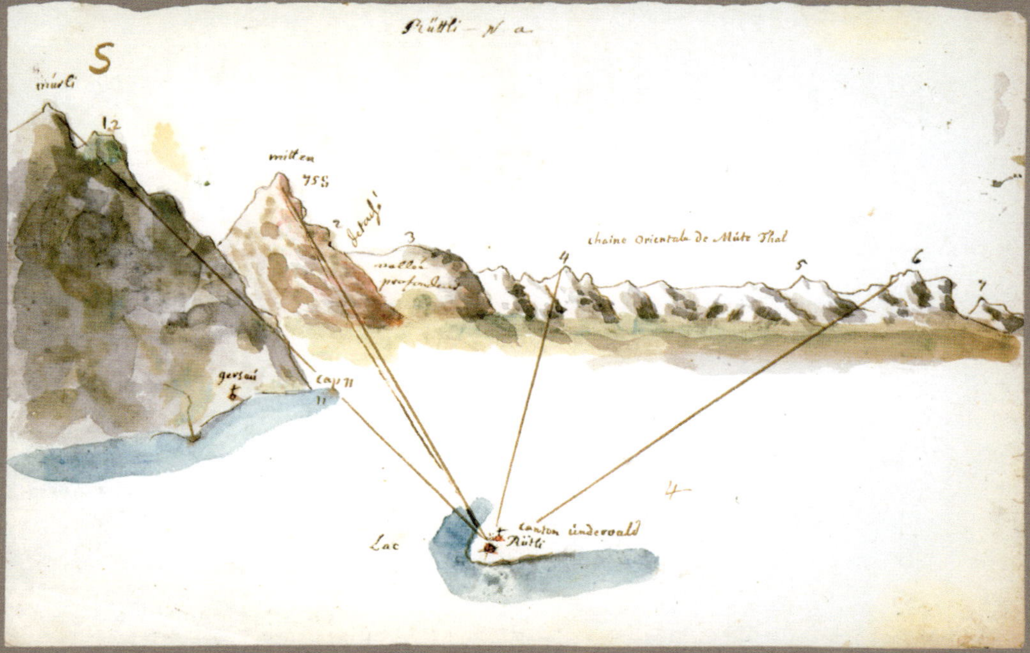


9 *Rüttli – IV a*; the location is not Rütli but Ridli near Beckenried.
Watercolored drawing in pencil and India ink, ink inscription (20.5 × 31,5 cm)
Illustration: Zentral- und Hochschulbibliothek, Lucerne

10 *paroisse brunnen N° 4, ingelbol*; Haken is the old name for the Mythen.
Watercolored drawing in pencil and India ink, ink inscription (21 × 34 cm)
Illustration: Zentral- und Hochschulbibliothek, Lucerne

11 The *Relief der Urschweiz* from the north. Hand-colored outline etching by Christian von Mechel, 1786
Illustration: Archiv Gletschergarten Luzern

## Hunters and Collectors:

# CURIOSITY AND AMBITION

The development of the European tree nursery is closely linked with the great voyages of discovery and the history of colonialism. Adventurous journeys around the globe and conquests of land resulted in the discovery of numerous plants that significantly enriched Europe's flora, which had been particularly impoverished by the continent's glacial periods. Moreover, exotic plants were regarded as a new, previously unknown manifestation of divine power and were coveted by many, not only physicians and botanists. These plants were passionately collected and displayed in nature cabinets, arboretums, greenhouses and gardens. Seeds, fruits and even living plants were brought from abroad and cultivated in the greenhouses of botanical gardens and small tree nurseries. The nineteenth century was a time of extremely intensive acquisition of and trade in new plants. Apart from propagation, the cultivation of new varieties by means of constantly improving techniques became a central activity of ornamental tree nurseries.

"Le Dirigeable," canopy expedition, French Guiana, 1996
Photo: Roman Kaiser, Givaudan Schweiz AG

# THE CONQUEST OF FLORISTIC REALMS

## HOLARCTIC PALEOTROPIC NEOTROPIC CAPE AUSTRALIAN ARCTIC

**European plant hunting from the sixteenth until the middle of the twentieth century basically involved plant collectors from Central Europe advancing into other floristic regions and—unsurprisingly—finding new plants. Rich pickings were to be expected given that Central Europe is certainly not a "hot spot" in terms of biodiversity. Of the 250,000 flowering plant species found throughout the world only 2500 occur in Germany, Austria and Switzerland, just one percent of the world's flora.**

Essay by Heinz Schneider

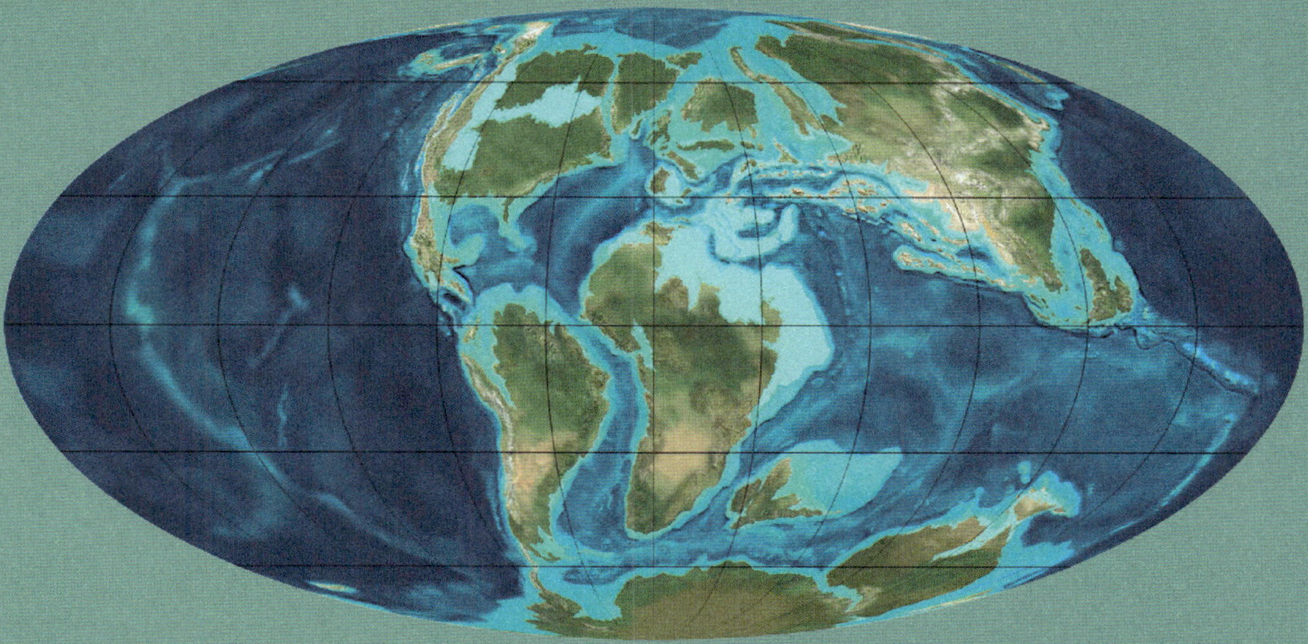

1

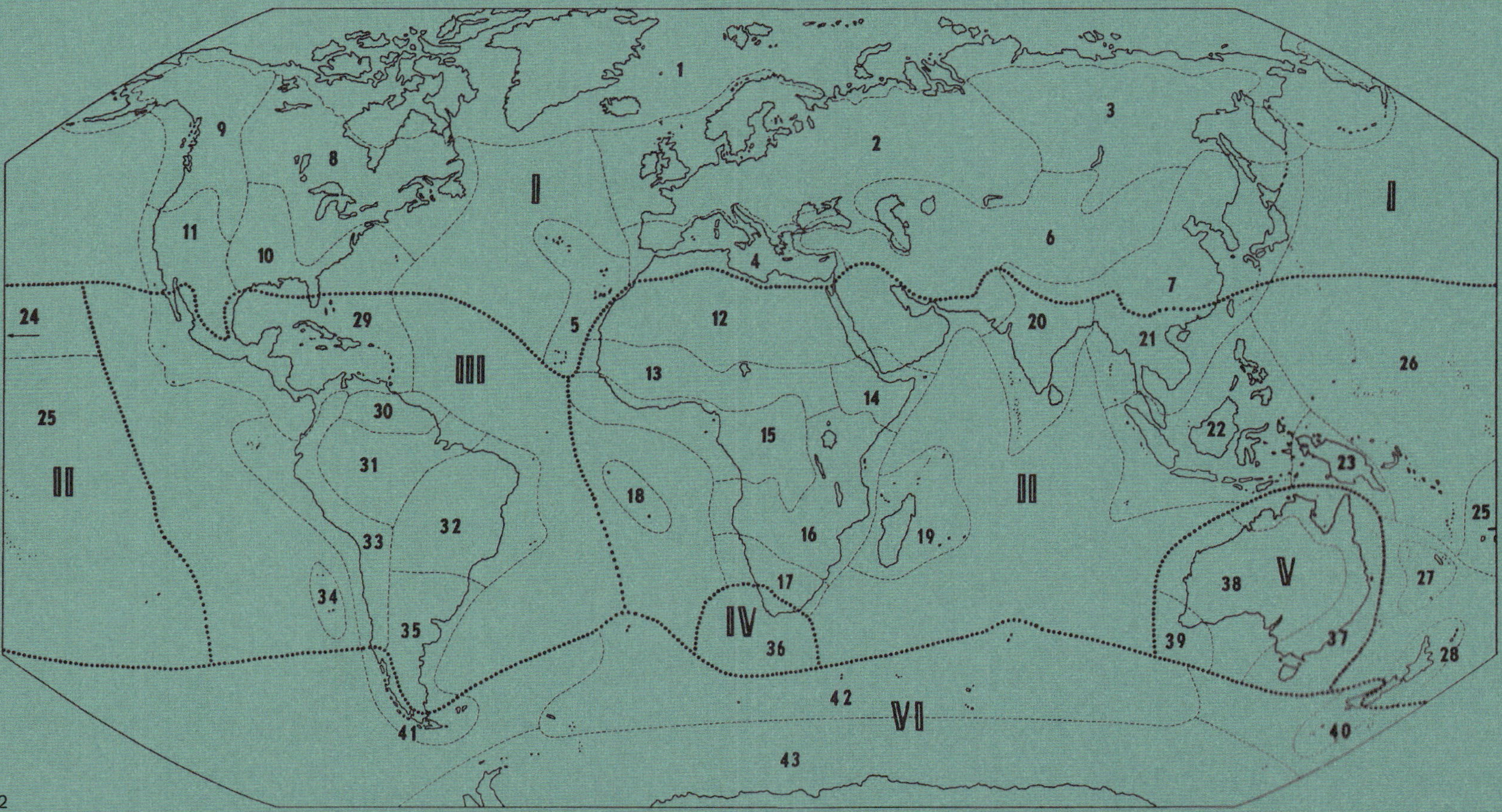


2

1 Plate tectonics, location of land masses at the time of the emergence of flowering plants (Albian, uppermost Lower Cretaceous, 105 million years ago)
Illustration: Ron Blakey, 2009

2 Overview of the Earth's floristic realms and floristic regions
Floristic regions:
I Holarctic
II Paleotropic
III Neotropic
IV Cape
V Australian
VI Arctic
Illustration: based on Adolf Engler, *Syllabus der Pflanzenfamilien*, Borntraeger: Berlin, 1964

| Year | Discoverer/collector | Region | Plants | Floristic region |
|---|---|---|---|---|
| 1519 | Hernán Cortés | Mexico | *Solanum lycopersicum* | 29 |
| 1555 | Konrad Gesner | Pilatus/Switzerland | *Carlina, Doronicum, Gentiana, Pinguicula, Saxifraga, Veratrum* | 2 |
| 1576 | Carolus Clusius | Lisbon | *Dracaena draco* | 4/5 |
| 1595 | Giovanni Pona | Monte Baldo/Italy | *Papaver alpinum* | 2 |
| 1773/4 | Francis Masson | South Africa | *Strelitzia reginae, Encephalartos altensteinii* | 36 |
| 1791–1795 | Archibald Menzies | Expedition to South America and Australia | *Araucaria araucana* (Chile), *Cephalotus follicularis* (Australia) | 41, 39 |
| 1799–1804 | Alexander von Humboldt, Aimé Bonpland | Central and South America | *Dahlia* | 29 |
| vor 1816 | Thaddäus Haenke | South America | *Victoria amazonica, Puya raimondii* | 31–33 |
| 1815–1818 | Adelbert von Chamisso | South Seas | *Eschscholzia californica* | 11 |
| 1823–1829 | Philipp Franz von Siebold | Japan | Numerous Japanese plant species, hydrangeas | 7 |
| 1823–1834 | David Douglas | New England | *Pseudotsuga menziesii, Mahonia aquifolium, Lupinus polyphyllus, Abies grandis, A. procera* | 8 |
| 1887–1941 | Carl Albert Purpus | Canada, USA, Mexico | Cactaceae, *Ceanothus, Cornus, Ilex, Kalmia, Paxistima, Penstemon* | 11, 29 |

3

4

3 Several plant collectors, their botanically or horticulturally important discoveries and the relevant floristic regions

Table: based on Adolf Engler, *Syllabus der Pflanzenfamilien*, Borntraeger: Berlin, 1964

4 The state of knowledge of flora in 1979 (based on David G. Frodin, *Guide to Standard Floras of the World*, 1981). The darker the area, the more extensive the knowledge of its flora.

Illustration: based on David G. Frodin, *Guide to Standard Floras of the World*, Cambridge University Press: Cambridge, 2001

## THE HUNDRED-MILLION-YEAR EVOLUTION OF FLOWERING PLANTS

Flowering plants constitute one of the indispensible biological foundations of our existence and comprise some 250,000 species worldwide. The evolution of this immense diversity required a period of time equivalent to more than one million consecutive human lives: a dimension that is almost unimaginable. When the first flowering plants appeared around one hundred million years ago, in the middle of the Cretaceous period, the planet looked very different from the way it does today. Dinosaurs were the dominant animals, ferns and conifers the dominant plants, and the location of the continents differed greatly from where they are found now. The disintegration of the southern continent of Gondwana, which had already begun in the Jurassic period, was continuing, and the first fossilized flowering plants date back to the time when South America and Africa separated from one another (fig. 1). We can conclude that the origins of flowering plants go back to a phase in which Gondwana was still intact to some extent since plant families exist today that exhibit a classic Gondwana distribution. The Proteaceae plant family is a particularly well-known example. While Proteaceae certainly constitute a family, they have developed differently in their three main areas of distribution, viz., Australia, South Africa and South America.

The formation of the earth's surface, driven by plate tectonics over the last hundred million years, is a decidedly complex process, particularly in the region comprising Europe, the Mediterranean, North Africa and Asia Minor. It is difficult to describe in words when and where the numerous waterways and land bridges opened and closed that were decisive for the dissemination of plants. Many geography textbooks provide maps that visually represent this long process of development. The most instructive tools for beginners in this field are the animated maps that are increasingly being made available on line (these can be found on YouTube, for example, under the keywords plate tectonics, continental drift, Scotese, Ron Blakey).

However, the evolution of flowering plants is not only a product of shifts in the continental land masses but also a climatic history alternating between constant phases, fluctuations and abrupt changes. For instance, a little more than five million years ago the Mediterranean almost completely dried up. As a result, for a time plant migration routes were open that are now blocked.

All these processes have left traces and contributed to today's complex patterns of plant distribution.

## FLORISTIC REALMS

The Danish botanist Joakim F. Schouw's Fundamentals of General Plant Geography, which was published in Danish in 1822 and in German the following year, constitutes an early attempt to map and comprehend these patterns. Two later seminal German works by the botanists Adolf Engler *(Versuch einer Entwicklungsgeschichte der Pflanzenwelt,* 1879; A Tentative Developmental History of the Plant World) and Ludwig Diels (*Pflanzengeographie,* 1908; Plant Geography) developed the concepts of floristic realms and floristic regions that are still current today. In simple terms, floristic realms are characterized by distinct plant populations whereas floristic regions exhibit different as well as a range of shared elements. Endemics, that is, species restricted to a very limited area of distribution, play a particularly important role in these distributive classifications. The extensive synopsis by the Russian-Armenian botanist Armen Takhtajan (*Floristic Regions of the World,* 1986) and *Biogeography* by C. Barry Cox and Peter D. Moore (2005) also build on these fundamental concepts. Fig. 2 shows Engler's concept in an illustration from 1964, which delineates six floristic realms and forty-three floristic regions.

## PLANT HUNTERS

The modern interest in the plant world dates back to the sixteenth century and initially emerged among circles interested in botany and gardens in Italy, where the herbarium technique was invented and the first botanical gardens established (in a number of cities, including Padua, Mantua and Bologna). This period also saw the start of the great voyages of discovery. Already Columbus's travels were bringing an influx of plants from the New World. From around 1540 a wealth of scientific publications began to appear that sought to name and classify the new plants. A general ignorance of plant geography soon gave rise to a phenomenon that was to hamper botany for a long time to come and that involved the vain attempt to find among the very different flora of Central Europe the Mediterranean plants named by ancient authors like Theophrastus (regions 2 and 4 in fig. 2).

This is indicative of a more general state of affairs. European plant hunting from the sixteenth until the middle of the twentieth century basically involved plant collectors from Central Europe (region 2) advancing into other floristic regions and—unsurprisingly—finding new plants. Rich pickings were to be expected given that Central Europe is certainly not a "hot spot" in terms of biodiversity. Of the 250,000 flowering plant species found throughout the world only 2500 occur in Germany, Austria and Switzerland, just one percent of the world's flora.

The history of the discovery and importation of new plants can thus be structured and represented not only in episodic, biographical, chronological, national, horticultural and systematic terms but also with reference to floristic regions. Fig. 3 lists several prominent examples together with the numbers of the plant regions depicted in fig. 2. It goes without saying that a range of diverse factors has resulted in more intensive research in some areas than others. Fig. 3 shows the state of regional floristic knowledge. Even though a number of gaps have been filled in since 1979, we are still a long way from achieving a uniform degree of knowledge across all regions.

## GLOBAL AWARENESS OF NATURE CONSERVATION

The entire modern period, extending from the early voyages of discovery to the transformation of our awareness of nature and the environment in the seventies and eighties, could be summarized as the age of the plant hunters. Seen against the background of our current degree of mobility, the erstwhile "heroic exploits" of innumerable collectors, discoverers and researchers, who frequently took great risks, have often been and still are glorified, particularly in the British and American cultural sphere (a good example is *Flora mirabilis* by Catherine H. Howell, published in 2009). However, in most circles of botanical experts the patriotic viewpoint has now been replaced by an awareness of global responsibility. Many of today's practitioners of horticulture would surely agree with the sentiments expressed by Stefan Schneckenburger in 2001 when writing about the plant collector Albert Purpus (1851–1941): "It is doubtless a good thing that the age is now past in which plant hunters and botanists collected in great quantities. A range of laws and regulations relating to nature conservancy, the Washington Convention on International Trade in Endangered Species (CITES) and biodiversity conventions are, on the one hand, providing urgently needed protection for natural environments and individual species and, on the other, protecting the interests of countries in the use of their own natural resources. Just as it would be a mistake to condemn past collectors from a present-day perspective, we would also be in error if we were to cite their behavior as a standard for the twenty-first century at a time when nature is being wantonly sold off on a worldwide scale. Rather than regarding these plant hunters as a paradigm, we should see them as children of their day and age, when they collected the bounties of a seemingly inexhaustible natural environment, at times under extremely harsh conditions and economic constraints."

# TRADITIONAL BRITISH

## COLLECTING AND CULTIVATING

**The naturalization of exotic trees in gardens and parks, forests and cities has a long tradition in Europe that stretches back to antiquity. In England, the land of plant hunters, the landscape offers a plethora of foreign and extravagant trees. Since the settlement of Central Europe new plants have been introduced through the immigration of people from other countries. Species that were brought in prior to the fifteenth century are referred to as archeophytes, while those that came later and are partly naturalized are called neophytes.**

Photo series by Dominique Ghiggi

1

According to a 1995 study published by Ingo Kowarik, a professor of plant ecology at the Berlin Institute of Technology, 220 species of woody plants in Europe were indigenous while 3150 had arrived from elsewhere over the centuries. Particularly in the last two hundred years, European flora has undergone fundamental changes. During this period numerous plant species, including many tree species, have been introduced to Europe under the most hazardous conditions. Without the expeditions undertaken by numerous plant collectors, our plant world would be a great deal poorer.

During the nineteenth century the English were particularly active in acquiring foreign plants. From around 1850 onwards, an enormous increase in the number of woody plants can be observed. They are described as sorts, varieties, hybrids, anomalies, bastards and variations. The larger the area in which a species naturally occurs, the more variations exist and the more varieties can be bred. For instance, the range of the maple lies within the temperate zone of the northern hemisphere and stretches from America to East Asia, as can clearly be seen on a map. Today the maple is represented in practically every tree-nursery catalogue throughout the world in a diverse assortment of varieties from many different regions.

In the nineteenth century the English firm Veitch and Sons, also known as Veitch Nurseries, was probably the largest family-run tree nursery in Europe. The firm's business model owed its success in part to the policy of employing its own plant hunters, who collected exclusively for this one tree nursery. Between 1840 and 1910 the firm sent out twenty-two plants hunters. By the outbreak of World War I, the Veitch tree nursery had introduced 1281 plants into cultivation that were previously unknown or newly bred varieties, including 232 orchid species.

The "Traditional British" photo series shows individual examples of trees from the Sir Harold Hillier Gardens and Arboretum near Romsey in the southern English county of Hampshire. The arboretum was founded as a tree nursery in 1953 on a one-hectare plot. Some of the trees were collected by Sir Harold, who is since deceased, over a thirty-year period in China and Japan and subsequently planted around the Victorian farmhouse. Others were purchased by botanical gardens and well-known plant collectors. All these species have been used to produce new varieties in the conservatory; they have later been shifted to the arboretum for display. Many of them have now become indigenous to the British Isles and are referred to as traditional British.

1 *Robinia pseudoacacia* "Coluteoides" (black locust)
2 *Metasequoia glyptostroboides* (dawn redwood)
3 *Carpinus betulus* "Fastigiata" (European hornbeam)

2

3

4

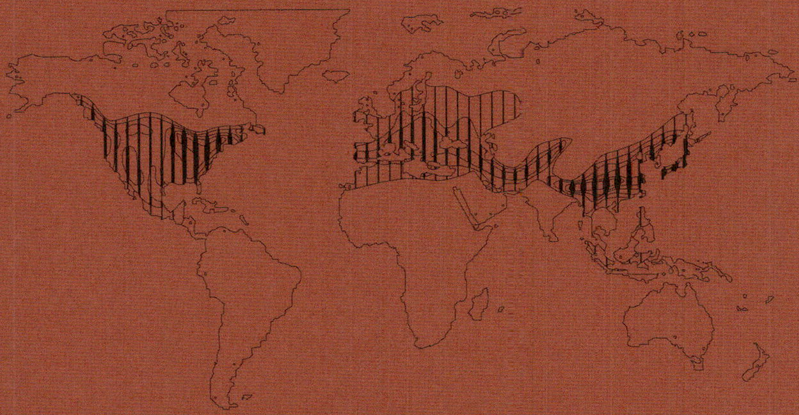

When we observe the form and location of the areas colonized by different species in Europe and the rest of the world, it becomes clear that these areas lie in different climatic zones—some species are found in oceanic zones, while others congregate in continental or tropical zones. These differences are connected with the very specific requirements of species. It is therefore understandable that related species within the same genus that are closely related in genetic terms generally exhibit similar dispersal tendencies.

In the case of maple species (genus Acer), two areas of origin, or genetic centers, have been identified, one in eastern North America and the other in Southeast Asia. In historical terms this is a consequence of the glacial period. The overall area corresponds to the family of the Aceraceae, which is found through out the temperate zone of the Northern Hemisphere but is restricted to mountain areas in the tropics.

Illustration: based on Heinrich Walter, *Allgemeine Geobotanik*, UTB: Stuttgart, 1986

4 *Eucalyptus dalrympleana* (white mountain gum)
5 *Lithocarpus henryi* (Henry's stone oak)
6 *Picea breweriana* (brewer spruce)
7 *Magnolia campbellii* 'Darjeeling" x *M. denudata* (Cambell's magnolia)

5

6

# DARWIN IN SWITZERLAND

**Charles Darwin, the preeminent naturalist and founder of the theory of evolution, also had ties to Swiss scientists. And one of them, an important plant researcher, could have even closed the biggest gap in the theory of evolution.**

Aperçu by Christoph Keller

Before Darwin, there were other researchers dealing with questions relating to evolution; in fact, they were evolutionary biologists *avant la lettre.* One of them was Johann Jakob Scheuchzer (1672–1733), originally a doctor in Zurich, who began his career as a naturalist in 1695 with an appointment as Director of the Zurich Kunst- und Naturalienkammer (Cabinet of Artifacts and Curiosities) and its wide-ranging contents. Surrounded by a collection of natural finds that was extensive even for its time, Scheuchzer was inspired to devote all his energy from then on to the exploration of his home country.

For twenty years his travels took him to the farthermost corners of Switzerland; he collected, annotated and systematized the finds he made, which consisted primarily of many varieties of petrifications. Scheuchzer, however, influenced by the scientific spirit of the Renaissance, also went to great lengths to dispel some of the deep-seated myths held by the population of the time. He disproved, for example, the view that the storms on Lake Pilatus in the canton of Lucerne were caused by demons disturbed by people or by objects thrown into the lake. "I myself," he wrote in 1714, "in the presence of herdsmen, who laugh at these fables, have thrown stones, wood and other objects into this pond on more than one occasion, without harm or danger."

The supernatural and the laws of nature—like Charles Darwin a good century later, Scheuchzer was interested in discovering what it is in nature that is actually determined by physics or biology and what is determined by God's hand. Scheuchzer, who today is considered the founder of paleobotany, did more than study fossils and petrified plants. In his comprehensive work *Physica Sacra oder Geheiligte Natur-Wissenschaft* (Physica Sacra or Sacred Natural Science), he attempted nothing short of the scientific proof of the existence of God by, among other things, showing that some of the stories of the Bible, the Great Flood for example, did in fact take place.

With this approach, however, the Zurich naturalist fell out of favor with the Swiss—they refused to print the *Physica Sacra.* Consequently, the four folio volumes, with a total of 2098 pages and 750 elaborate copperplate engravings, were published in Augsburg beginning in 1731, with the final volume being published posthumously in 1735. Yet despite the resistance he faced, Scheuchzer was the pioneer of this "natural science," and with his extensive collections of fossils and petrifications, he was an inspiration for many who followed in the quest to discover where we come from. Among them, for example, was the Genevan zoologist Charles Bonnet, who already in the eighteenth century had established a step-ladder model of all "natural things"—corals and fungi at the very bottom, humans at the very top. It was a notion of evolution well before Darwin's time. Specifically, Bonnet surmised that there must be a kind of family tree in evolution, a "perpetual and more or less slow-moving progress of all species towards greater perfection."

But for whatever the reason, Bonnet hesitated to pursue his idea with the required perseverance—he hesitated, as did other Swiss scientists. Take, for example, the botanist Oswald Heer from Saint Gall, a profound expert on Alpine flora who corresponded personally with Charles Darwin, carrying out a lively exchange with the preeminent Englishman; despite this, in the end he still dismissed the latter's ideas. Also vehemently opposed to Darwin when it came to evolution was the Fribourg glaciologist and naturalist Louis Agassiz, who earned great merit in the study of the Ice Ages. Instead, he was a supporter of polygenesis, the idea that humans descend from completely different sources, that blacks and whites therefore do not stem from a common ancestor. Agassiz, who was transformed into a racist during a stay in the United States and who classified blacks as "servile and groveling" and Mongols as "sly, devious and cowardly," spent the rest of his life espousing a disquieting racial ideology that blinded his scientific view of evolution. Charles Darwin, it is no wonder, did not like Louis Agassiz.

In the botanist Carl Wilhelm von Nägeli (1817–1891), Charles Darwin found another intellectual counterpart altogether. Nägeli, a student of Oswald Heer's, took on a professorship of botany at the University of Zurich as early as 1849. He then moved to Freiburg im Breisgau, then back to Zurich to the ETH, before finally taking a teaching position in Munich in 1857. Nägeli studied chromosomes, fungi, microscopy, in other words, a wide-ranging field. At the heart of his research, however, was always the problem of evolution; in 1865 his first book, *Entstehung und Begriff der Naturhistorischen Art* (Origin and Concept of Natural Historical Species), was published.

On June 12, 1866, Nägeli received a letter from Charles Darwin in which the great naturalist wrote, "I have just finished reading your work *Origin and Concept,* and it interested me so much that I have taken it to be translated into English." Darwin's interest in Nägeli's findings is not surprising for in his work the Swiss botanist deals intensively with the question of whether, in addition to what Darwin called the "natural selection" of species, there is also something like an "inner" mechanism that drives the development of species. And this quest for an "inner" law of evolution occupied Darwin as well—both of them, Darwin and Nägeli, suspected that there must be something akin to "mechanics" that controlled the transfer of characteristics from one generation to the next. Both were grapling with the mechanism of hereditary transmission, which they didn't understand; both were dealing with the laws of genetics.

And yet… At the time of Nägeli and Darwin's correspondence, one person had not only recognized the basic laws of genetics, he had also proven them through experimentation, namely, the Augustinian monk Gregor Mendel, who in 1866 had sent his paper on hereditary mechanisms in peas to Nägeli with the words "the experiments were carried out on different types of peas and led to the outcome that the hybrids form very peculiar sequences." These "peculiar sequences" represented precisely what Charles Darwin and Carl Wilhelm von Nägeli surmised, i.e., that there must be certain physical laws at work in the process of hereditary transmission.

Unfortunately though, Nägeli did not take the monk from Brünn seriously, not even later, despite the fact that Mendel sent him treatise after treatise. Nägeli was dismissive, he put him off, he left his letters unanswered—for it was unfathomable to our learned scientist that a man of the church could have possibly been able to unravel the mystery of heredity.

In retrospect, we can speculate about what would have happened if the great botanist Nägeli had recognized the significance of Mendel's findings. He would have likely incorporated them into one of his papers or shared them with Darwin in his correspondences with him. Darwin would have then had to correct his theory of selective breeding, taking into consideration that not only environmental factors and adaptation to these factors lead to changes within a species, but instead that there are complicated hereditary mechanisms at work. These in turn result in the fact that characteristics do not simply disappear (for example, by preventing the reproduction of the carriers of these characteristics), but rather that these traits can still remain in effect generations later. Given this insight, the racist theories propagated in the twentieth century might not have been able to circulate as widely as they did, and it would not have been possible to indiscriminately apply the idea of "selective breeding" to human beings. Buttressed by Darwin's authority, the understanding of hereditary transmission would have come much earlier: heredity as a manifold, complex and ungovernable process that cannot be simply suspended.

It is also likely that there would have been more rapid advances in plant breeding as well. It would not have taken until 1900—when the botanist Carl Correns, the geneticist and botanist Erich Tschermak and the plant physiologist Hugo de Vries rediscovered Mendel's Laws—for geneticists to realize that heredity is a complex game that is difficult to control, a puzzle that can result in unforeseen things like mutations or, by the same measure, homogeneous, outwardly identical offspring. The great advances in experimental research made by a Joseph Muller with his mutation research around 1907 could have been made much earlier as well. Or, to quote the great geneticist Adolf Portmann, the departure from a world of "thinking in analogies, in pictures" and from a way of perceiving the world "in grand imaginations" would have occurred much earlier. And as for the ignorant eugenicists and racial hygienists, perhaps their ideas would have fallen on less fertile ground, if only Carl Wilhelm von Nägeli had taken the scientific work of an Augustinian monk more seriously

This article is based on a report the author did in 2009 for the Swiss radio broadcaster DRS 2.

1

# RHODODENDRON MANIA

**A century and a half after the period of widespread rhododendron mania in England, the Belgian gardener Koen van de Moortel spent ten years photographing an enormous number of flowering rhododendron varieties in his country's most famous parks and gardens. The varieties of the rhododendron exhibit differences as diverse as its habitats, which range from coasts to high mountains and from tropical rainforests to the subpolar tundra.**

Photo series by Koen van de Moortel

The Kalmthout and Hemelrijk arboretums located north of Antwerp were renowned far beyond the borders of Belgium for their extraordinary collections of often rare plants, which Jelena and Robert de Belder collected from all over the world. The property in Kalmthout was originally a tree nursery, which was managed in 1856 by the renowned tree grower Charles van Geert and later run by Antoine Kort. The latter bred many rhododendron varieties, which he planted between conifers in the sandy soil of the tree nursery. The tree nursery was closed during World War I. It was only in 1952 that the brothers George and Robert de Belder purchased a piece of the overgrown land and began to restore it. In 1954 they were joined by Jelena Kovacic, who later became Robert's wife and remained a passionate and tireless plant collector and breeder until her death in 2003. In 1979, thanks to Jelena's inspiration, Philippe de Spoelberch established an arboretum as part of the Wespelaar Park, constructed during the nineteenth century in the English landscape style.

Rhododendron varieties from the Kalmthout, Hemelrijk and Wespelaar arboretums in Belgium.

1 *Azalea* "Gloire de Belgique"
2 *Rhododendron odoratum*
3 *Rhododendron yakushimanum*
4 *Azalea* "Barbecue"
5 *Rhododendron yakushimanum* "Hydon Dawn"
6 *Rhododendron yakushimanum* "Golden Torch"
7 *Azalea* "Barbecue"
8 *Azalea* "Goldlack"
9 *Azalea* "Chocolate Ice"
10 *Rhododendron* "Albatross x Lodaurie"
11 *Rhododendron* "Blaney's Blue"
12 *Rhododendron* "Furnivall's Daughter"

2

3

4

5

6

7

8

9

10

11

12

# SCENT SEEKER

## TAKEN FROM THE TRAVEL DIARY WRITTEN BY ROMAN KAISER

**Roman Kaiser is one of the best-known fragrance researchers in the world. After studying chemistry, he soon became an excellent botanist as well. He has always devoted himself to the world of natural scents, so it was only fitting that plants, the main natural source of scents, would become his second great passion. By studying plant scents he discovered many new scent molecules for the perfume industry. In order to do so, however, he does not have to resort to exploiting the flora, as the heroic plant hunters of old once did. At the Swiss company Givaudan, he developed a system that allows him to capture plant scents in a non-destructive way. Again and again his affinity to fragrances and to the living natural habitat takes him to distant lands to make new discoveries. Over the past 10 years he has studied the scents of hundreds of highly endangered plant species from all over the world.**

Introduction by Dominique Ghiggi
Photographs by Roman Kaiser, Givaudan Schweiz AG

Until the middle of the last century, the only source for the raw materials used in perfumery were extracts from scented flowers or other parts of plants and, to a lesser extent, animal secretions. It is not surprising then that with the development of organic chemistry, scientists began to examine the composition of these so-called essential oils and related natural extracts. As a result of this ongoing research activity, the perfumers now have at their disposal not only some five hundred regularly used natural products for their creations, but at least twice as many synthetic fragrance compounds that, in one way or another, were derived from such natural products. In this context, a research team from Givaudan, the world's largest manufacturer of flavors and fragrances, investigated over the past thirty years the scents of 2500 individual plant species by using the so-called headspace technology, which makes it possible to capture the fragrance of individual flowers or plants in a quality as perceived by the human nose and without destroying the plants themselves in any way.

*"Nature has always set the standard for our olfactory judgments and, therefore, it is only logical, even a must, to search in nature for new scent molecules and new scent concepts and to use them as leads in fragrance research."*

Roman Kaiser

## OLFACTORY SCENARIOS

However, as Givaudan has shown, this nondestructive approach to trapping, investigating, and reconstructing natural scents is not only designed for studying of specific flower, herb, fruit, and wood scents, but can also be applied to the investigation of entire olfactory "scenarios" perceptible in a particular environment such as a Scandinavian sauna, a maquis biotope on the Ligurian coast or a forest biotope at the incomparable Sequoia National Park in California. It is well understood, however, that the absolute amount of fragrant material in the air of such scented surroundings is almost never sufficient to retrieve reasonable samples just by drawing the air through an adsorption trap. The entire scenario has to be broken down into its individual scent-contributing building blocks, which can then be studied and subsequently reconstituted by the established procedures. Finally, the whole olfactory scenery may be reconstituted by recombining the individual building blocks. Givaudan has recently gone from reconstructing individual concrete fragrances to reconstructing entire olfactory scenarios (fragrance landscapes). This development began in 1980 with the wish to recreate the characteristic fragrance that typically comes about when sauna-goers in Scandinavian countries cool down by slapping themselves with birch tree branches. Other olfactory scenarios followed, including the typical smell of Sequoia National Park or the olfactory impression of a tobacco shop, to name just a few. As a technical aside it should be mentioned that it normally does not suffice to merely capture and analyze the air of a fragrance scenario, as the concentration of the individual components contained therein is usually far too low. Instead, the scenario must be analyzed in its individual parts and subsequently reconstructed. [1]

## THE RAINFOREST AS OLFACTORY TREASURY

It is estimated that roughly eighty to ninety percent of all plant, animal and fungus species are to be found in the rainforests, which currently make up thirteen percent of the earth's surface. According to another estimate, seventy to eighty percent of those species—in other words, approximately sixty percent of the planet's entire biodiversity—inhabit, for ecological reasons, the treetop regions of these forests, the so-called canopy. This zone, located forty meters or more above the forest floor, constitutes one of the least explored biospheres on earth. Of course it was the dream of many biologists and botanists to develop suitable means to gain access to this world. As has been shown in television documentaries or articles in magazines

such as GEO, National Geographic or the New York Times Magazine, researchers already have various highly developed systems at their disposal that allow the exploration of the secrets of the canopy.

## TO THE CANOPY BY DIRIGIBLE

The system which arguably gets closest to nature and might also be the most effective has been developed by a team led by Professor Francis Hallé of the Institute of Tropical Botany at the University of Montpellier. It consists of the following three main components: first, a zeppelinlike dirigible measuring fifty-one meters in length and twenty meters in height, with a volume of 8.5 million liters ("Le Dirigeable"); it is additionally equipped with a diesel engine for fine maneuvering. The balloon can carry a load of 750 kilograms, making it the largest vehicle of its kind in the world. Secondly, there is a triangular platform (luge or skimmer), the sides of which measure 5.5 meters in length. It is suspended approximately ten meters below the balloon, so that an experienced pilot can maneuver it accurately towards the trees. And thirdly, a hexagonal platform with an area of six hundred square meters which can be placed onto the treetops of the rainforest at a height of thirty to fifty meters. This platform can be disengaged from the dirigible for stationary studies over longer periods of time.

## BACK INTO THE TREES

After this system had proven itself on three test expeditions, it was decided to make it accessible to the scientific community as well as interested parties from the industry. As a result, ProNatura International, a Paris-based, globally active nonprofit rainforest preservation group, contacted Givaudan under the reasonable assumption that new natural scents could be discovered within the rainforest canopy. After the company was guaranteed exclusivity within the fragrance and flavor industry as well as the copyright for a film project, the management signed the contract. Givaudan thereby became the first company in the business to take part in such an endeavor. For logistical, scientific, ecological and security-related reasons, an area of the rainforest of Lower Amazonia belonging to French Guiana was chosen as the research destination.

This spectacular opportunity to study a largely unexplored biosphere containing such an unparalleled degree of diversity, from an olfactory standpoint, nicely dovetailed with the company's idea of studying and reconstructing entire olfactory "scenarios" perceived in a particular environment as well as new individual natural scents.

Participants in the mission were the fragrance chemist Dr. Roman Kaiser, the accomplished fragrance researcher Kent Lombard and Jean Guichard, creator of many famous fragrances. The explorations in the canopy, the understory, the forest floor and the adjacent savannas were documented by a film team led by Yves Bourgeois. It was turned into the documentary *A New Scent Trek Adventure, Expedition Canopy* 1996.

1 An introductory article on this topic by Dr. Roman Kaiser was published in: *Perfumer & Flavorist*, Vol. 22, 1997, pp. 7–18.

The first mission was undertaken by Roman Kaiser and Kent Lombard. A film team led by Yves Bourgeois documented their explorations in the canopy, the understory, the forest floor and the adjacent savannas.

Previous double page:
"Le Dirigeable," a zeppelinlike dirigible measuring fifty-one meters in length and twenty meters in height, with a volume of 8.5 million liters and equipped with a diesel motor. It was developed by a team led by Professor Francis Hallé of the Institute of Tropical Botany at the University of Montpellier.

Following double page:
discovery of an orange-red flower of the genus Noranthea (Marcgraviaceae) during a research flight

Photo on the previous double page and following dirigible photos: Philippe Schaff, photographer, Paris

**FRENCH GUIANA, FALL 1996**
On September 29, we met with the film crew at the Novotel in Cayenne, one of the five biggest hotels in French Guiana. The next morning, after spending a final night in an urban environment, we took the N1 (properly numbered, despite the fact that it is the *Departement's* only highway) towards Sinnamary. A hundred meters past kilometer marker 101, we found, just as described, a small sign with the abbreviation CIRAD pointing into the forest. Only fifty meters further, the scene looked just like a European would imagine a rainforest: on both sides of the reddish dirt road, bushes, overgrown with lianas, soon giving way to an Amazonian type of forest; in the trees, shrieking monkeys and colorful birds, bright blue morpho butterflies; and from deep within the forest, the typical call of the screaming phia bird, here known as vociferans, which perhaps characterizes Amazonia like no other birdcall. It was to be our faithful companion over the next fourteen days. At 2:30, we finally reached the clearing where our camp was located; it consisted of three covered shelters with rectangular wooden floors. Two of these shelters were furnished with hammocks, in which people were taking their siesta; the third contained a long wooden table, which still bore the traces of an extensive lunch. As we would soon realize, we had, immediately after our arrival, been confronted with two essential ground rules that enable people to handle the strains of such a mission in the heart of the tropics: eat and drink in abundance, and comply with the law of the siesta. At 3:30, the camp came alive as the head of the mission, Professor Francis Hallé, greeted us and introduced his extraordinary team: Dany Cleyet-Marrel, designer and pilot of the dirigible, in whom we would place our full trust over the following two weeks; Gil Ebersold (how nice the ring of the French version of this Bernese name!), architect and designer of the "Radeau des Cimes," the detachable platform; Jean, the Provençal copilot, who took off his straw hat only to sleep, and who had a pertinent dictum for every situation; François, who was responsible for all administrative affairs and always looked out for our well-being; and finally the youngest member of our team, Laurant, from the deepest Midi, strong as a lion and an asset in any situation.

We then proceeded to the dirigible's launching and landing pad, a forty-by-seventy-meter clearing created during the World War II, from where the enormous logs of giant trees were formerly transported out of the rainforest. The first mission was thus taking place in an area that had once been witness to destructive human contact. This area was meticulously cleared of the underbrush that had begun encroaching on the white sand again, and then covered with a giant plastic tarp to prevent any damage to the sensitive skin of the dirigible or to the technical equipment, particularly the burners. From the head of the mission to the hired hands, everyone worked together shoulder to shoulder, the sweat flowing in rivulets—of course their water supply had to be replenished. But the look on the faces of all those involved was one of good-natured anticipation; everyone felt that something unique was about to occur. Francis estimated that preparations would take at least two more days and proposed to give us greenhorns an introduction to the surrounding forest and the nearby savanna in the meantime. Just half an hour later we were among the giants of the rainforest, lianas and vines hanging and climbing in all directions, with no apparent end or beginning.

**RAINFOREST GENTIANS**
Epiphytes along the tree trunks, in this case mainly Araceae and Bromeliaceae; where the forest is less dense, young palm trees stretching their fronds towards the light; leaf-cutting ants carrying their giant loads into underground nests; everywhere you look, fungi on rotting wood, and in between, brown leaves and toads in perfect camouflage among the leaves; then three deep-blue blossoms completely devoid of green, typical saprophytes belonging to the family of gentian plants and exuding an intense, refreshing rose scent. Luckily I was carrying the necessary equipment in my backpack that allowed me to take the first fragrance sample, *Voyria caerulea* FG6. The following two hours necessary for collecting the scent were used for a crash-course in "tropical biology." Francis explained to us the basic principles of tropical rainforest architecture and, using the example of ant colonies, the incredible complexity of symbiotic systems. At one spot an old, giant tree had fallen, creating a lane in the canopy that allowed the sunlight to reach the ground again: here the all-important influence of light was strikingly evident.

In the stifling heat, breathing was like inhaling steam. Suddenly a quiet drumming sound began and rapidly escalated; a minute later, we were caught in our first afternoon tropical rainstorm, the intensity of which almost took our breath away and left us soaked to the bone in a heartbeat. We found shelter in the expansive buttress roots of a giant tree. But the deluge was soon over, the first sunbeams broke through the pierced canopy of the clearing and the leaves glistened as if they were studded with diamonds. Quickly the forest came alive again with three vociferans chirping in a concerto grosso style—two in unison, one whistling echo! The forest was teeming with toads and tree frogs, and even the snakes were easier to see now. Dusk was quickly approaching and it was time to return to the camp. For the novice, an overwhelming experience: in the evening light, all the colors give off one last warm radiant burst. Meanwhile, the regular evening concert began, which would reach its crescendo in terms of tonal diversity and force between the hours of eight and ten o'clock. As Romain, an entomologist from the Musée national d'Histoire naturelle in Paris, explained to me, the concert is mainly performed by frogs and toads, supported of course by cicadas and monkeys. The latter either pay homage to the beautiful song or keep rhythm by drumming on tree trunks. Under the starriest sky that we novices had ever seen, we arrived at camp, where the canopy

1

2

team was working under floodlights to prepare for take-off the morning after next. François, a cook from Kourou, some thirty-five kilometers away, brought us an evening meal from the main kitchen. As exquisite tropical appetizer *cœur de palmier* (young leaf buds of Euterpe oleraceae), followed by *lapin à la mode Guyane française,* and for dessert, cheese and fruit salad with a shot of white rum as a tropical touch. This gourmet menu was accompanied, as always, like a faint reminiscence of the distant homeland, by a carafe of Côtes du Rhône. We were joined for dinner by Pascal Petronelli, a forester who had grown up in the French Jura and had spent the past sixteen years at Camp Parakou. He has adapted to the rainforest and lives with it like no one else I know. Over the course of the next days, he often guided us through woods and savannas, opening our eyes to many small wonders that we would otherwise have passed by without taking notice. He reduced his verbal communication to a minimum, often just a word or two, sometimes a fragment of a sentence; he was a master of sign language. His constant companions were a Doberman, grateful for every token of affection, and his machete, with which he could even open cans. Of course he mostly needed it to clear paths through the forest, but frequently he also cut a piece of bark out of a tree trunk which he wanted to identify by the bark and wood structure.

Roman Kaiser on the detachable platform designed by Gil Ebersold

1 *Pachira insignis*
2 *Phragmipedium* sp.
3 *Anthurium jenmannii*
4 *Clitoria guianensis*

3

4

**SAVANNA LANDSCAPES BETWEEN RAINFOREST AND THE ATLANTIC**

The next morning we had already left the camp by dawn for a savanna region roughly forty kilometers away, from where we started a three-hour hike at seven o'clock, avoiding the nearly unbearable midday heat. This landscape, shaped by annual wildfires, is troublesome to pass. As a consequence of the annual fires, every grass plant has developed into a sharp cone, which results in the sensation of walking on a bed of nails, and all this without protection from the scorching sun. Here, even the traditional French wine drinkers began to dream of a cool beer. But our hardships were rewarded with extraordinary plants. Apart from the savanna palms, protecting themselves from the fires with a thick bast layer, there are even some deciduous trees that survive, always arranged in groups to ensure protection from the wildfires. The resin of such a Burseraceae *(Protium heptaphyllum)* continues to pose a special challenge to our laboratory. Back at camp, there was no time for recovery: after our siesta, a training session was scheduled. We learned climbing techniques and practiced mounting headspace equipment to trees on a shaky foundation (the record was six minutes; under real conditions on the canopy, this turned into a full seventeen minutes).

**FINALLY, THE TEST FLIGHT**

Well before dawn, the dirigible envelope, which is neatly packed away after each flight, was unfolded and blown up using a fan. The burners were tested, as was the GPS (Global Positioning System, controlled by satellite, to allow us to locate trees of interest again on the following day). After the burners were turned on, the dirigible inflated, radiant in its rainbow colors; we slipped into our harnesses, pulled on our killer-bee protection nets and our helmets and took our places in the raft. We slowly took off, just as the eastern sky became immersed in a glowing carmine, and reached the treetops as the first sunbeams were breaking through the morning fog—beside us, startled parrots flying away; in front of us, 2500 kilometers of green ocean. Accustomed as we were to European proportions, the sight of this fantastic expanse and its sheer beauty left us virtually speechless. A vast array of different shapes in all conceivable tones of green, interspersed with the splashes of colorful blossoms, which gave off wafts of fragrance that we could smell! Already at a quarter past seven, however, we had to start thinking about the return, since from around eight o'clock the thermal conditions become unfavorable and flying is not advisable. Cut loose from earth's gravity, the sense that you've drunk a glass of champagne among friends, no problems whatsoever, no abnormal sounds from the burners, not a trace of vertigo, absolute trust in a team of individualists, who all had only one goal in mind.

**RESEARCH FLIGHTS**

During the following research flights, we were constantly overwhelmed by the diversity of the rainforest. Standing at the forwardmost point of the raft, I kept an Argus-eyed watch. "Over there, Dany! See that tree with orange-red blossoms at ten o'clock? Those blossoms are going to have a strong smell of carotenoid metabolites, beta-ionones and isomers!" And the balloon promptly turned in the desired direction. Dany managed an unbelievable maneuver and the raft came to a standstill directly in front of the splendid flowers, without breaking a single branch. At this point I discovered that these magnificent blossoms were completely devoid of odor, and after further examination this made sense: while the inflorescences of the Noranthea guianensis, as this tree is called, have a brilliant color that indeed comes from carotenoid pigments, these do not metabolize into a fragrance. This specimen of Marcgraviaceae is visited and pollinated by hummingbirds, and since these are attracted by brilliant colors rather than by odor, there is no reason for the tree to produce a scent.

The dirigible's launching and landing pad near the camp, which was located in a clearing

5

6

Unbeknownst to us, we had taken an ant colony aboard our raft. These creatures, plentiful in number and variety, were our constant companions and often had us performing wild dances. Soon a greenish white veil hovering above the treetops attracted our attention, and an extremely distinctive herbal, but also floral fragrance became perceptible. Dany understood at once and steered towards the finely structured liana, an Apocynaceae, which was covered with thousands of small blossoms. It was the perfect opportunity to try out what we had practiced. Gil seized a thick branch to stabilize the sled, while I set up the headspace equipment. Seventeen minutes—an extremely tricky task for the pilot, to hover in place for so long. That morning, after we had identified the location of the tree—after all, we had to find it again to recover the apparatus—we docked at two more trees with blossoms that gave off fascinating fragrances.

For the next five days, between six and eight each morning, we embarked on more of these flights, which were unique in every respect. We explored an area around Parakou of approximately twenty kilometers in radius.

The film crew shot footage from all conceivable angles, from within the raft or from the gondola, from a chair hanging from a cable, and even with the help of a helicopter. Then the balloon crew needed a day off. For us, that meant another and this time more extensive excursion into the forest. Led by Pascal, we wandered through a variety of different biotopes, crossed small rivers on fallen tree trunks and explored bat caves.

Two days later, another highlight: the six-hundred-square-meter platform, the so-called *Radeau des Cimes,* was lowered onto a suitable spot on the treetops, allowing us to spend an entire day climbing above the treetops, examining fragrant blossoms or branches. Interestingly enough, in contrast to being in free flight on the raft, here the glance back along the safety rope did result in a certain feeling of dizziness. On the whole, the mobile raft that could be lowered from the dirigible onto the trees proved to be the most efficient means for our investigations.

On October 16, the time had come: all the equipment had to be packed up in trunks and we embarked on our homeward journey. On October 18, we were already able to begin the analysis of the forty-two headspace samples.

5 *Passiflora racemosa*
6 *Swartzia panacoco*
7 *Aristilochia gigantea*
8 *Aechmea* sp.

7

8

9

10

11

12

16

17

18

19

23

24

25

26

30

31

32

33

13

14

15

20

21

22

27

28

29

34

35

36

9 *Lecythidaceae* sp.
10 *Crinum erubescens*
11 *Epidendrum medusae*
12 *Couroupita guianensi*
13 *Passiflora quadrangularis*
14 *Clusia grandiflora*
15 Euglossine bee in the flower of a *Mabea piriri*
16 *Couma guianensis*
17 *Anthurium jenmannii*
18 *Curatella americana*
19 *Lecythidaceae* sp.
20 *Passiflora glandulosa*
21 *Bignonia* sp.
22 *Cochliostema odoratissima*
23 unidentified species
24 *Clitoria ternata*
25 *Qualea mori-boomii*
26 *Noranthea guianensis*
27 *Coryanthes macrantha*
28 *Couroupita guianensis*
29 *Philodendron megalophyllum*
30 *Cyphomandra divaricata*
31 *Macoubea guianensis*
32 *Noranthea guianensis*
33 *Rodriguezia secunda*
34 *Voyria caerulea*
35 *Coryanthes* sp.
36 *Pachira aquatica*

Following double page:
"Le Dirigeable," canopy expedition
French Guiana, 1996

The English landscape parks of the eighteenth century constitute three-dimensional *Gesamtkunstwerke* produced at a time when landscape gardeners and landscape painters were influencing one another. However, in the period that followed, garden design gradually began to be targeted by critics, who dismissed gardens as dissimulation and purely artificial, man-made works. Around 1800 the German philosopher August Wilhelm von Schlegel even argued that garden design should no longer officially be recognized as one of the fine arts.

Today, in an age of land art events and garden exhibitions, the artistic character of gardens has once again become a focus of discussion.

But what is a garden? We characterize a garden as a small part of nature that is contained, tamed, fenced in and, where required, altered. A garden creates an antithesis; it generates a relationship between the raw nature of the environment and a cultivated piece of land within it. The garden as a refuge, an idyll free of chaos and a vision of paradise is one of our society's fundamental myths. The garden of modernity constitutes part of the self-perception of the upper class. The dynamic character of the garden—growth and decay—requires patience and time in a way that is divorced from the rapid pictorial production and informational flood associated with the avant-garde.

It is above all the unfamiliar climate that first strikes visitors when they enter the Masoala Rainforest Eco-Conservatory, where everything is enveloped by warm, humid, heavy air. The level of precipitation inside is twice as high as Zurich's normal rainfall, and this contributes to the perception of a completely different climate zone. Humidity permeates everything. The constant change from the musty smell to the heavy scent of flowers confuses the senses. The sonorous hiss of the waterfall gradually grows louder until the cascade itself becomes visible in the distance between the trees. Chirps and twitters blend into this acoustic background, intimating the presence of cicadas and birds. Enticing fruits hang from the trees but only the animals succumb to the temptation. What is visible is only part of this strange environment. The customary understanding of our familiar everyday world is questioned. Our gaze becomes dispersed among delicate palm fronds, powerful tree trunks and the constantly changing play of light and shade. The basic principle of the jungle, a multilayered, luxuriant and chaotic composite of plants, is intensified by the topography and the network of waterways and paths. Rubber plants and dragon trees have been so densely planted and in such dimensions that they take on an unfamiliar appearance. They provide homes for birds, reptiles and lemurs, freed from bars and cages. The "raree show" principle so often characteristic of zoos and botanical gardens is replaced by visitors' direct participation as actors. They discover swampy glades that provide a biotope for innumerable frogs. The path leads them on to the waterfall, where birds hunt fish and bathe in the spray. Walking and climbing paths lead into the depths of the forest and invite visitors to take a closer look at individual biotopes. However, as is normally expected of guests, the visitor should keep to the prescribed walkways. The process of change is part of the concept. As is always the case in the initial phase of vegetation development, the ground is composed for the most part of mineral material rather than earth. In the case of the Masoala conservatory this material is lava stone. Over the course of time leaves and branches will form a jungle floor. The different stages of development allow patrons to participate in a natural process that only becomes comprehensible over several visits.

## HOW A VISION BECAME REALITY

The design for the Masoala Rainforest Eco-Conservatory was first developed over ten years ago. Dieter Kienast, and I were responsible for the concept and the conservatory's inner workings. Several members of my office staff in Zurich found my passion for Masoala infectious and helped me to realize my vision of reproducing a rainforest that would offer visitors a unique experience of nature.

Is it possible to create an exact copy of a rainforest? No, all we can do is try to imitate reality as closely as possible. Our first task was to become acquainted with the unique flora and rainforest environment of Madagascar. In this endeavor we were ably assisted by local botanists and foresters during our extended exploratory tours in the rainforest of Masoala. There we studied the specific composition and structure of the forest as well as the courses of streams and the appearance of waterfalls. We compared the knowledge we acquired

# TREE JOURNEYS

**Is it possible to create an exact copy of a rainforest? When stepping into the Masoala Rainforest Eco-Conservatory in the Zurich Zoo, one is first struck by the unfamiliar climate. Warm, humid air envelops both the visitors and the plants. The latter are all native to the Madagascan rainforest and were gathered in an intensive search through large-scale plant nurseries in Malaysia, Thailand and Florida.**

Essay by Günther Vogt
Photographs by Vogt Landscape Zurich

Masoala Rainforest Eco-Conservatory, Zurich
Photo: Olafur Eliasson

**MASOALA NATIONAL PARK**
When Benyowsky, a Hungarian nobleman, was running his trading post two hundred years ago on the Onive River, the Maoala Peninsula was completely covered with thick vegetation. No one dared to venture into the mysterious, almost impenetrable jungle world. The inhabitants were confined to a few villages along the coast, where they lived from fishing and rice cultivation in their immediate surroundings. Around the turn of the century Masoala, like the entire east coast of Madagascar, was still covered by uniform areas of rainforest. At this time scientists were already drawing attention to the unique features of the region. In 1927 this 5200 km² region was declared the country's second protected area by the colonial administration. When the French left in 1960, only ten hectares of forest had been cleared. However, following Madagascan independence, the region was reclassified and opened to logging. In addition a large palm oil plantation was established in the area. From then on the region was left completely unmonitored. In 1991 only 3660 km² of forest remained. Today a mere four percent of Madagascar's original secondary forest is still standing. Every year Masoala loses a further six percent of its forest stocks. Nowadays Madagascar's largest interconnected forests are only thriving within the 2300 km² covered by the Masoala National Park, which was founded in 1991. This national reserve contains not only rainforests but also mangrove swamps and coral reefs.

Masoala, Madagascar
Photo: Modis Web satellite image, NASA

*"Nature is what we see in it."*

on these trips with experiences we had already gained in other regions of the world. When observing a waterfall in Switzerland, for instance, the view is dominated by the water, whereas in Madagascar the cascade itself contains relatively little water with the result that the eye is drawn to mosses, lichens and ferns. We repeatedly encountered remarkable and unique plants, for example, a species of palm that only occurs within a circumference of five hundred meters and is found nowhere else in the world. There are around one hundred types of such rare palms on Madagascar. These and other memorable experiences convinced us to abandon our original idea and to base the design of our conservatory as closely as possible on the characteristics of the Masoala rainforest.

Actually collecting the plants we needed was perhaps the most exciting part of the project. Intensive searches in large-scale plant nurseries in Malaysia, Thailand and Florida eventually yielded a range of species originating from Madagascar. In a highly complicated process, trees of up to twelve meters in height were transported in green houses by ship to Holland, where they were gradually acclimatized. After several months in quarantine, their journey continued to the Zurich Zoo. In this way we were able to assemble five hundred different species of plants.

Seedlings were also cultivated in the Zurich Zoo plant nursery, which was constructed on the edge of the Masoala rainforest in Madagascar especially for the Zurich Masoala conservatory. We have planted some of these seedlings beneath the conservatory's larger trees, whose canopy is providing the protection they need to grow and thrive until they can gradually replace the initial plantings. A number of logistics experts were of invaluable help with the transportation of the plants and their acclimatization in Europe.

Planting forest of this type requires large spaces. The gigantic dimensions of the Masoala Rainforest Eco-Conservatory give an impression of just how much space is required. With the exception of the lighting, we have simulated all original rainforest conditions such as the air humidity and temperature the plants require. The natural rainforest floor is poor in nutrients and the same kinds of conditions are required in the Masoala eco-conservatory if the plants are to thrive. The earth is made of tiny lava stones, with larger clumps underneath that are covered by ever-smaller stones and a top layer of fine pumice and tuff. This base is covered by a finger-thick layer of peat.

One of the greatest challenges facing us at the outset was pest control. In order to avoid endangering the animals that would later inhabit the conservatory and its visitors, we could not chemically treat any of the plants we had acquired. As a result, many plants were attacked by pests which are commonly found in tropical green houses but do not significantly inhibit plant growth. Our insect specialists subsequently found an organic method of control for each of these unwelcome guests.

We are far more familiar with artificial alternative worlds than we are with simple natural interrelationships. The dynamic character of nature—the cycle of growth and decay—vanquishes all that is ephemeral; it demands a more expansive temporal horizon. Nature can only be really enjoyed by those who have the patience to embed themselves in it and attempt to understand it. In this sense visitors to the rainforest have the opportunity to see themselves as spectators of the most natural of all processes, the transience of life and ultimately of the self.

Zurich Zoo tree nursery on Masoala. Transfer from open ground to pot cultivation. The zoo runs a tree nursery on Masoala, where it produces plants for the Masoala Rainforest Eco-Conservatory and for local use. It is thereby providing support for the sustainable use of forest resources. The knowledge accumulated through the project regarding the cultivation of indigenous plants is contributing to the protection and reforestation of Madagascan rainforests.

**Although it is located on Africa's doorstep and only separated from the continent by the four-hundred-kilometer-wide Strait of Mozambique, in both floristic and plant-geographic terms Madagascar exhibits links not only to Africa but also to India and the Indo-Malaysian Archipelago. Two hundred and seventy million years ago the gigantic southern continent of Gondwana was home to an extremely uniform type of vegetation that was fundamentally different from that found in the Northern Hemisphere, and rich deposits of this Gondwana flora have been found on Madagascar in Carbono-Permian drift coal deposits. However, due to the early isolation of the Madagascan land mass, its flora developed independently and gave rise to a form of vegetation that, while exhibiting relationships to that of Africa and Indo-Malaysia, also has its own specific features and is characterized by a high degree of endemism. Madagascar probably has the highest rate of endemic animal and plant species in the world.**

Photo: Modis Web satellite image, NASA

## endemic: native to a particular location and only found there

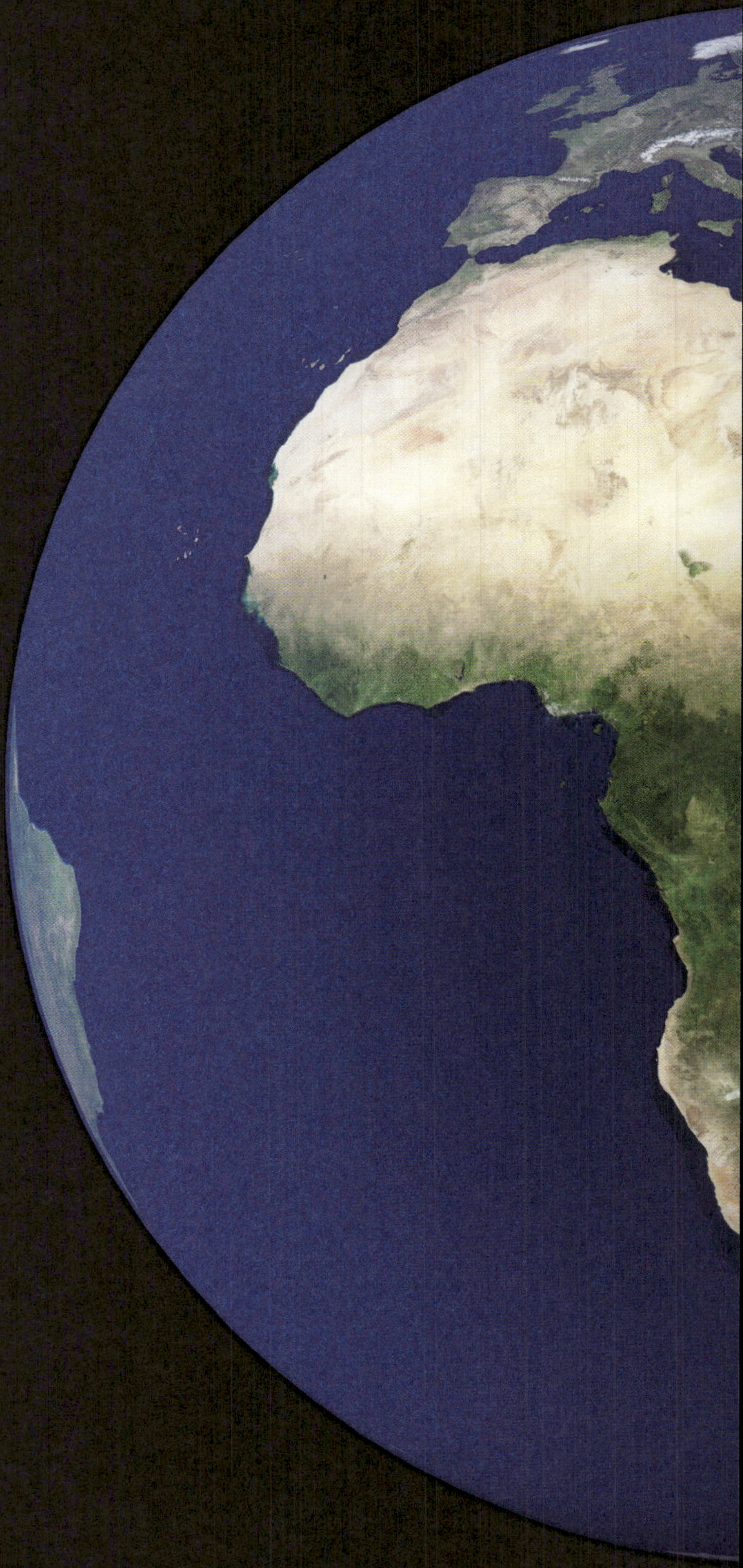

## exotic: introduced, nonnative

## Biodiversity on Madagascar

Area: 2 percent of Africa
Species diversity: 25 percent of African species
12,000 plant species, 86 percent of which are endemic
4,220 tree species, 96 percent of which are endemic
170 palm species, 98 percent of which are endemic

## Biodiversity in Masoala

Over 2,400 plant species
502 tree species, 63 palm species

## Most common tree families

Sapotaceae, Euphorbiaceae, Rubiaceae, Burseraceae, Strelitiaceae

## Most common tree species

*Albizia lebeck, Avicennia marina, Canarium madagascariense, Calophyllum inophyllum, Diospyros graoilipes*

## Biodiversity in the Masoala Rainforest Eco-Conservatory

260 plant species
105 tree species, 14 palm species
2,100 planted trees, 500 lianas

## Plant formation

Evergreen lowland rainforest
Three levels:
1. Tree height: 25–30 meters
*Ravenala madagascariensis, Terminalia catappa, Canarium subulatum*
2. Tree height: 8–18 meters
*Bucida buceras, Dypsis lutescens, Garcinia subelliptica, Gardenia carinata*
3. Herb and shrub layer: 3 meters
*Cissus antartica, Mussaenda incana, Stephanotis floribunda*

# indigenous: native to one or more locations and naturally occurring there

## Masoala Peninsula

Area: 5,200 square kilometers
Temperature: 24 °C (min. 20 °C, max. 30 °C)
Rainfall: 3000 millimeters per year
Relative humidity: 80–100 percent

## Masoala Rainforest Eco-Conservatory

Area: 11,000 square meters
Steel construction: 90 × 120 meters
height: 30 meters
Foil roof: 14,000 square meters, UV-permeable, three-layered
Cost: 50 million Swiss francs
Temperature: 25 °C (min. 18 °C, max. 35 °C)
Irrigated with rainwater (17–20 °C),
Tank with 80 cubic meters per day
Relative humidity: 65–100 percent
Mineral lava substrate

## 1999–2001

Inventory and purchase of trees on Madagascar, in Florida, Thailand and Malaysia

## December 2001

Loading into 120 containers
Shipping to Rotterdam
Duration: 3–4 weeks

## January 2002

Acclimatization in six tree nurseries in Holland and Belgium
Transplantation and maintenance

## October 2002

Loading into truck containers
Journey to Zurich

## March 2003

Planting completed

# naturalized: introduced and capable of dispersal without human intervention

## 1999–2001: Inventory and purchase of trees

**MADAGASCAR:** bamboo

Bamboo

*Ravenala madagascariensis*

*Platycerium* sp.

*Ficus* sp.

Bezoek jungle

Tree measurement (G. Vogt)

*Artocarpus lakoocha*

Tree section 3

*Ficus benjamina* "Exotica"

Tree root stocks

*Veitchia* sp.

*Ravenala madagascariensis*

*Bismarckia nobilis*

*Eugenia platyphylla*

Quality check

*Cyathea* sp.

*Vitex pinnata*

**THAILAND:** *Barringtonia* sp.

*Ficus altissima*

**FLORIDA:** *Ficus benjamina* "Exotica"

Delivery code

Tree section 1

Tree section 2

In the greenhouse

*Ficus nitida*

**MALAYSIA:** *Ficus nitida*

*Ficus nitida*

*Delonix regia*

*Elaeis guinensis*

*Ficus* sp.

Tree crane

December 2001: loading into 120 containers, shipping to Rotterdam, duration three–four weeks

January 2002: acclimatization in six tree nurseries in Holland and Belgium, transplantation and maintenance

October 2002: loading into truck containers, journey to Zurich

**March 2003: completion of planting**

## Tree Factory:

# PRODUCTION AND AESTHETICS

**Trees, including fruit trees, ornamental plants and forest plants, are cultivated on open land or in greenhouses, where they are either lined out in nursery rows in the earth or grown in containers and transplanted as required until they have reached a certain size (tree quality), when they are passed on for resale or sold to end users. The rapid growth of cities has resulted in a high demand for a wide range of trees of differing qualities that can be produced in a short time and at a low price. This development has had a profound effect on the tree industry and its established traditions. Production centers have grown significantly and many have specialized to meet the demands of a particular market sector. In addition, production has been rationalized through the introduction of automated and systematized processes and it has—to some extent—become independent of the prevailing climate. Nevertheless, the great passion that numerous family businesses have for cultivation and the handicraft associated with it remains evident and visible to the naked eye.**

Single trees transplanted eight times, Bruns Pflanzen, Bad Zwischenahn, Germany
Photo: Dominique Ghiggi

**Pistoia**
Photo series by Olaf Unverzart, photographer and artist, 2005

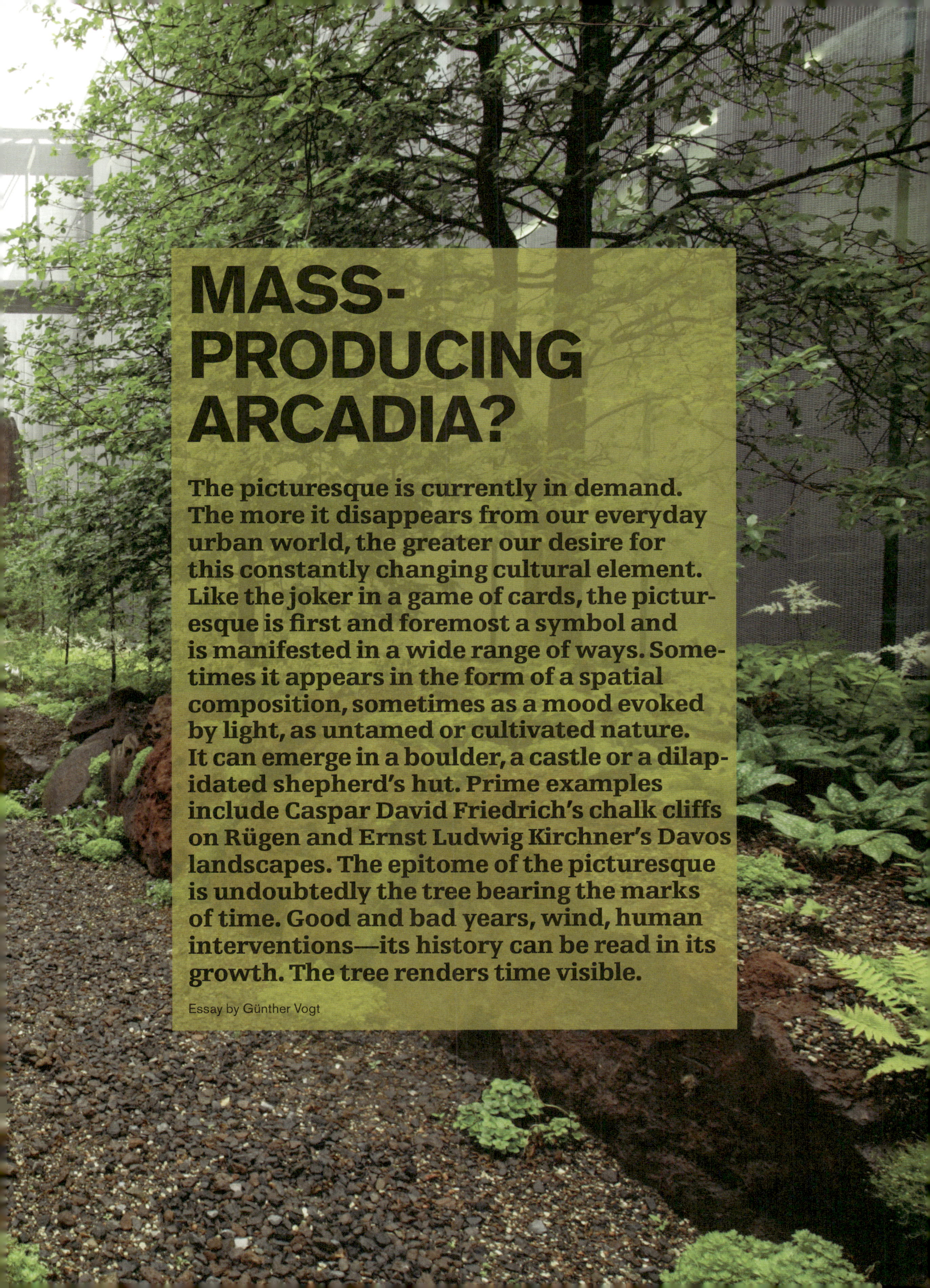

# MASS-PRODUCING ARCADIA?

**The picturesque is currently in demand. The more it disappears from our everyday urban world, the greater our desire for this constantly changing cultural element. Like the joker in a game of cards, the picturesque is first and foremost a symbol and is manifested in a wide range of ways. Sometimes it appears in the form of a spatial composition, sometimes as a mood evoked by light, as untamed or cultivated nature. It can emerge in a boulder, a castle or a dilapidated shepherd's hut. Prime examples include Caspar David Friedrich's chalk cliffs on Rügen and Ernst Ludwig Kirchner's Davos landscapes. The epitome of the picturesque is undoubtedly the tree bearing the marks of time. Good and bad years, wind, human interventions—its history can be read in its growth. The tree renders time visible.**

Essay by Günther Vogt

Models with wrinkles and curves have always proved more appealing motifs for artists than slim, flawless youth. The picturesque is an individual, a personality with edges and a history. What better symbol to represent this than a tree?

For the old masters and landscape painters as for garden designers, and from the English landscape garden until today, the gnarled old tree has stood for rootedness and constancy, for the tenacious struggle against the adversities of existence. Surrounding the tree with a shepherd and his flock proved a popular addition. And when we find the obligatory lion joining the peacefully gazing herd, then we know that we have come to the symbolically and thematically laden world of Arcadia. This world is an expression of a sociocultural ideal that still nourishes our image of the picturesque. If a dilapidated Greek temple is also visible shimmering through the trees behind a small lake, and if the lions and lambs are replaced by sleek cattle in the background, then it is highly likely that we are in a three-dimensional translation of the Arcadian dream, namely, an English or French landscape garden.

The centuries-old olive tree, enthusiastically imported into the gardens, courtyards and roof gardens of the better-off in today's globalized world, does not represent some sort of preparation for global warming or for a life of self-sufficiency in the next crisis. The transplantation of the ancient olive tree from its homeland into the gardens of Central Europe and the United States is rather an expression of a new era of the picturesque, one characterized not by the ancient oaks and lindens of village squares but by olive and fruit trees, by the idealization of cultural history rather than history's glorification. The olive tree, formerly an everyday part of a harsh rural life and an agricultural "production unit," has become, at least for the urban individual, a decorative symbol of the romantic ideal of a simple life close to nature in the sunny south—and in the process takes this idea to an absurd extreme. The literally uprooted tree, bereft of content and context, has become an empty shell, pure form, for in Western culture the picturesque lives in and from its individual history and thus essentially points not to the future but to the past.

With the olive tree the well-off owner not only purchases a beautiful plant. They also get a story and a reference to history, for the picturesque tree represents a manifestation of compressed time. It touches on fundamental human experiences with which the modern world has lost touch. It shows us an image of aging that does not simply allow a physiognomy—whether of the tree or the human—to age without differentiation; rather it draws certain features and characteristics with more definition and thus emphasizes what life has made out of and with the individual. It brings the themes of aging and dying, which in our society have literally been forced to the periphery, into hospitals and rest homes, back into our reality and lends them individuality and dignity.

Just as the image of the picturesque tree expresses compressed time, so the imported olive tree expresses borrowed time: the time of other people, cultures and ways of life. To this extent it is nothing other than a living counterpart to the artificial temple ruins in the English landscape garden—a status symbol. It seems to refer the life of its owner to a longer, more significant history, for the authentically picturesque bears with a cultural content. This picturesque emerges where the interaction of different forces of nature finds expression and retrieves some secret that it has visibly lived through and experienced. The young supple birch above all needs one thing to become the bleak tree bowing and bent by life on the moor, worthy of a picture for the painter or photographer and a second glance from the passing traveler on foot. It needs time. However, like man, this is exactly what modern trees do not have. For example, in Holland a street tree survives for an average of fifteen to twenty years and then usually has to give way to the next construction project—too little time to grow into an impressive old grove with its fellows. And even contemporary parks, squares and gardens—and the plants in them—seldom reach maturity due to the increasing demand for functional space. The ancient tree giants that dominate our traditional parks and squares have a succession problem. Most of the trees planted today are replaced long before they can attain their individual shape and be deemed worthy of protection.

Nevertheless, or precisely for this reason, landscape architects and tree nurseries are now more than ever being confronted with the demand for the picturesque image that old trees embody. The people of the globalized, urbanized world crave roots and identification points, individuality amidst international shopping chains with their unitary corporate design and the standardized greenery of urban roadside plantings. Rather than young, slender trees that can barely be distinguished from their neighbors, the city-dweller expects parks to provide a landscape characterized by imposing trees, cozy niches, and shady corners—if possible on the first day after planting.

And while ancient forest giants and old cultivated plants are transported over thousands of kilometers and transplanted in order to meet this demand, outside the professional world the (seemingly) immobile tree is nevertheless understood as an epitome of rootedness in the local context, as a reliable value within a turbulent world. It is not without reason that the bookshops are full of books about trees: coffee-table books, Celtic tree calendars, specialist works on botany and morphology, works on the mythology of trees and their mysterious powers. The picturesque tree is a heterotopia in the sense employed by Foucault—a land without place that nevertheless exists in our minds and is linked with quite specific sentiments, ideas and conventions, a real place "outside of all places," as Foucault puts it. The Sleeping Beauty castle of our imagination is not covered by one-year-old, bright green Morning Glory or exotic climbing plants, but by brittle, old rambler roses in all their morbid, awkward beauty. In Italy we do not want to be guided to the entrance of a rural estate by the friendly avenue of lindens from a German folksong but by dark columns of cypress. And we do not want to see symmetrical growth in the Swiss stone pine that offers protection to the chamois on the high alpine ledge, but rather a gnarled form with branches bent by the constant wind and perhaps a trunk split by lightning.

Of course the number of naturally grown, picturesque olive trees and other centuries-old originals that can be transported around the world is limited. Moreover, in many places there are also laws and protective measures designed to hinder this form of selling off our natural and cultivated heritage. However, the yearning for a distinctive quality remains and is growing into a global phenomenon. Satisfying this longing and cultivating the heterotopia of the picturesque tree is one of the challenges facing tree nurseries. But can Arcadia be mass-produced? Is the mass-production of the distinctive an oxymoron? Can individuality and history be grown?

It is one thing to design plans or models for a hilly landscape in the courtyard of the warehouses in Saint Gall featuring wind-bent sycamores or for a forest tilted by a landslide and featuring skewed trees that have partly grown into one another on the Novartis Campus. However, it is quite another thing to translate these designs into reality, to find tree nurseries that have foreseen the unusual wish for skewed trees or other unconventional growth forms, or have the capacity to cultivate such trees within a reasonable timeframe. It is in the nature of things that tree production cannot respond to trends and specific wishes from one day to the next since even the most rapidly growing tree requires a minimum growing time. Planners cannot simply select what they want from a botanical textbook—they have to work with the species and forms that have been cultivated by tree nurseries over recent years. Supply determines demand. On the other hand, the interests of the planners can be detected in the assortments actually offered by tree nurseries. Alongside forest nurseries and those that focus on offering a special assortment, nurseries have emerged that are devoted to the provision of single trees featuring unusual, distinctive growth forms that contrast with the EU-standardized street trees that are cloned in their thousands.

Of course, like the street tree, the picturesque nursery tree is the product of an industrially organized, automated and rationalized business sector—albeit a masterly one. Its scars and crooked growth have not been generated by its history but by the skills of the tree-nursery staff. Its forms do not speak of wind and weather, lightning

Previous double page:
TREE SCULPTURES IN THE COURTYARD OF FIFA HEADQUARTERS IN ZURICH
The picturesque as an expression of a compressed history of time and life. Three years after being installed, each of the sixteen-ton statues began to be colonized by mosses and ferns.
Photo: Christian Vogt

Model of a model. Studies by Vogt Landscape Zurich for the development of the sculptures on a small scale.
Photo: Vogt Landscape Zurich

strikes, dry years, attacks by pests, the signs of lovers in its bark or the feet of dancers on its roots. The history of the nursery tree is told far more quickly. It is grown in a greenhouse, first in pots, later transplanted again and again in carefully laid out rows on the grounds of the nursery, and sometimes, through precise cutting and other measures, coaxed into producing an irregular form. Professional care and optimal supplies of water and nutrients ensure the fastest possible rate of growth.

In nature the picturesque tree develops its singularity on the basis of its solitary position, the advantages, deficits and particularities of its location. On the one hand, the fact that it stands alone means that it is supplied with light, air and space from all directions and thus, in contrast to the forest tree, presents an impressive appearance from every perspective. On the other hand, it is far more exposed than forest trees to erosion, wind, storms, sun, parasites and other negative influences. Tree nurseries though have learned to mass-produce distinctiveness under optimal conditions and in a relatively limited space. The range of extraordinary plants resulting from these efforts is astounding. Of course we can ask ourselves whether these plants with their artificially formed picturesque appearance are authentic. In fact, given the prevailing zeitgeist, they are probably more authentic than we might wish. Like an old olive tree or an ancient linden, nursery trees tell the history of their time: a time without time.

And yet they do not only satisfy an important and justified need for the distinctive. Paradoxically, these living artifacts also contribute to preserving the variety of forms in our plant world. Single trees that hinder farm machinery have become a rare site in our fields and unusual growth forms are not desired in our forests. Forked, multistemmed and unusual trees are worthless to the forest industry, and, other than in inaccessible locations, they have become rare. By contrast, due to the great demand for the picturesque, imperfection has become a valuable commodity in nurseries specializing in solitary trees. The artificial growth forms in the tree nursery thus have the potential, as it were, to continue the wealth of natural forms. Whether this is relevant in the sense of ecological diversity is a secondary concern here given that we are not dealing with scientific values but with an image, an atmosphere, the convention of so-called beauty—in short, with the picturesque.

In pragmatic terms, from the point of view of both the tree and the person, it is irrelevant if the desired image is produced in the rows of the tree nursery or has been formed by chance and nature. It does its job. Even if it is not exactly what they are looking for, what people find here is clearly at least a satisfactory alternative. And for the tree it is always agreeable when people provide it with an optimal habitat and keep down the competition from lawnmowers and hedge trimmers. Is the solitary nursery tree a copy and an artifact, or is it a plant like any other? Or is it in fact ideally suited as a fixture for our equally artificial parks and squares? Anyone searching for the true Arcadia or substitute nature in our parks will be disappointed, like the zoo visitor hoping to catch a glimpse of the authentic Africa from the giraffe enclosure. However, the dialectic of the natural and the artificial as a theme in the design of urban green spaces has also become outdated. Both idealistic viewpoints have given way to a reality that is far more complex but also more interesting, and that is presenting design and plant production with new themes and new challenges. And in this context, too, tree nurseries and planners will have to deal with the demand for the picturesque.

COURTYARD OF THE WAREHOUSE AREA
IN SAINT GALL
The picturesque in its adolescence—a paradox as design element: sycamores bent by the wind draw attention to the absence of this weather element. Arbor, an illustrious tree nursery in Belgium, was able to respond to the designer's unusual request. The sycamores were deliberately grown by the tree nursery in a wind-exposed location without support, thereby creating their skewed form.
Photo: Christian Vogt

# ANCIENT GIANTS

**Since the initiation of the Chinese government's policy of "reform and opening up," the country has seen a growing trade in old trees. Even though most cultivated areas are dominated by mass plantings of single varieties, old solitary trees have been enjoying an ever-increasing popularity since the more prosperous social strata have been able to afford their own houses with private gardens and the state has been promoting the construction of public green spaces**

Travelogue and photographs by Christine Zimmerli

A ginkgo tree *(Ginkgo biloba)* about one thousand years old in Tianmushan, Zhejiang province

Mrs. Zhao has been extremely successful as a buyer and retailer of old trees. Born in a rural part of Zhejiang Province, she moved to Shanghai in the nineties and initially worked there as a domestic maid. In Shanghai Mrs. Zhao witnessed the emergence of new and luxurious housing developments and quickly realized that these were creating a need for plants and trees. Together with her husband, she began to transport old trees from Zhejiang to Shanghai and to build up an extremely lucrative business selling them there. Digging up and removing old trees does not appear to be subject to strict legal regulations, and Mrs. Zhao budgeted for insurance costs and possible fines as part of her business expenses. Today she is a wealthy woman and owns over a dozen houses in Shanghai.

The problematic nature of digging up old trees and replanting them is obvious. China has only a few areas of natural forest, for example, in the provinces of Sichuan, Guizhou and Yunnan. According to Alex Abke, a German landscape architect in Shanghai, "Many old trees are brought to Shanghai from the neighboring provinces, for example, camphor trees *(Cinnamomum camphora)* from the province of Anhui. Dealers pay the farmers, dig up the trees, lop off the crowns and replant them here. They are not concerned with whether the trees survive transport." Chen Yu Peng from the Shanghai forestry authority is also critical of the practice, pointing out that the removal of trees from old forest stocks is actually illegal but there are no strict controls.

Recently a small number of protective regulations have been introduced. For example, the removal of trees with over twenty-five centimeters DBH (Diameter at Breast Height) is now prohibited. Certain regions have also been declared protected zones, such as Tianmushan, a hilly area some 250 kilometers southwest of Shanghai, which has a long religious tradition. The area contains stocks of thousand-year-old ginkgo and cryptomeria trees which are assumed to have been planted by monks.

## TREE NURSERIES AROUND GUANGZHOU

In the area around Guangzhou in southern China many tree nurseries specialize in old trees. The specimens I have come in search of are originally natives of the hilly provinces further north and are transported to Guangzhou, where the climate is mild and the soil fertile.

Guangzhou is located in the province of Guangdong (Canton), around two hours by train from Hong Kong. This harbor city was already an important trade center during the Tang Dynasty (618–907) and was connected by commerce with the Middle East and South Asia. Today Guangzhou still draws people from all over the world and its population includes quite a high number of Brazilians and Africans compared with Beijing or Shanghai.

Henry Ruan and his brother run a business here that mainly involves the export of Chinese banyan trees (Ficus microcarpa) to Europe. He has good contacts with the tree nurseries around Guangzhou. He says that southern China is the best place to buy old, high-quality trees because people here are specialists in the transplantation and sale of them.

The weather in Guangzhou is already hot and humid in spring. "We have a tropical summer and an English winter," says Ruan as we drive with his brother out of the city into a tree-nursery district. With an annual rainfall of 1696 millimeters, the climate in Guangzhou is very wet. The vegetation is thick and the city appears luxuriantly green. Particularly noticeable are the banyan trees with their aerial roots, which grow along the roadside and sometimes even in the middle of the street.

There are more than a thousand tree nurseries around Guangzhou. The region has now established itself as a production and distribution center even though the market for trees, particularly for old trees purchased to stand alone, has only developed in the last five to ten years. Most of the tree nurseries were founded in the nineties and do not have any established tradition.

Rapid economic development in China, particularly since the nineties, has given rise to a stratum of extremely prosperous people. In the large cities on the east coast signs of this new wealth are clearly visible. Many Chinese who have earned a great deal of money in a short time regard a valuable tree as a status symbol and the purchase of their own home and a car is often followed by the acquisition of a particularly fine specimen. Such trees do not come cheap, some costing upwards of tens of thousands of dollars. Certain kusamaki trees *(Podocarpus macrophyllus)* from Japan can fetch between 250,000 and 350,000 dollars. Apart from newly rich private customers, the clients of the region's tree nurseries include luxury hotels in Guangzhou, Beijing and Shanghai. However, nurseries seem to rely above all on the large demand coming from nearby Hong Kong, where they supply major customers such as the city's airport and Hong Kong Disneyland. The new Hong Kong International Airport, which began operations in 1998, was exclusively supplied by one tree nursery with nine forty-foot containers per day for a period of seven years for the design of the airport's exterior spaces. The airport project also included the building of an entire new city, Tung Chung New Town.

The soil around Guangzhou tends to be acidic and is therefore ideal for the cultivation of all types of plants. Trees from northern China thrive in the south, although the reverse usually does not apply. Ruan says that a large number of the trees used for Expo 2010 in Shanghai also originated from the Guangzhou region.

We drive first to New World Garden, one of the prime tree nurseries. It is located in Ao Tou, one hour's drive north of the Guangzhou city center. The air quality here is better, because the industrial zones are located in the south. The company's premises cover an area of around one hundred hectares.

The area used to be covered with rice fields. The tree nursery, which was established just over ten years ago, now has fifty employees. The owner had to build up the expertise necessary to run such a business himself since traditional knowledge was not passed on during Mao's rule. The enterprise focuses exclusively on production and does not conduct any research in areas such as the development of new varieties through selective breeding. The trade in seeds is also regarded as relatively unimportant.

Dozens of tree varieties are transplanted and lined out at the tree nursery. The majority of them are Chinese trees but there are also varieties from Southeast Asia and a few from Europe, for example palms from southern France. The selection is based entirely on demand. Indigenous trees cultivated at the nursery include different banyan varieties as well as the camphor tree *(Cinnamomum camphora)*, a broadleaf evergreen, and sweet osmanthus *(Osmanthus fragrans)*, which blooms in October and gives off an enchanting scent. Both species are also highly popular and widespread around Shanghai.

Many trees in this nursery are over one hundred years old and come from the mountainous regions in the provinces of Guizhou, Sichuan and Yunnan. The nursery owner travels through these regions in search of high-quality specimens, purchases the selected trees for some tens of thousands of RMB (several thousand dollars) and transports them back to the nursery, where they are nurtured for two to three years. The sellers are often farmers on whose land the trees are standing. Not everyone in China is happy about this trade, and many regard it as illegal and destructive. But the state seems unwilling to intervene. Ruan argues that his business is based exclusively on private sales and has nothing to do with the illegal clearing of natural forests. He points out that in any case there are practically no natural forests left in China as a result of the campaign of industrialization in the fifties, when huge forest stocks were cut down throughout the country.

We drive southwest to another tree nursery district. The road is lined with eucalyptus trees, as well as lychee and mango trees, which provide fruit that is sold at the roadside. Ruan explains that this diversity is relatively new and that in the sixties Guangzhou was almost completely dominated by eucalyptus trees, which were used above all as a source of wood. We visit Luo Han Song Garden, a business devoted exclusively to old kusamaki trees *(Podocarpus macrophyllus;* or *Luo Han Song* in Chinese) imported from Japan. China is practically the only foreign market for Japanese dealers, because the export of old kusamaki is only possible over short distances. Differing from the Chinese variant, these trees (also referred to as Buddhist pines) are often over one hundred years old and are considered extremely valuable since they cannot be easily propagated. Ruan says that the Japanese sometimes joke that all their trees have now been dug up. However, he thinks that this market could well last another twenty to thirty years.

*"Dealers pay the farmers, dig up the trees, lop off the crowns and replant them here."*

The trunk of an old Chinese cedar *(Cryptomeria fortunei)* in Tianmushan, Zhejiang Province

Indian banyan trees *(Ficus benghalensis)* are a feature of the streetscape in Guangzhou

Old transplanted *Ficus* trees in a nursery near Guangzhou

Old kusamaki trees *(Podocarpus macrophyllus)* from Japan can sell for as much as 350,000 dollars

Certain palm varieties are imported from southern France

Transportation of an old Chinese banyan tree

*"The Japanese sometimes joke that all their trees have now been dug up."*

**THE SYMBOLIC MEANING OF PLANTS**

In China many trees, flowers and shrubs have a symbolic meaning. For instance, some trees have a religious significance, such as the sacred fig *(Ficus religiosa)*, also known as the bodhi or bo tree. This evergreen grows in southern China, is a close relative of the banyan and originally came from India. Legend has it that Siddhartha Gautama, the historical Buddha Shakyamuni, first achieved enlightenment while sitting under a sacred fig tree.

Religious meaning is also attributed to the ginkgo *(Ginkgo biloba)*, which is traditionally planted in temples. This tree is indigenous to China and known there as a "living fossil." It has been used to line the Expo Boulevard at Expo 2010 in Shanghai. In some regions planting ginkgo in the domestic context is taboo because the plant is associated with temples and monks. Since the latter are also linked with "childlessness" the ginkgo is not regarded as an appropriate domestic plant in a culture in which "home" and "family" mean the same thing. Traditional Confucianism regards procreation as one of the most important filial duties.

Modern Chinese has only a limited number of sounds (monosyllables) but a great many written characters, and therefore the language is full of homophones, i.e., words that are pronounced the same (though they may differ in the tone applied, since Chinese is a tonal language). Thus some plants are considered taboo because their names evoke unpleasant associations, such as the pear (pronounced like the Mandarin word for "abandon"), the red date (pronounced like another word meaning "premature," which can be associated with premature death), and the mulberry (pronounced like the word for "burial").

By contrast, other plants are regarded as symbolic of good character. Bamboo is seen as symbolizing strength and steadfastness because the plant does not break during storms. In addition the Chinese characters used to describe it ("hollow interior") are equated with open-mindedness and modesty.

Pine, bamboo and plum are known as "three friends in winter" on account of their robustness, and they are often found in Chinese art. The design of the Expo park also alludes to these three plants, which are regarded as symbolizing the character of China.

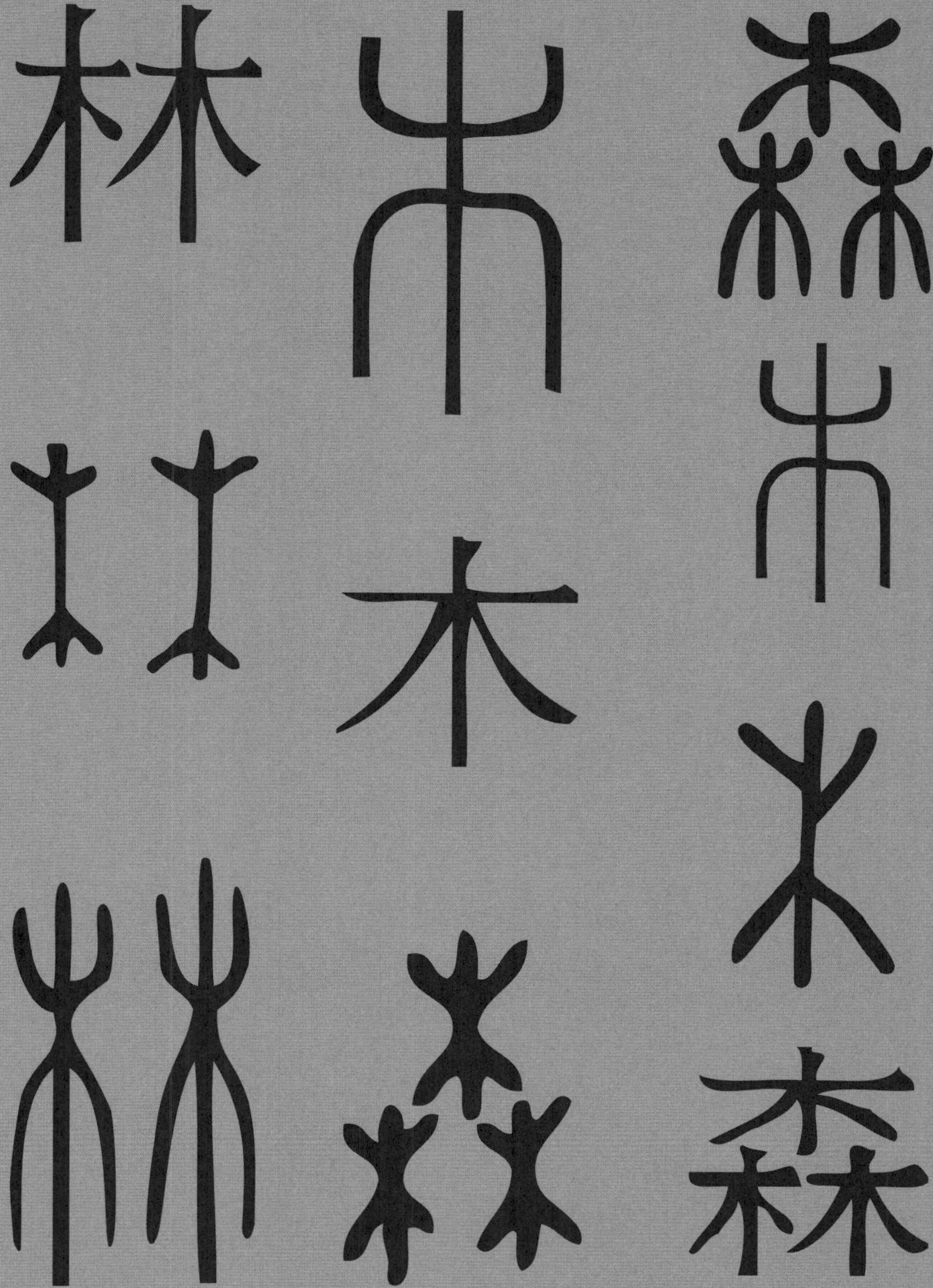

The Chinese characters 木 (wood), 林 (forest) and 森 (forest) in old and modern script. The words for forest consist of a multiplication of the ideogram for wood.

# SYSTEMATICS AND AESTHETICS: A CHRONICLE

**Over the millennia, mankind has produced an enormous variety of cultivated plants by means of selection, breeding and propagation. Furthermore, special production sites have evolved in Europe whose range of products, structures and processes have reflected the zeitgeist and its underlying agenda. To this day, cloister gardens, botanical gardens, greenhouses, arboretums and nurseries continue to provide an important foundation, both for the production of plants and for designing exterior spaces and urban areas.**

Photo essay and photographs by Dominique Ghiggi

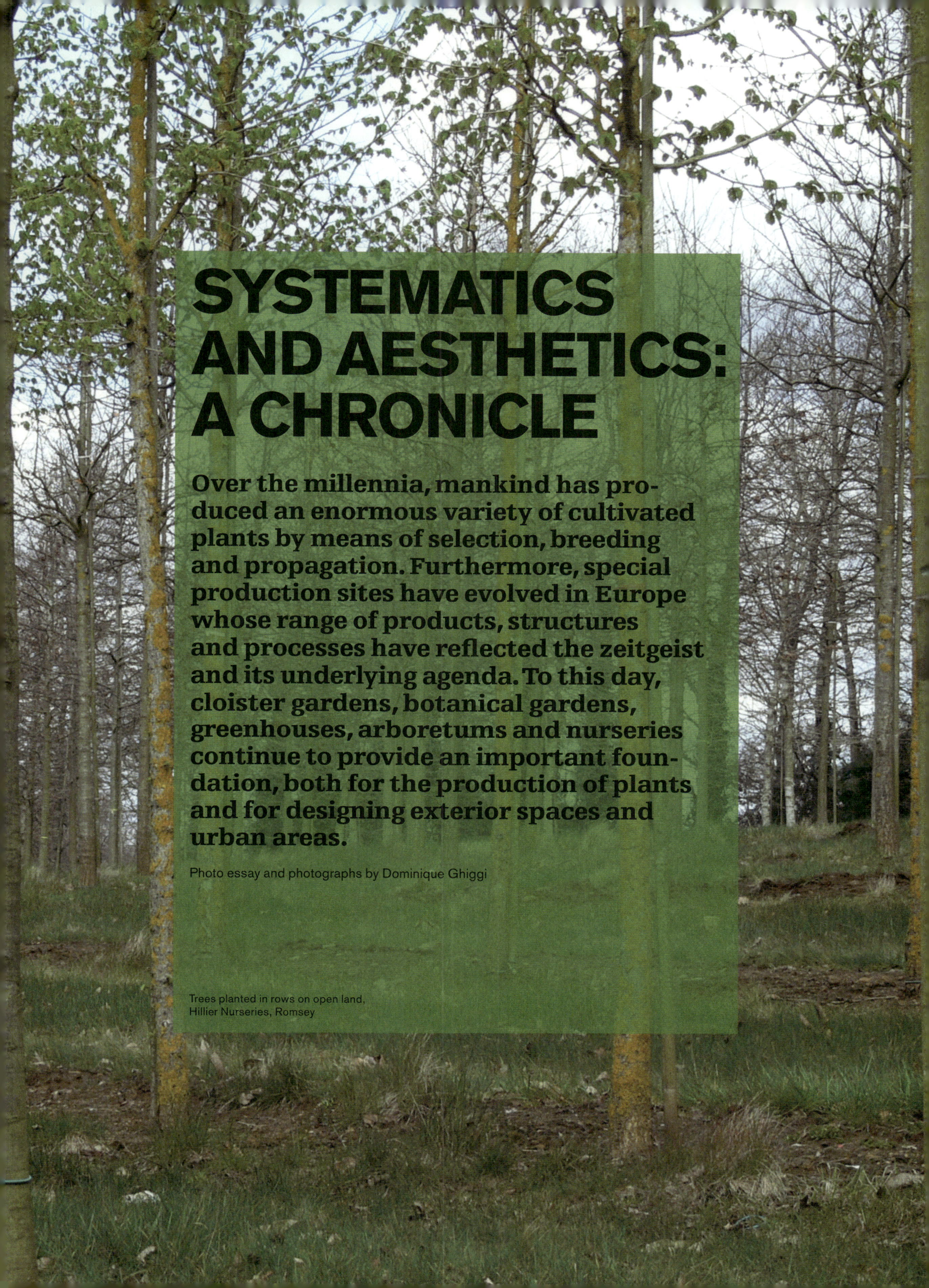

Trees planted in rows on open land,
Hillier Nurseries, Romsey

Throughout the history of plant production, particularly given the changes in garden styles, people have always favored new tree species, varieties and forms, and cultivated them in large quantities. But starting with industrialization, trees were no longer produced for gardens and parks alone. Over time, tree production has increasingly been adapted to the scale of the landscape—initially to that of forests and later to that of the growing cities. Over the last hundred years, a greater number and variety of trees have been cultivated than in previous centuries.

Yet one thing has not changed since the first trees were planted: the need to create a suitable basis for the cultivation and care of plants in order to achieve optimal growth. Whether in fields, beds, pots or greenhouses, soil tillage continues to be the most important condition for success. This factor has gained special significance through the growing depletion of soil worldwide due to intensive farming, as well as increasing desertification and urbanization.

Saint Gall cloister plan, with the enlarged section of the Hortulus according to the specifications by Walahfrid Strabo
Illustration: Cod. Sang. 1092, Stiftsbibliothek Saint Gallen

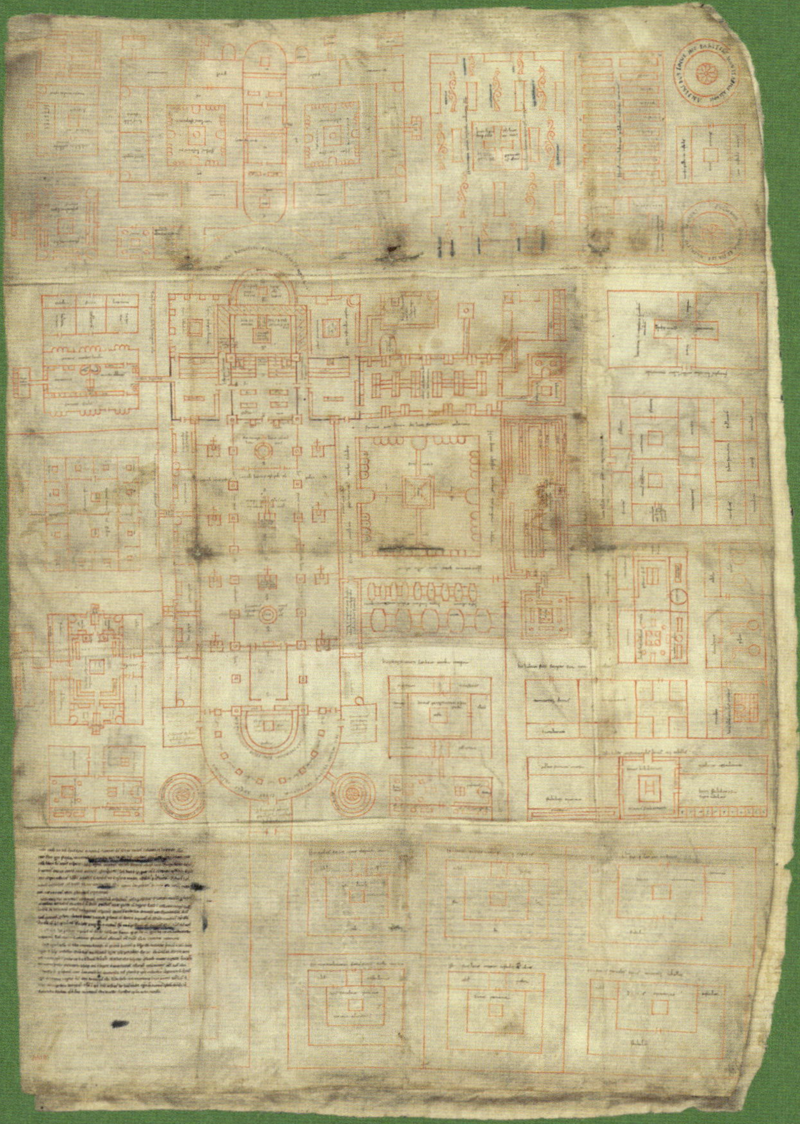

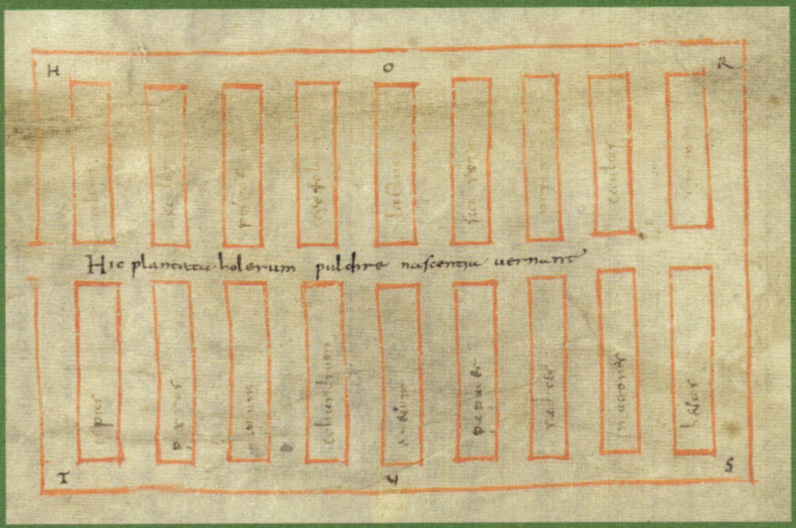

# Cloister gardens: symbolism and structure

"Cloister"—from the Latin claustrum—refers to a self-contained community. The word was originally used to describe the covered colonnaded paths that are typical of monasteries in the Western world. In languages such as Dutch, German and English, it later came to refer to the entire complex of buildings.

Within the monasteries' originally self-sufficient structures, plants were grown in gardens and processed mainly for the residents' own use. Since they carefully documented their activities, the monasteries had a profound influence on the development of agricultural cultivation and the dissemination of economic plants throughout Europe, particularly herbs, medicinal plants, vines, and native fruit trees. The monasteries' use of grafting, a traditional form of cloning, played an important role in propagating fruit trees.

As the plan of the Carolingian Abbey of Saint Gall illustrates, the square was considered the ideal form for a monastery complex. Depending on the region, agriculture and viticulture were practiced outside the monastery walls, where meadow orchards were also located. According to the sixth-century *Rule of Saint Benedict*, everything that was necessary for living, such as water supplies, mills, gardens, etc., was supposed to be located inside the monastery. The gardens shown on the Plan of Saint Gall include not only cloister, herbal and vegetable gardens but also orchards. Each garden type has a rectangular shape. The rectangular beds are bordered by wooden planks and laid out in rows for vegetables and herbs. The cloister gardens and orchards consist of square courtyards on empty grounds, usually without paths. Each plant was meticulously categorized according to its use and significance. For example, the beds for medicinal plants were systematically arranged on the basis of the plants' healing powers, one species per patch. The monks described the plants' benefits and medicinal effects, as well as their symbolic powers.

***HORTULUS*** **BY WALAHFRID STRABO**
Walahfrid Strabo, the young abbot of Reichenau Abbey on Lake Constance, wrote his famous horticultural poem in the first half of the ninth century. Entitled *De cultura hortorum*—abbreviated as *Hortulus*—it describes his observations and practical experiences in the cloister garden he tended. His garden primarily contained medicinal plants and consisted of twenty-three beds, each containing one species. In the poem Strabo introduces each plant in a new stanza, praising its benefits, medicinal effects, beauty and symbolic powers in hexameters. Along with the Plan of Saint Gall and Charlemagne's regulations on estate management *(Capitulare de villis)*, the *Hortulus* is considered one of the earliest medieval documents on horticulture in Germany. Its par-ticularity lies in the description of experienced reality of the plant life in a small garden that actually existed in Central Europe. Today the twenty-three plants, described in great detail, are still cultivated in regions of the temperate Central European climate zone.

***DE VEGETABILIBUS*** **BY ALBERTUS MAGNUS**
Saint Albert the Great was an important ambassador of the European plant kingdom in the High Middle Ages. A German scholar and bishop, he paved the way for the Christian Aristotelianism of his age. Under his direction, the Cologne monastery school gained an excellent reputation around 1250, attracting students from all over Europe. Endeavoring to reconcile Aristotle's natural philosophy with the Christian faith, Saint Albert the Great acquired an encyclopedic knowledge in the fields of theology, philosophy, medicine and the natural sciences. However, he did not succeed in presenting this knowledge in a self-contained system—this task was only completed by his student Thomas Aquinas. Saint Albert the Great's most famous work on plants is *De vegetabilibus*. It was published in 1260 and was the first detailed treatment of Central European flora including geographical descriptions.

This drawing of the Saint Gall cloister by someone named Lasius was copied in 1876 for the book *Geschichte der Bildenden Künste in der Schweiz* (History of the Fine Arts in Switzerland) by the Zurich historian Johann Rudolph Rahn (1841–1912). The original drawing no longer exists.

* Kloster Sanct Gallen nach dem Grundrisse vom Jahre 830. (Lasius).

# Botanical garden: systematics and biodiversity

Almost all cultures have enclosed gardens where plants are grown for food or ornament, or which serve as places of recreation or as symbols of power. Yet botanical gardens used for the study of plants, or more precisely botany, are a relatively recent phenomenon. They go back to the budding Italian universities in the mid-sixteenth century and the beginnings of the golden age of the natural sciences. The world's oldest botanical garden was founded in Padua in 1545—the Orto Botanico di Padova.

Botanical gardens were initially referred to as *hortus medicus* and used to train doctors and pharmacists. Like medieval monastery gardens, they contained the medicinal, poisonous and spice plants known at the time. However, in contrast to cloister gardens, their gardeners came to arrange the plants according to biological relationships. Since the Church was against any attempt to classify plants as part of evolutionary lineages, any in-depth study of the systematics of the plant kingdom was neglected for centuries. When research finally began, the first studies concentrated on the useful and medicinal plants indigenous to Europe. The new species that plant collectors brought back to Europe from their journeys around the world, including many trees, were only studied later. The constantly growing diversity of species resulted in a complexity that required urgent "decoding," using clear and objective criteria. In two works entitled *Species plantarum and Systema naturae,* published in 1753 and 1758 respectively, the Swedish naturalist Carl von Linné established the modern classification system based on genus and species that continues to be relevant to biological nomenclature to this day. In this system, the scientific name of every plant, in Latin, includes a noun for the genus and an adjective for the species, followed by the complete or abbreviated name of the author who conferred the name, e.g., *Fagus sylvatica L. (L* = Linné).

With the ongoing discovery of new botanical species from all regions of the earth, botanical gardens grew richer in species. In the seventeenth century the demand from different social classes increased and the propagation of foreign plants no longer took place primarily in the conservatories of wealthy families. Botanical gardens thus became important centers for research into foreign botanical species and their introduction into new countries. They also evolved into hubs of international exchange. Trees were initially grown in orangeries and later in greenhouses; their seedlings, bulbs or seeds were traded.

Between the sixteenth and eighteenth centuries, botanical gardens were constantly expanded to include new sections. Their exterior facilities evolved from the meticulously laid-out geometric beds common in the Middle Ages to the symmetrical Renaissance gardens, from ornamental Baroque gardens with shaped hedges and trees to the landscaped gardens of the eighteenth and nineteenth centuries. In these landscaped gardens, trees were planted on lawns, either individually or in groups, in a seemingly natural design.

**THE HORTUS BOTANICUS LEIDEN**
The botanical garden of Leiden University in the Netherlands, often referred to simply as the Hortus, is the second oldest in Europe after the botanical garden in Padua. It was built on the Rapenburg Canal in 1590. Visitors enter through an archway next to the monastery church, which was converted into a university in 1575. Two names are closely associated with the garden's history, Charles de l'Écluse, often called Clusius, and Philipp Franz von Siebold. Both men were doctors, botany professors at Leiden University, plant breeders and collectors.

It was Clusius who planted the first tulip in the Hortus Clusianus, a garden that he built in 1594 and which today makes up just one section of the botanical garden. Having developed the garden for scientific purposes, he laid it out in the typical Renaissance style with four squares subdivided by rectangular beds. More than a thousand of the botanical garden's species were originally planted in the Hortus Clusianus, which offered a mix of useful, medicinal and exotic ornamental plants from the Mediterranean region, Central Asia and America, including the famous tulips from Turkey. Clusius's garden was later destroyed and reconstructed on a nearby site in 1933. The new garden was restored in 1990 and then moved back to its original location in front of the Hortus in 2009.

European scholars regard Philipp Franz von Siebold as the scientific discoverer of Japan. Around 1830, after his first six-year stay on the small artificial island of Dejima in the bay of Nagasaki, von Siebold identified and described the botanical species he had imported to the Hortus. Today, a variety of Asian species, especially orchids and ferns from Southeast Asia, have become one of the Hortus's special focuses. Botanists continue to study their pollination methods, their evolution, biological relationships and propagation. Most of von Siebold's plants can be found in the greenhouses and gardens in the park area, which has been open to the public since it was founded.

There are many interesting sights in the garden for both plant experts and plant lovers, including the Von Siebold Memorial Garden, designed by the Japanese landscape architect Makoto Nakamura; the orangery for Asian and Mediterranean potted plants, built between 1740 and 1744 based on plans by the French architect Daniel Marot; the arboretum, in which trees are grouped primarily by families; the new greenhouse for semitropical potted plants, designed by Hubert-Jan Hanging and home to the Hortus Shop and a restaurant; and, finally, the Systematic Garden, the heart of the Hortus botanicus. It was designed to show the evolutionary lineages of the entire plant kingdom, and students visit this garden to learn how to identify plant species. In the rear is a small tree nursery in which trees were still bred well into the twentieth century.

Today the Hortus still focuses on preserving and expanding botanical variety. Its researchers are especially interested in plants known to have originated in the wild, rather than in hybrids. Many new species are collected from natural stocks worldwide and kept on site. However, the national and international regulations on protecting endangered species are so strict in most countries that they greatly impede efforts to collect and import plants. The mere exchange of seeds is an unsatisfactory alternative because it provides fewer and fewer new species.

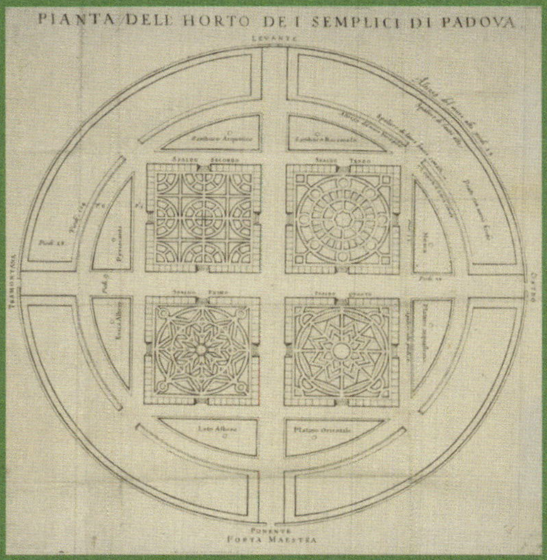


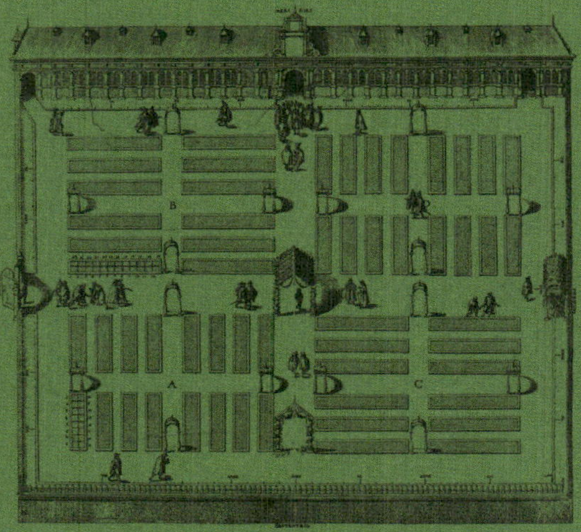

GIACOMO ANTONIO CORTUSI (1513–1603)
"L'horto de i semplici di Padoua, oue si vede primieramente la forma di tutta la pianta con le sue misure: & indi i suoi partimenti distinti per numeri in ciascuna arella, intagliato in rame. Opera che serue mirabilmente alla memoria de gli studiosi / \ Giacom'Antonio Cortusi!". *Venetia: appresso Girolamo Porro,* 1591 . – [72] c., [5] c. di tav. ripieg.: ill. ; 8°.
Illustration: generously provided by the Biblioteca dell'Orto Botanico, University of Padua

Plan of the Hortus botanicus Leiden by Jacques de Gheyn II
Illustrat on: from Pieter Paaw, *Hortus Publicus Academiae Lugduno-Batavae*, Leiden: Officina Plantiniana, 1601

Leiden Botanical Garden
1 Systematic garden, the heart of the Hortus botanicus
2 Arboretum
3 Orangery for Asian and Mediterranean tub plants, designed between 1740 and 1744 by the French architect Daniel Marot
4 The Clusius Garden, reconstructed in 1993
5 Greenhouse for subtropical tub plants designed by Hubert-Jan Henket Photo: Hortus botanicus Leiden

2

3

4

# Greenhouses: acclimatization

The nineteenth century was marked by intense efforts to acquire and exchange plants from foreign countries. Long journeys were required to import living plants from overseas, and many plants died on the way. In many cases, the exotic species introduced into Europe first went to England, where the development of greenhouses was at its peak, garden magazines were becoming increasingly popular, and the Wardian case had just been invented. Like their predecessors, the winter gardens, greenhouses were developed to grow plants that were accustomed to different climates. Offering optimal climatic conditions in transparent glass structures, they enabled people to acclimatize and to grow a wide variety of plants. Huge greenhouses were sometimes built for tall trees. Victorian greenhouses, which often contained tree ferns and palms, were the most famous and elegant of the period. Their steel-and-glass structures were richly decorated in the contemporary fashion and became a distinguishing element of nineteenth-century architecture; it spread across the entire European continent. Glass greenhouses and palm houses also became a characteristic feature of botanical gardens.

**THE WARDIAN CASE: TRANSPORTING EXOTIC PLANTS**

An accidental observation by the London physician Nathaniel Bagshaw Ward led to the invention of the Wardian case in 1829. Ward was a passionate naturalist who bred ferns in his leisure time, but he had little success when he attempted to cultivate the ferns in a specially built stone garden. He was also interested in moths and butterflies, in their development and metamorphosis, and in the summer of 1829 he put a hawk moth cocoon in moist humus into a wide-necked glass bottle, and sealed it with a lid. He noticed that the moisture released during the heat of the day condensed on the glass surface and ran into the soil. This cycle kept the soil moist. Before the final stage of the metamorphosis, a tiny fern and a blade of grass had appeared in the humus. Ward was astonished. The ferns that had not grown in his garden suddenly grew in the bottle all by themselves. He built a special small green house and over the course of four years observed the magnificent development of the fern, which produced three to four new fronds a year. Ward put his observations to good use: He designed the "Wardian case" for the cultivation and transport of tropical plants, with low sides, a glass roof and a perforated watering pipe attached below the roof.

Interior View of the Crystal Palace, Hyde Park, showing the Opening of the Great Exhibition in 1851 (litho)
Illustration: Guildhall Library, City of London/The Bridgeman Art Library

Variants of the Wardian case
Illustrations: from Nathaniel Bagshaw Ward, On the Growth of Plants in Closely Glazed Cases, London: John Van Voorst, 1852

# Arboretum: collecting and breeding

By definition, an arboretum (plural: arboreta or arboretums) is a collection of trees growing outdoors. According to the eleventh edition of the Encyclopaedia Britannica, published in 1911, the term was coined by John Claudius Loudon in 1838, in a book on trees, but the world's oldest example—the Arboretum of Trsteno near the Croatian city of Dubrovnik—already existed in 1492.

Starting around 1850, trees were increasingly arranged in groups according to precisely defined criteria. In systematically laid out arboretums, the tree species or varieties were grouped together in genera or families based on their biological relationships, much like in classical botanical gardens. Or they were arranged on the basis of morphological traits such as the color or form of their blossoms, leaves, or of the trees themselves. In geographical arboretums, trees were grouped according to their regions or countries of origin. Forest arboretums, by contrast, consisted of groups of the same tree species, which were selected on the basis of wood productivity.

Arboretums focused on breeding and propagating the trees in order to create new varieties. Various trees with striking morphological or physiological traits—such as special robustness or a particular size, shape or number of blossoms/leaves—were selected and crossed until the desired characteristics emerged. Subsequently, the daughter plant was propagated vegetatively, that is to say cloned. Many new ornamental tree varieties came into being, particularly in the nineteenth century. It was generally the gardeners and nursery staff who, thanks to their trained eye, discovered divergent forms and propagated them, employing the cutting and grafting methods developed for fruit trees in the late seventeenth century. Today, scientists also use smart breeding methods that are based on genome research instead of the outer features of the plant. The plants' genetic makeup is extensively analyzed in order to select suitable partners for crossing. The time advantage achieved thereby is an important advancement over classical selection breeding.

The boom in botany between the sixteenth and nineteenth centuries left an indelible mark on garden design and led to the rise of the picturesque English gardens. The single tree, combinations of several trees forming a group, and the colorful gradations of different kinds of shrubs—none of these could be shown to best advantage in the rigid forms of French gardens. Supported by the growing enthusiasm for the wonders of foreign lands, the population took an interest in viewing the unique beauty of natural tree growth. Groups of trees called "clumps" were one of the most important elements in English landscape gardens. They embodied the principle of a natural landscape whose diverse and picturesque impressions were pleasing to the eye—much like "a landscape painting one could walk into."

**THE ARBORETUM TERVUREN**

The public Arboretum of Tervuren in Belgium is a magnificent park where visitors can discover the world's forests. Charles Brommer, the conservator of the National Botanical Garden in Meise and professor at the Free University of Brussels, created this geographical arboretum in 1902, encouraged by A. Dubois, the director-general of the water and forestry administration. The arboretum covers about one hundred hectares in the Kapucijnenbos (Capuchin Woods) near Brussels and boasts 465 different tree species. The groups of trees have been planted with unobtrusive signage in several plots according to their origins and the type of soil suitable to each species. The different species are arranged in the plots on the basis of ecological affinities. Today, each group of trees forms a small forest consisting of different representative species. Clearings and avenues separate the plots, creating pleasant perspectives. A walk through the arboretum takes visitors on a trip around the world, with stops in Europe, Asia and the Americas: the eastern section contains the plants of the Old World and the western section the species of the New World. The principal forest types native to the temperate regions of the earth, including the American West, Europe and Asia, have been reproduced on a small scale; a short excursion to the southern hemisphere is also included.

In the past, the Arboretum of Tervuren's main aim was the long-term growth of the trees it had imported, which one day were to be used in forestry. It also experimented with these trees. In the course of the arboretum's hundred-year existence, certain tree species that were incapable of adapting to local conditions have disappeared, but many have prospered, produced seeds and multiplied. The success of reforestation is ensured by Belgium's mild Atlantic climate and fertile soil. Today the arboretum still carries out experiments on tree planting and adaptability, and supplies many forest tree nurseries with the seeds of commercially and ecologically important coniferous and deciduous species, including the American Douglas fir and local oaks and beeches.

English landscape garden from the facsimile of the colored atlas by Prince Hermann von Pückler-Muskau, panel III, Inv.-no.: IV/56/1362

Illustration: Hermann von Pückler-Muskau, *Andeutungen über Landschaftsgärtnerei: verbunden mit der Beschreibung ihrer praktischen Anwendung in Muskau*, edited by Harri Günther, Stuttgart: Deutsche Verlags-Anstalt, 1987; Fürst-Pückler-Museum Park and Branitz Castle Foundation

**THE ARBORETUM WESPELAAR**
Wespelaar Park in Haacht, Belgium, consists of four different sections that are owned by the aristocratic de Spoelberch families. The arboretum encompasses the ten-hectare Herkenrode Garden, built primarily in the mid-nineteenth century, and a twenty-hectare area called Wespelaar Arboretum that Philippe de Spoelberch created in 1979 on the basis of the park, which had a rich plant life. A chemist trained in the agriculture industry, de Spoelberch developed an interest and passion for trees, which finds full expression in his tree collection. The arboretum is mainly used for scientific and educational purposes and is the second-most important documented collection of trees in the country. It can be visited as part of a guided tour.

The arboretum consists primarily of landscaped islands, and a small section in the Herkenrode Garden is made up of geometrically arranged plots, each with one tree genus. The magnolias and rhododendrons are among its most important plant collections.[1] The locational preferences of the tree species were taken into account when determining where the trees were to be planted, either in the shade of evergreen or deciduous populations, or under the open sky. But aesthetic considerations also play an important role in Wespelaar. De Spoelberch carefully studies the color compositions created by the groups of trees, and trees that are not in the right place because of their color or forms are removed and planted elsewhere.

Right next to the main building, behind a high evergreen hedge, stands a small greenhouse in which tree species are bred for the arboretum. Its goal is to create species that bloom faster and bear larger blossoms. In comparison to tree varieties, tree species require longer to bloom and often produce many small blossoms. Small quantities of the new tree varieties are also sold in the retail trade. Philippe de Spoelberch principally believes in guiding the progress of nature and is a firm advocate of using genetically modified useful plants in the fight against world hunger.

The breeding house forms a small private tree nursery together with the other propagation areas, which are suitable for all stages of growth. First, seeds are sown in a bed protected by a plastic sheet or cuttings are planted in the earth. Then, during the second year, the young plants are potted and acclimatized for twelve months in a hothouse. The trees are subsequently allowed to grow in the open for two to five years until they are finally transplanted to the arboretum. Some of the seedlings are also grown in the adjacent beech forest, where they have adequate protection against the wind and direct sunlight.

1 The complete list of trees and shrubs can be found in the catalogue section of the arboretum's website at www.arboretumwespelaar.be.

Beech grove in the Geographic Arboretum in Tervuren near Brussels, Belgium

Wespelaar Arboretum in Haacht, Belgium:
1 Herkenrode Garden from the mid-nineteenth century, part of the Wespelaar Arboretum
2 Philippe de Spoelberch conducts regular teaching tours through his arboretum
3 Geometrically arranged islands, each of which is devoted to one tree species
4 Flowering ornamental fruit tree placed in the shadow of deciduous trees
5 The small breeding house stands next to the main building of the complex, behind a high, evergreen hedge
6 Tree varieties are cultivated for the arboretum in the small greenhouse
7 In the nursery next to the greenhouse young plants are initially cultivated in beds for one year before being transferred to pots
8 The potted plants are acclimatized for one year in a glasshouse

1

2

3

4

5

6

7

8

## Tree nurseries: trade and production

Tree nurseries that are run as commercial businesses and dedicated to the production of large numbers of trees have existed in Europe only for about five hundred years. Other countries have a much longer tradition in tree production and trade. In Egypt this tradition extends back to the age of the Pharaohs; in China it has been ongoing for 4000 years; and in Turkey it began in the twelfth century. The Japanese also acquired extensive knowledge of the cultivation and transplantation of old trees early on in their history, and they continue to apply this knowledge today.

However, a distinguishing feature of European tree nurseries is the degree of specialization that they have achieved, particularly since the nineteenth century. From the original fruit tree nurseries of the fifteenth century to the forest tree nurseries of the eighteenth, from the first large nurseries with a wide assortment of the nineteenth century to the container nurseries developed over the last hundred years, a great deal has changed.

In terms of production, the primary change has been in the number of trees sold and, consequently, the size of company structures. Thanks to technical measures, basic activities such as breeding, cultivation, harvesting and the sale of plant products have been standardized and separated in terms of their logistics. But one thing has not changed: most nurseries continue to be run as family businesses, and despite the use of machines and standardized processes, they still require expertise in horticulture and manual labor.

In the eighteenth century, European tree nurseries were still rather small because they only supplied trees for the local market. The majority were affiliated to monasteries, large estates or palaces. In the course of the nineteenth century, most of the companies grew rapidly, along with the cities. A large number of tree nurseries were established close to cities because it was easy to supply the market there. In conjunction with industrialization, the railway and road systems expanded, which allowed trees to be delivered over longer distances. During this time, larger tree nursery areas were established and soon began to dominate the European market. Today the areas used for agriculture around the tree nursery regions are continually shrinking, while new companies have been founded and steadily expand. Over the last five hundred years there has been a huge increase in the number of plant production sites, some of which have now assumed vast dimensions. The small and medium-sized tree nurseries in the landscape turned the landscape itself into a vast production site.

Regarding the plant trade, the market has expanded beyond national borders and has become more complex due to the formation of large nursery centers. As a result, precise knowledge of the current market conditions has become essential. To keep up to date, companies send their employees on annual trips so that they can meet with their customers—mostly private or state-run nurseries and a growing number of garden centers—and incorporate their requests into upcoming production cycles. Visits to tree fairs and seminars on current market developments are also important. Conversely, the tree nurseries regularly receive visits from landscape and structural architects, who influence plant production through the plants they select for large projects. In general, most of the trees produced in Europe are native species adapted to the climate zone and soil of the respective countries. Additionally, several nurseries in Holland have specialized in acclimatizing and selling tropical and semitropical trees.

Multistemmed single trees awaiting transplantation. Bruns Pflanzen, Bad Zwischenahn, Germany

Dispatch area. Bruns Pflanzen, Bad Zwischenahn, Germany

Production of young deciduous trees. Sylva forest tree nursery, Waarschoot, Belgium

FENDT

# Forest tree nurseries: ecology

Although the first deciduous and coniferous tree plantations are mentioned in sources dating from the thirteenth and fourteenth centuries, forestation and tree nurseries did not acquire greater economic significance until much later. The destruction of forests by humans throughout history, particularly in the eighteenth and nineteenth centuries, was gradually reversed by targeted forestation efforts beginning in the late eighteenth century. However, with the increase in barren cleared areas, it was no longer possible to undo the large-scale destruction of forests—the result of industrialization—by harvesting saplings from the forests and replanting them. Young forest plants had to be cultivated in tree nurseries in order to meet the demand for trees. During this period, North American trees were used for the first time to reforest extensive areas in Germany. In the period up to the early twentieth century, the world's largest continuous tree nursery region emerged in the district of Pinneberg near Hamburg. Today replanted forests make up a large part of our natural environment.

During evolution, the original forest trees spread over long distances. Various populations of different tree species emerged and continually adapted to the climatic conditions in the various regions. The genetic makeup of every tree allows us to make deductions about its origins. Modern forest nurseries are characterized by the fact that they pay strict attention to questions of origin and are interested in propagation material that does not only conform to high standards in terms of morphology and physiology, but also in terms of genetic quality. In Europe it is in principle only permitted to cultivate plants whose origin is authorized.

**SYLVA AND SYLMA**

The Sylva forest nursery has operated as a family-owned Flemish business since 1750. Over the years, the proprietors—the van Hulle family—have expanded it to encompass more than eighty hectares. The present-day company, based in Waarschoot, was founded in 1936 as "Tree Nurseries van Hulle-Coppens and Company." At the time tree nurseries had begun to produce mainly coniferous species. When the sons took over the company in 1972, they founded Sylva Limited, which specializes in producing young deciduous trees in open land, particularly beeches and oaks. Today the company employs forty-five people, nearly half of whom come from Poland and Romania.

Flanders is particularly well suited for the cultivation of forest trees. The soil is sandy and the temperatures are mild, ranging from minus five to plus thirty degrees Celsius. Root growth is more vigorous in light soils, which makes it necessary to replant the trees more frequently, but it brings the advantage of preserving the delicate root system near the trunk. This is why the region has been particularly successful in planting forest trees of different origins. Nevertheless, although the conditions in Flanders are optimal for extensive forestation, the amount of land covered by forests—only 150,000 hectares—is small and the level of investment is low because of the high price of land (50,000 euros per hectare). The situation is different in Wallonia, where 600,000 hectares of land are covered by forest and the price of land—20,000 euros per hectare—is much cheaper by comparison. In France prices even run as low as 5000 to 10,000 euros per hectare.

The seedlings grown in fields—around twenty million a year—are delivered to other tree nurseries in Belgium and abroad at a maximum age of four years. Sylva receives orders from countries and private businesses throughout Europe, and less frequently from North America. These customers supply the nursery with seeds; it stores large quantities in a seed warehouse—some in boxes stacked on shelves, others in bags in a separate cold storage area. To reforest its own land, Sylva harvests seeds itself. For example, many of its beech and oak seeds come from the Zonien forest in Brussels. Government institutions inspect its fields and products on a weekly basis.

The one-meter-wide beds, which are arranged in rows, are a maximum of three hundred meters long. One important point is that beds are laid out so that the machine-based work processes are not disrupted by varying distances between the rows or by different plant care requirements. This means that different tree species requiring the same amount of time to grow can be grown in the same section. In other words, species do not play a decisive role in determining the arrangement of plants.

Each season is characterized by specific processes. In spring the seedlings are sown and transplanted; in summer the trunks, branches and roots are pruned; and in autumn the trees are dug up. The mild climate also makes it possible to work in winter, and in this season the seedlings are dug up and sorted. Before the plants are sold, they are stored in a cool warehouse where the seedlings are sorted according to species and height, and tree nursery staff carefully check the root system, the robustness and straightness of the trunk, the branch attachments and the proportions of every plant. The production cycle from sowing to sale lasts an average of two to three years.

With the increase in reforestation in the south of Europe, there has been a greater demand for forest plants cultivated in greenhouses and containers. These developments required changes at Sylva, and in 1992 it founded its subsidiary Sylma. Under the management of the young Christof van Hulle, this company has specialized in cultivating young forest and ornamental trees in pots and hydroponic systems in greenhouses. Sylma grew to four times its original size in the period up to 2002 and has since been an independent business. In comparison to Sylva, its production cycle is shorter and restricted to one to two years. This is one reason why Sylma was able to quickly adapt to the European market.

1–2 Sylma, Lovendegem, Belgium. Cultivation of young forest and ornamental plants in pots and hydroponic systems in the greenhouse

3–8 Sylva, Waarschoot, Belgium. Forest tree nursery on open land
3 A mild climate and sandy soil are well suited to the cultivation of forest trees
4 Young plants cultivated in fields
5 Seedlings under a protective sheet
6 One-year-old beeches
7 Seed storage room
8 Sorting according to species and heights in the warehouse

1

2

3

4

5

6

7

8

## Assortment tree nurseries: quality

In contrast to forest tree nurseries, assortment tree nurseries—which sell a wide range of products—are horticultural enterprises. They emerged in the nineteenth century as garden culture spread throughout France and England, creating a demand for a large variety of species and forms. The leading tradition-steeped businesses in Europe are Hillier Nurseries in England, Arbor in Belgium, Bruns, Lappen and von Ehren in Germany, as well as Vannucci Piante in Italy. All these nurseries produce trees for different-sized gardens, offering large quantities and a great variety. For around fifty years demand for plants has increased in the expanding, densely populated areas in and outside Europe.

Producing trees for streets is an important line of business for these nurseries. The aim is to grow identical-looking tall trees cultivated in batches. For decades there has been a trend toward standardizing trees, which to some extent has degraded the trees to the status of a mere product. In terms of appearance *(habitus)*, tree production is heavily oriented toward the standards and directives prescribed in the individual countries. There are, for instance, precise definitions regarding trunk height, crown base and the shape of the leading shoot. In Germany alone producers have to follow a multitude of directives and standards.

Some few nurseries—of which Bruns in Europe is the most important example—grow specimen of large-size trees (solitaries) and trees that require meticulous care for several years. This group includes trees clipped into particular shapes and those that grow in especially picturesque forms. The demand for such products has been on the rise for the last few years. In contrast to the market for forest plants, where customers are mainly interested in purchasing young trees, the demand for ornamental trees is quite large. The price of a plant is based primarily on its quality. A distinction is made between young deciduous trees (transplanted twice); multistem shrubs (transplanted at least three times); trees with straight cleaned up trunks (transplanted at least three times), avenue trees (standards to be planted along streets, with an especially high crown) and large-size trees (transplanted at least four times in an especially wide bed, not more than four years old). Most companies specialize in a specific phase of "tree raising," such as the production of seedlings, the growth of seedlings into large trees or the production of trees for sale and export. Wide-assortment tree nurseries may have an entirely different appearance depending on their specialization. For instance, more extensive areas are needed for growing large trees than for smaller ones.

Most trees and standards are cultivated by sowing seedlings, with the success of cultivation mainly depending on their quality. The most robust seedlings with upright leading shoots provide the best guarantee for the successful propagation. For many trees, though, a thin bud means unsatisfactory further growth. Different-aged tree species can have the same quality. There are some species, such as ashes, that reach a certain size more quickly than others, in contrast to the rather slow-growing oaks.

**HILLIER NURSERIES**
Hillier Nurseries near Romsey in the English county of Hampshire was founded as a family-run business in 1864 and is one of the most famous tree nurseries in the world. Up to a few decades ago, it was by far the largest wide-assortment nursery, selling 12,000 different varieties. Situated amidst the hilly cultural landscape in southern England, the nursery area is sometimes evocative of a landscape park. The fencing along the boundaries of the area, put up to protect against theft and wild animals, is discreet and unobtrusive. Once inside, visitors can move freely among the various fields of trees, which are interspersed with old tree stocks.

Propagation operations were outsourced years ago. Since then, the seedlings are purchased from special propagation companies in the surrounding area. Hillier has evolved from a wide-assortment nursery with a rich tradition in plant collecting[2] into a commercial nursery specialized in growing seedlings into standards on open land and in pots and containers. The company, which employs fifty people, lines out around 750,000 trees each year. These trees are transplanted in a single long season, lasting from November to April. On the European mainland, which has severe winters, the trees are transplanted in two seasons, usually in November and December, and March and April.

The layout of the fields at Hillier Nurseries is quite dynamic and is planned anew every year. Trees of different varieties and qualities alternate in the various fields, even within one year's planning.

Hillier Nurseries, Romsey, England. Wide-assortment tree nursery with a long tradition amidst the undulating landscape of Hampshire

Wide fields of young plants are bordered by a low hill, and on the other side are long rows of standards which have already been transplanted three times. Birches stand next to maples, willows next to cherries, etc. The production cycle from seedling to salable standard can last five to eight years (sometimes less, depending on the species). As a result, it takes longer to respond to certain trends. However, Hillier attempts to take these trends into account by meeting special customer requests at an early stage. It sells the trees it produces primarily to customers in Great Britain, where there is the greatest demand for standard products. Due to this demand, it does not cultivate large-size trees but favors uniform street trees. Tree adaptability is generally the most important criterion for the selection of varieties. Resistant trees with a low susceptibility to disease—including birches, hornbeams and maples—are always popular and have been included in the product range for more than one hundred years. A new development is the increased demand for trees bearing edible fruit.

Given the labor-intensive processes of transplanting and transporting trees, market prices for trees are far too low, as a consequence of the fierce competition. This is one of the main reasons that Hillier—like many other large companies—has expanded into garden centers. The market for garden centers developed in Manchester in the sixties and has grown ever since, particularly in the seventies and eighties. The sale of large and small potted plants to private customers provides an additional source of income for the nurseries.

2 See Sir Harold Hillier Gardens and Arboretum in "Traditional British." (p. 68 ff.)

# Container tree nurseries: industry

Vannucci Piante, Pistoia, Italy
Loading area with automatic irrigation and lighting

Pot cultivation with guided irrigation system

Loading area

The Greeks and Romans already cultivated different-sized trees in pots. They mostly mixed substrates from soil and added compost. During the Baroque period, almost all the major palaces, including Versailles and Sanssouci, featured an orangery with fruit-bearing and scented exotic specimens. However, most trees were grown in ground until the mid-nineteenth century.

The origins of the industrial pot and container culture go back to the early sixties in the United States. The term "container" refers to a vessel with a capacity of up to two liters that is used for the mass production of plants. The Monrovia Nursery in California was an important pioneer in this field and has served as a model for the development of many container tree nurseries in Europe. From its origins in the U.S., the container culture has grown into a production sector with great economic significance in all of Europe. The percentage of container and potted plants in tree nursery production has constantly increased as far as both forest and garden plants are concerned. The trend has been reinforced by the use of in vitro propagated plants, which are best suited for cultivation in containers.

From the perspective of the tree industry, container culture represents an important step forward. Firstly, the use of substrates eliminates the companies' dependence on local soil quality. Secondly, containers simplify and give independence to the transplanting processes, blurring the lines of the traditional planting seasons in spring and fall. The introduction of machine- and system-controlled processes streamlines workflow, which accelerates production processes, especially those related to the transport and irrigation of plants. As a result, plant prices are generally determined by the length of production periods.

On the other hand, container cultivation can be cost-intensive and detrimental to the environment, particularly when it uses peat or produces additional garbage, such as disposable plastic pots and containers. To remedy these problems, some companies have begun to use recyclable and ecologically friendly materials instead of standardized plastic products. Furthermore, organic components in substrates have been found to promote rotting and decomposition processes that have a highly disadvantageous effect on the growth and development of plants. It therefore pays to use mineral-based substrates that contain little organic matter.

**THE PISTOIA TREE NURSERY CENTER**

Well into the nineteenth century, most of Tuscany's tree nurseries were located in Pistoia's city gardens. In this favorable spot near the sea, the owners grew fruit and citrus trees for the famous villas of the Medici family. As the city began to grow, the tree industry flourished and plant production was moved to a plain surrounded by hills on the city's periphery. Italy's largest tree nursery area soon emerged. Boasting a production area of around six thousand hectares, one thousand companies and eight thousand employees (or nearly nine percent of Pistoia's population), it is the most important in Europe today. Thanks to the favorable Mediterranean climate with its short frost period, one hundred rainy and 250 sunny days a year, Pistoia supplies trees to all of Europe, the Mediterranean region and Central Asia.

Cypresses on which the tree nursery center has gained a monopoly, are the city's hallmark. Arranged in rows, they form a cultural landscape that is interspersed with gently rolling hills and features vineyards, scattered vegetable and grain fields, as well as a vast expanse of different colored tree nursery crops. Everything is ordered, and even the overgrown niches seem to be part of the overall design. This is the work of the tree nursery staff, who have developed a great sense of aesthetics along with their many other skills.

Although Pistoia has fertile soil, the price of land has risen so dramatically over the last few years (one square meter costs twenty-five euros) that the companies have become more dependent than ever on container production. Switching to pot and container plants is advantageous because more trees can be cultivated per hectare. Production usually takes place in two phases. Seedlings are planted in open areas and transplanted to pots after a period of two to three years. Due to the heavy clayey soil, rainwater remains in the deeper layers of the plain for a longer time, and the seedlings in the open land only require limited irrigation, even in summer.

**VANNUCCI PIANTE**
In 1938 Vannino Vannucci Senior founded a *vivaio* (tree nursery) in Pistoia on less than one hectare of leased land. Now, just over seventy years later, it grows plants on 403 hectares and employs seven hundred people—half for the whole year and the other half depending on the current requirements. The tree nursery extends outward in all directions from the center of operations, encompassing a large number of small plots on which the occasional old farmhouse can be seen. The nursery has swallowed up a growing number of the surrounding agricultural fields, with which it forms a mixed landscape of traditional farming, viticulture and tree nursery crops. Some families live in the *vivaio* as if it were a small town. Indeed, the avenues of palms and cypresses, the many squares, the parklike road lighting and the picturesque houses are reminiscent of a holiday village.

The company propagates and grows a large assortment of trees, palms, shrubs and climbing plants. A total of 191 hectares is used to grow seedlings on open land, 167 hectares are available for container cultivation, and forty-five hectares are devoted to protected crops such as tree ferns and other plants that require shade and are sensitive to frost, and must therefore be kept in greenhouses and shadehouses. In 2009 its product range included 4.5 million container plants, with two million kept in two- to seven-liter containers, two million in ten- to eighteen-liter containers and half a million in twenty- to 1500-liter containers. The largest containers are used for large-size trees that are cultivated in the open land and transplanted and potted between November and mid-April each year. Vannucci also sells one-hundred-year-old palms and olive trees. A special section next to a brook contains olive trees that are up to 1500 years old and stand like giants with their pruned branches. These trees originally came from Calabria, were transported to Pistoia and have stood in pots in the nursery for four years. As Vannucci's competitor Enzo Margheriti explains, they were allegedly saved from being cut down when a street was built.

The tree nursery also produces different hedge forms (topiary), clipping the branches into shapes such as dinosaurs and swans. The development of new varieties is no longer of great importance, but there are plans to build an arboretum over the next few years in cooperation with the garden designer Enzo Enea. It will be located in an overgrown area where a tree nursery was once founded around 1830.

Thanks to its size and efficiency, the company is able to sell nearly all of its products all year round. The most important plants are displayed in a 3000-square-meter greenhouse. Often the customers—usually garden center representatives, landscape architects and exporters—stop by personally to select their plants and draw up orders together with their salesman. The company is very proud of these business relations, which are based on mutual trust and often go back many years. It is also proud of its technological progress over the last twenty-five years. It has more than 125 tractors and forklifts, over four thousand metal boxes, a 3.8-hectare loading area with automatic irrigation and lighting, as well as two modern loading halls in which eighteen trucks can be loaded at the same time. As a result, it is able to execute orders very quickly. A number of important and ingenious innovations are still used to this day, such as special shopping baskets, ditches for loading goods, bridges, and the famous terracotta vessels for container cultivation—the *vasi rossi* of the Linea Vannucci.

Vannucci Piante, Pistoia, Italy
1 Hundred-year-old olive trees brought from Calabria to Pistoia
2 Tree ferns and other plants that are sensitive to frost and require shade in shadehouses
3 Creation of different hedge forms (topiary)
4 Cypresses, the hallmark of the Pistoia tree nursery center
5 Yard with special baskets for loading plants
6 Housing within the tree nursery complex
7 A 167-hectare area for container cultivation
8 Overgrown area where a tree nursery was founded around 1830. An arboretum will be established here in the coming years.
9 Former farmyard where part of the substrate mixture used for pot cultivation is now stored

1

2

3

4

5

6

7

8

9

# THE HISTORY OF PHALAENOPSIS SP.

**Aalsmeer, March 31, 2009.**
**Here, south of Holland's Schiphol Airport, is where my two-day tour begins, investigating the production of the Phalaenopsis sp., the Marilyn Monroe of orchids—a unique beauty serially propagated in the laboratory. Once an epiphyte growing wild in the tropics, it has been used to breed 25,000 hybrids since 1886 and has become one of the world's most beloved indoor plants. The enormous demand is based on its low prices and on the availability of variants to suit every taste. Every year two to three hundred new cultivars are produced.**

Travelogue and photographs by Dominique Ghiggi

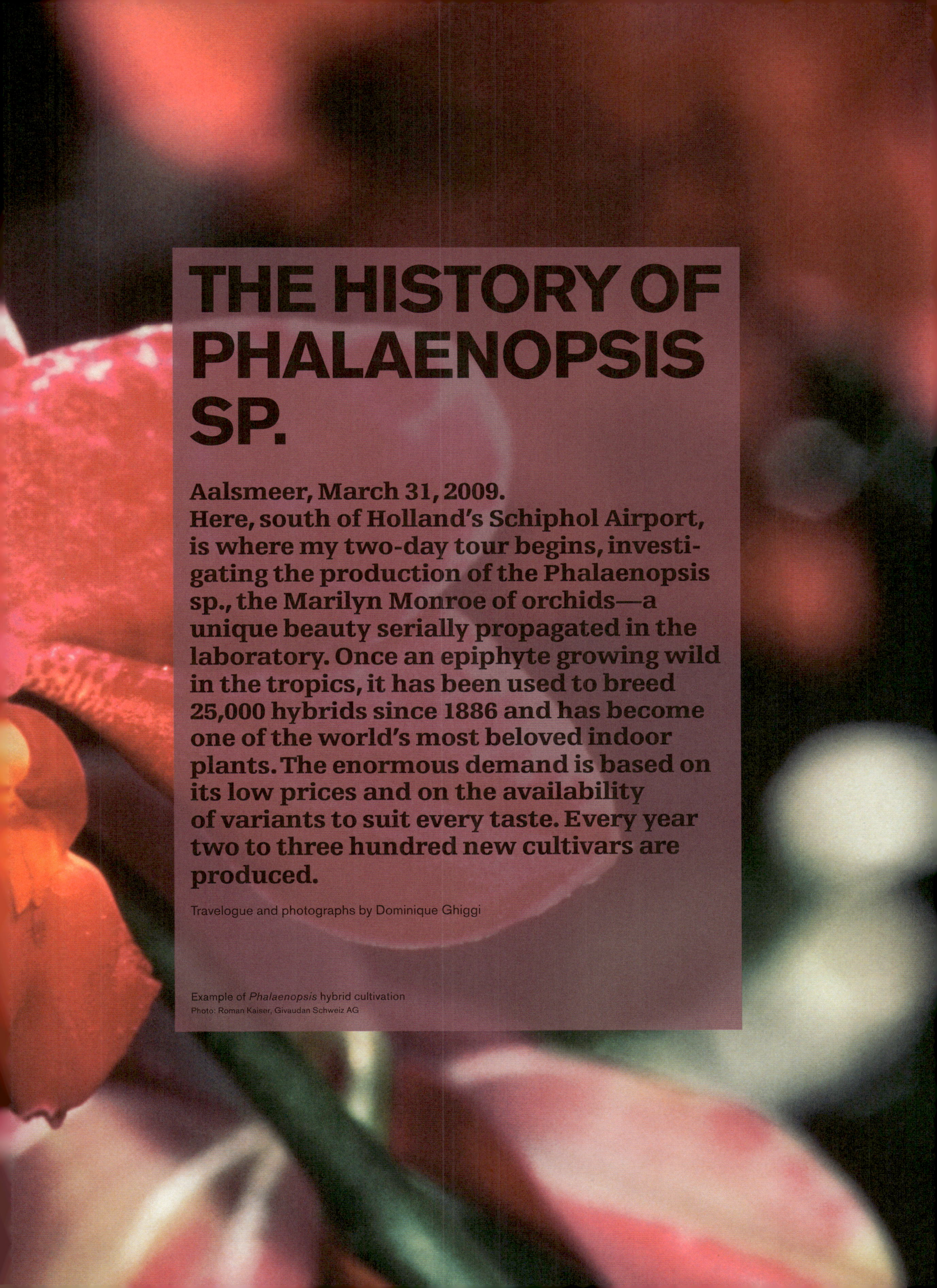

Example of *Phalaenopsis* hybrid cultivation
Photo: Roman Kaiser, Givaudan Schweiz AG

I had actually intended to spend my two-week trip through Germany, Holland, Belgium, England and Italy tracking the production of trees in order to gain an insight into the tree industry in some of Europe's traditional horticultural countries. Trees have always interested me more than shrubs or herbs. In my childhood I already began drawing trees, and later, as a biology student, I began to research them. In my current profession as a landscape architect I have also learned to value them as elements of spatial design. The production aspect fascinates me precisely because in our profession and in society at large it receives so little attention, although it is fundamental to landscape architecture, whether in one's own garden, in parks or on the street. Its process says something about the prevailing zeitgeist and in particular about our discipline as a whole.

The natural home of the much coveted pot plants of the genus *Phalaenopsis* is in fact on trees in the tropics. It was this information that aroused my interest in the methods used to reproduce them, particularly in Holland, the center of Europe's *Phalaenopsis* industry.

## ORIGINS OF THE WORLDWIDE TRADE IN PLANTS

Holland is the biggest international hub of the plant trade. An enthusiasm for all things new has a long tradition here. During the great voyages of discovery, plant collectors discovered an ever increasing array of new species in foreign regions. As a result, a diverse range of exotic ornamental plants was brought back to Dutch gardens and greenhouses. Auctions selling imported tulips from Turkey were already being held in Holland in the late sixteenth century. One of the first people to recognize the enormous commercial potential of ornamental exotic plants was Emanuel Sweerts, a Dutch plant trader, whose well-known drawings of bulbs and exotic plants were published in his work *Florilegium amplissimum et selectissimum* in 1612. This was the first commercial catalog of plants to be produced in Holland and perhaps marks the beginning of the worldwide trade in tropical plants.

In the region around Aalsmeer, horticulturalists have specialized in the production and export of bromeliads, orchids, cacti, carnivores, tropical trees and indoor plants, and I visited a number of these businesses after completing my research in the *Phalaenopsis* production centers. Each business has focused on its own special niche, since the rarer the plant species the greater the guarantee of its success. This is all the more important today, when plant prices are generally low due to keen competition in the sector.

A number of enterprises in the region are specialists in the transportation and acclimatization of tropical plants. Hans Nieuwkoop was the first gardener in Aalsmeer to import tropical plants and ceramic pots from China. He personally selected his plants, which often included gigantic trees, in tree nurseries in Florida, Costa Rica, Brazil, Thailand, Japan and China and also arranged their shipment. Some twenty-five years ago, he developed special ocean shipping containers for this purpose, known as reefers, in which temperatures were maintained at a constant 18 °C. This improved method of plant transportation played a significant role in the expansion of his family business.

Other businesses focus intensively on the cultivation of new hybrids. One example is the firm Corn.Bak in Assendelft, only a few kilometers away from Aalsmeer. Corn.Bak mainly produces bromeliads and carnivores in greenhouses and annually breeds around two thousand hybrids, of which only one or two species are subsequently produced for the market.

## THE FLORA HOLLAND

Apart from inquisitiveness, the notable characteristics of Dutch plant production are the self-confidence and efficiency with which businesses are run. This is particularly the case in Aalsmeer, where I was told a good deal about the workings of the plant industry.

About one hundred years ago, horticulturalists demanded their own auction houses in order the better to represent their own interests in when facing the traders. As a result, in 1912, at a time when horticulture had already acquired a highly significant status in the area, the plant auction houses Bloemenlust and Centrale Aalsmeerse Veiling were opened in the east and center of Aalsmeer respectively. In 1972 they amalgamated to form Verenigde Bloemenveilingen Aalsmeer. New auction halls were built not far from Schiphol Airport, providing Dutch horticultural businesses with better access to the American and Japanese markets. In 2008 a further fusion led to the creation of Flora Holland, which, with almost two million square meters of space and an annual turnover of two billion euros, is the world's largest flower and plant auction company. Over the last few years China has established its own large-scale plant industry and become Holland's biggest competitor. As a result, Dutch exports to Asia have fallen off.

At the beginning of my exploration of the *Phalaenopsis* world, I visited Sander Kroll at his firm Ki Plant in Aalsmeer. He filled me in on a number of aspects of the plant export business and was kind enough to invite me to attend an auction the following day. Sander has been involved in the import and export of tropical tub plants for over fifteen years and has built up an international marketing network in the sector. He is obviously acquainted with most of the plant producers in the region and was able to help me map out a sensible route for my research and gain permission for me to visit several businesses.

## AN INSIGHT INTO THE PRODUCTION CENTERS

Propagation, breeding and preparation for sale are all located close to one another, and I am allowed an insight into all these aspects within a single day. Peter, a Polish builder working for Ki Plant, takes me around to the different centers in his old Volkswagen van and, on the way, tells me about his life in Aalsmeer, his Polish friends in Amsterdam and his family, who are still living in Poland. We first drive to Assendelft, one of two Floricultura locations, a family business and a specialist in the orchid trade since 1933.

The landscape we drive through around Assendelft looks almost pastoral, as if from another age. Until we reach Zaandammerweg, the road is bordered by green meadows where sheep are grazing. By contrast, Aalsmeer is conspicuously urban, subdivided into small sections and dominated by the innumerable greenhouses that line its streets. Almost every resident seems to have their own small green island on which they diligently cultivate trees, shrubs, flowers and fruit.

## PROPAGATION

We soon arrive at the big orchid enterprise known as Floricultura. Peter waits for me in the car and directs me to René Schoone, who is already walking over to greet me. He and his brother Kees took over the family business from their parents five years ago. René first takes me on a tour of the greenhouse, where young plants and new hybrids are grown. We then visit the laboratory in which the orchids are propagated.

The family business originally occupied six hundred square meters but now covers an area of twelve hectares, on which it employs a staff of 650. The magical formula behind Floricultura's success derives from the synergy between René's mother, a trained laboratory technician, his father, a horticulturalist, and René himself, who studied business management and logistics. In recent years the company has established itself as one of the international market leaders in the production of young orchid plants. Its chief foreign markets are the USA, Japan and Brazil.

The species of the genus *Phalaenopsis* occur naturally for the most part on the Philippines and the islands of Indonesia. Besides from the threat to their habitat by deforestation and slash-and-burn, these species are also depleted by excessive unchecked gathering to meet the enormous demand for them throughout the world. In light of this situation, the controlled propagation of the plants in greenhouses represents a plausible strategy—apart from the amounts of energy required. Germany and Holland are the world's biggest producers, followed by Indonesia and Taiwan.

As we walk through the gigantic greenhouse, René shows me the orchids from the firm's main assortment. Most of them are hybrids of the genera *Epidendrum, Zygopetalum, Cymbidium, Dendrobium, Miltonia, Odontoglossum, Paphiopedilum* and *Phalaenopsis*. They are almost indistinguishable from one another because the plants are still very young and in most cases have not yet flowered. They form a vast green carpet made up of different varieties. One of the staff is responsible for monitoring room temperature and humidity, checking whether pests have settled between the young plants, and ensuring that enough water is provided. These tasks are all vital to prevent diseases in the process of cultivation.

We then reach the mother plant hall, where the firm uses its own as well as purchased plants and seeds to breed new orchid varieties, which are subsequently propagated in large quantities in the laboratory. Six sections are devoted to a range of experiments involving different amounts of light, fertilizers, substrate, $CO_2$ and differences in temperature. In contrast to the previous hall, we are here confronted with a magnificent, colorful ocean of orchids. Even on first sight, it is easy to imagine how new varieties in a wide range of colors and forms will emerge from this orchid jungle.

The orchids sold on the market are all new cultivars bred from species that originally grew in the wild. These species and the primary hybrids play only a limited role in economic terms, unlike the multihybrids, which are bred over years to increase flowering and robustness. And the diligent and passionate search for even more beautiful genotypes continues. Breeding is based primarily on repeated cross-breeding and the subsequent cloning of daughter plants. The first artificially produced hybrid, the crossbreed *Phalaenopsis aphrodite x Phalaenopsis equestriserste*, bloomed in the United Kingdom in 1886 at the firm of Veitch and Sons, also known as Veitch Nurseries. Breeders even go so far as to use x-ray and neutron radiation as well as cold and heat shocks to trigger mutations in genes or to genetically modify plants.

We leave the greenhouse, and René asks me to don a white coat and to cover my shoes with white plastic bags before entering the laboratory. Here, the plants are propagated by vegetative means: between 10,000 and 100,000 young plants per orchid variety annually, in total around six million plants per year. The aim is to pass on the targeted features of a new cultivar in identical form and thus to preserve the purity of the variety. In the case of traditional cloning,

Examples of *Phalaenopsis* hybrid cultivation

Photos: Roman Kaiser, Givaudan Schweiz AG

The species comprising the genus *Phalaenopsis* occur naturally for the most part in the rainforests of the Philippines and Indonesia

root stocks are planted either directly in the earth (cuttings) or transplanted onto another plant (grafting). However, for more than thirty years now a more modern method has been used, so-called in vitro propagation. It is also referred to as meristematic propagation because it proceeds via the tips of shoots, or meristems. The great advantage of this method is that this youngest part of the plant tissue is not vulnerable to viral diseases. Moreover the method is far quicker than propagation using seeds. Meristems are taken from the best-quality plants in the mother-plant hall and cultivated in sterile culture cells—so-called laminate airflow cabinets—on a germfree nutrient medium to produce young plants. Plant hormones are added to stimulate the growth of side shoots. Each individual Petri dish is accurately labeled with the name of the grower responsible, the composition of the nutrient medium, the plant species and the cell number so that the process can be retraced and the cause of potential problems identified. The medium is renewed every ten to twelve weeks. A total of 450 people work in the laboratory and each of them has to undergo a training period of two months before they can work independently in a cell. The staff is made up mostly of women, many of whom come from Asia or Eastern Europe.

The final stage before the young plants are sold involves potting the plantlets and acclimatizing them in the greenhouse. The overall production cycle from meristem to young plant takes two years. René tells me that they have to decide at least three years in advance which varieties will be the next to be introduced onto the market. In order to keep the production time as short as possible and the size of the greenhouse area manageable, the two-year-old plants are sold on to other businesses. These attend to the cultivation and preparation of the plants until Flora Holland sends the *Phalaenopsis* out into the world to decorate window sills, bathrooms, living rooms and waiting rooms. Outside in the Floricultura forecourt, I say goodbye to René. In the meantime, Peter has been resting in his van for around one hour. We head back to Aalsmeer and continue our tour at Green Balanz, a firm that, among other things, further cultivates young plants from Floricultura.

## CULTIVATION AND PREPARATION FOR SALE

Green Balanz, which is still a family business, sells around two million orchids per year. On an area of ten hectares it further cultivates young orchids and prepares the plants for sale. A portion of these are supplied to Flora Holland, while another portion is sold directly to exporters.

Jacques van der Weijden has handed over management of the company to his son but is still active in the business and tells me about the most important developments in its operations. Since 2008 automated systems have been introduced, which allow the company to deal with larger quantities of plants. However, the processes involved are still the same as those in manual production. The young plants are first cared for and lined out in the greenhouse, where temperature regulation induces their magnificent flowers to grow. The growing orchids are subsequently sorted according to specific quality criteria and potted and sent via conveyor belt for final preparation, which involves numbering, packing and labeling. Only around ten women are responsible for this work. As in many other progressive companies, environmental awareness has become one of the hallmarks of Green Balanz, which has been consistently working to increase energy efficiency since introducing its automated systems.

Floricultura, Assendelft, Netherlands. Production of young orchids by means of plant tissue culture in the laboratory

Floricultura, Assendelft, Netherlands. The young orchids are potted before being moved to the greenhouse for acclimatization

Green Balanz, Aalsmeer, Netherlands. Following cultivation and preparation of the orchids for sale

**Phalaenopsis production:**

Schiphol Airport, March 31, 2009

Propagation: Floricultura, Assendelft

Cultivation and preparation for sale: Green Balanz, Aalsmeer

Auctioning: Central Aalsmeer Auction, April 1, 2009

## AUCTIONING

At six o'clock the following morning I once again meet up with Sander Kroll from Ki Plant. As arranged, he picks me up from the airport and we drive to the plant auction. The streets are broad enough for the 1500 trucks that bring plants to the auctions at Flora Holland every day. The company auctions both pot plants and large quantities of cut flowers. The former, including the *Phalaenopsis*, are mostly produced in Holland, whereas sixty percent of the cut flowers come from Europe and forty percent from Ecuador, Ethiopia, Kenya and China.

We have missed the sounding of the gong that marks the beginning of the auction. The public, which is composed for the most part of some two thousand Dutch representatives of smaller and larger export firms, is already sitting on the stands and observing the fresh wares being continuously presented on the catwalk while the numbers posted on the three monitors shift nervously back and forth. Mobile phones and laptops are within reach to provide information about when to push the button, while in the wings complex logistical processes are in full swing. Among the many plants on offer we spot them: white, pink, yellow, variegated and plasticized orchid flowers—an artfully deformed reminder of their tropical cousins or, should the price rise radically tomorrow, a legend soon to be forgotten in a consumerist world.

Plant auction: Central Aalsmeer Auction, behind the scenes

Epiphytes (from the Greek epi = upon, over; phyton = plant) are plants that grow on other plants. This term is used for both land and aquatic plants. On land, trees usually serve as the substrate for epiphytes, while aquatic epiphytes such as algae grow on higher aquatic plants. Attaching to a host in this way provides the plant with more light than would be accessible on the forest or sea floor. However, this evolutionary strategy also has a disadvantage in the sense that, because they are not embedded in soil, epiphytes are not always guaranteed continual access to water and nutrients. In the course of their evolution, epiphytes have therefore developed various morphological and physiological adaptive mechanisms that have made them independent of the water and nutrients provided by direct contact with soil. Many of the epiphytes occurring in the tropics form rosettes of stiff leaves that can accumulate not only rainwater but also falling plant material and dead insects, which decompose and provide the plant with nutrients.

## Epiphytic vascular plants

Ten percent of all vascular plant species
Mountain rainforests are inhabited by more epiphytes than terrestrial vascular plants
Occurrence: Tropics, subtropics; temperate zones: New Zealand, southern Himalayas

## Lower epiphytic plants

Algae, mosses, lichens
Occurrence: Tropics, subtropics, New Zealand, southern Himalayas, Europe

## Families rich in epiphytic species

Orchidaceae, Bromeliacea, Araceae, Polypodiacea, Cactaceae, Gesneriaceae

## Morphological adaptations

Trichomes, pseudobulbs, reservoirs, velamen, root networks, succulent leaves

## Most commonly produced epiphytes

*Tillandsia* spp., *Phalaenopsis* spp., *Vanda* spp.

# TREE NURSERY MARKET IN EUROPE

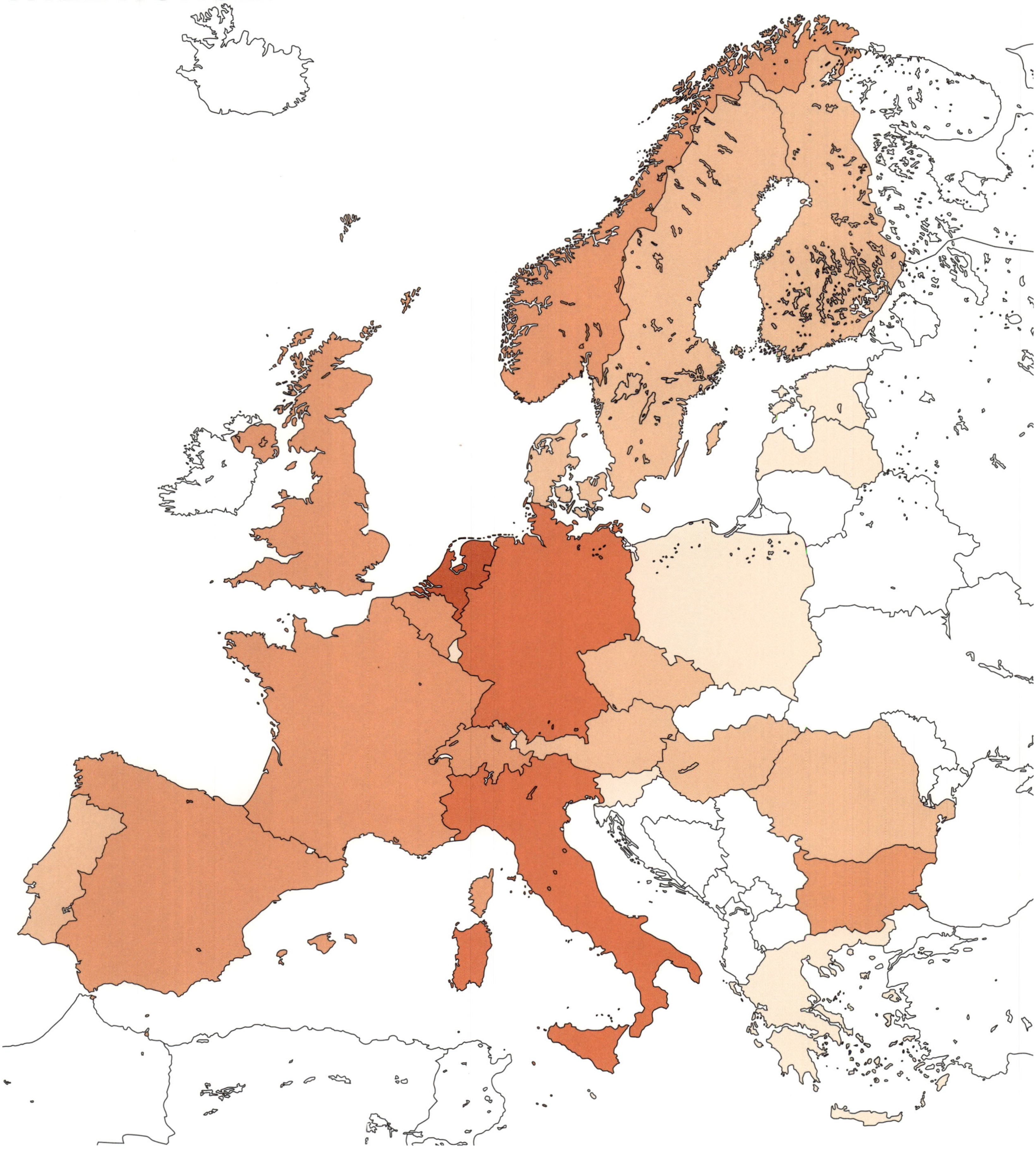

**Output value at producer prices (Million Euro)**

- 3000 +
- 1000–3000
- 100–1000
- 10–100
- 0–10

statistical data: based on http://epp.eurostat.ec.europa.eu/portal/page/portal/about_eurostat/corporate/introduction, Eurostat, Luxemburg © European Communities, 1995–2010
Illustration: based on "92.1 Politische Gliederung" (political structure), *Schweizer Weltatlas*, 2008 edition

# PLANT HARDINESS ZONES IN EUROPE

| Zone | °C |
|---|---|
| 1 | < −45,5 |
| 2 | −45,5 to −40,1 |
| 3 | −40,1 to −34,5 |
| 4 | −34,5 to −28,9 |
| 5 | −28,9 to −23,4 |
| 6 | −23,4 to −17,8 |
| 7 | −17,8 to −12,3 |
| 8 | −12,3 to −6,7 |
| 9 | −6,7 to −1,2 |
| 10 | −1,2 to +4,4 |
| 11 | > +4,4 |

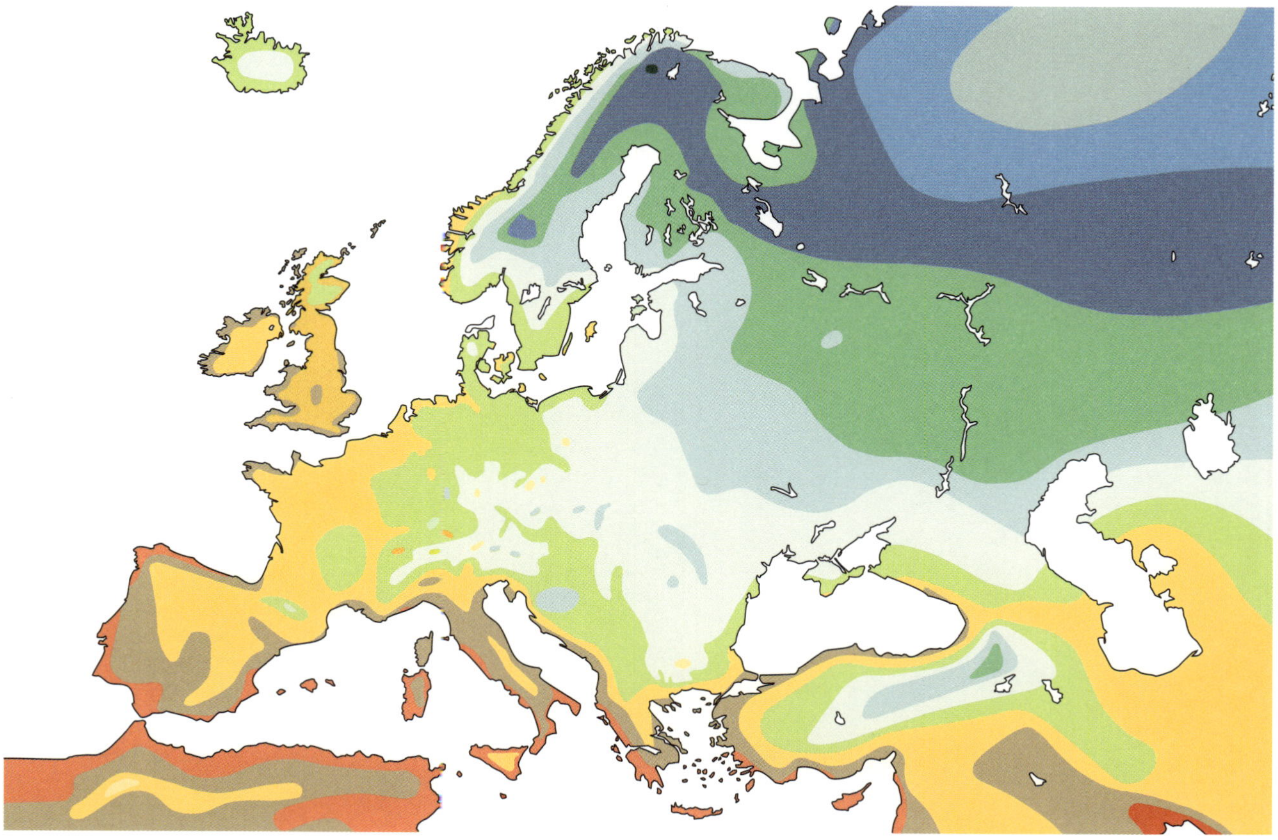

Illustration: based on W. Heinze, D. Schreiber, in Andreas Bärtels, *Gartengehölze*, Stuttgart: Ulmer, 1991

**BUSINESSES**
The largest tree nurseries in Europe have areas under cultivation of more than one hundred hectares. A number of them cultivate areas of over four hundred hectares and employ a workforce of around two hundred. For example, Bruns in Germany has a seven-hundred-hectare cultivation area, five hundred hectares of which are devoted to the production of specimen trees. In the USA some businesses have over a thousand hectares under cultivation.

Small businesses: one to two hectares
Medium-sized businesses: five to twenty hectares
Large businesses: more than twenty hectares

The majority of tree nurseries are family businesses that have a long tradition and produce a large range of ornamental plants, mostly on formerly leased farming land. The number of businesses is tending to fall, although the size of the area used by each business is rising.

**MARKET**
The German sales market is by far the largest in Europe, followed by the UK, France, Scandinavia, Austria and Switzerland. Germany imports far more plants from other countries and is the most important client for Dutch businesses. However, German tree nurseries also export significant quantities of plants, above all specimen trees and shrubs. By contrast, Dutch tree nurseries are purely export-oriented. Since there is a lot of land and good soil available in Eastern Europe, it is to be expected that competition from this region will increase in the future. Dealing in plants within Europe has generally become simpler than it was before, but this certainly does apply to import-export dealings with countries outside the EU. Plants must be delivered bare-rooted, which requires rapid transportation by air freight, and customs controls are bureaucratic and expensive. This explains why dealing with the Chinese market, for instance, still tends to be regarded as somewhat exotic by most European tree nurseries.

**SOIL**
In northern Germany and the Netherlands trees are mostly cultivated in light soils, whereas in southern Germany and in Pistoia, Italy, heavy soils are used. Root growth is more vigorous in light soils, which makes it necessary to replant trees more frequently. Transplantation and root-pruning allow for a fine root system to be preserved near the trunk. A tree transplanted three times exhibits far better crown formation and better developed roots.

**TREE NURSERY TYPES**
Distinctions are made between several types of tree nurseries: seed-breeding businesses are involved in seed propagation and the preservation of tree species, seedling tree nurseries produce young plants from seed, while wildling nurseries take young naturally regenerated plants directly from the forest. Cultivation businesses rear young trees to a particular height and trunk width, while businesses specializing in tall mature trees transplant them several times to produce avenue trees and, in some cases, specimen trees.[1]

**PLANT HARDINESS ZONES**
A plant hardiness zone refers to the area in which a particular type of plant is still able to withstand the minimum temperatures of the zone, i.e., the zone in which its cultivation area begins. All figures relating to hardiness zones are only guide values. The microclimate of some areas within a zone can deviate considerably downwards or upwards from the given values. Urban regions, for instance, are as a rule a half-stage warmer than rural areas. Large water surfaces as well as hillside locations and hilltops also have a beneficial effect on climate, whereas in hollows and valleys conditions tend to be less favorable. Protected locations in forests, on southern slopes or in cities often allow plants that are well tended to be planted in a zone where the temperature is generally too cold for the species concerned.

Plants can often grow in five or more zones. A plant from zone 2 can usually grow without problem in areas within zones 3–7 and possibly also thrive in zones 8 and 9. The zones listed here apply to every plant under optimal conditions and without any protective snowfall. Key figures for determining how well suited a particular zone is for particular species are the mean air temperature in January, the mean air temperature in July and the mean annual rainfall. The coldest average temperature in a year determines what zone an area is ascribed to. Probably one of the most important factors is the protection provided from cold and desiccating winds, which—above all in the case of evergreens—increase evaporation on the leaf surface, thus resulting in water loss that cannot be counterbalanced. The most effective protective measures in this regard are windbreak plantings or fine windproof netting.[2]

1 Gerd Krüssmann, *Die Baumschule. Ein praktisches Handbuch für Anzucht, Vermehrung, Kultur und Absatz der Baumschulpflanzen*, Berlin: Parey, 1997
2 Andreas Bärtels, *Gartengehölze*, Stuttgart: Ulmer, 1991

Most tree nurseries in Europe have specialized in a particular area. There are now hardly any firms that still cultivate single trees from seeding through to mature growth. In practice this means that today the growing of a tree takes place over several stages in a number of different business locations. Moreover, most tree nurseries are now increasingly purchasing trees and shrubs from specialist firms to complete their product range.

The tree nursery centers that emerged in Europe in the course of the nineteenth century were the result of a continual process of market-oriented development occurring at locations favorable to cultivation and trade. Thanks to their specializations, tree nursery areas have been able to remain competitive and supply ever more distant markets. Plant exchange between the different tree nursery centers is highly intense and complex. Most of the trees cultivated in a center are exported and, conversely, the majority of trees sold in the region around a particular center originate from abroad.

Over the last fifty years plant production has been strongly affected by the nature of a demand which required the delivery of trees in large numbers and varieties within a relatively short time span. Like all business sectors operating within the free market, the structure of the tree and plant industry has been influenced by the industrial model based on mechanized production. One example is the development of container tree nurseries from the sixties onwards, which produce trees in pots and containers and now constitute an important branch of the horticulture industry.

A tree nursery center primarily consists of a large number of independent horticultural businesses that form a network for their activities on the European market. The continuing existence of such structures can mainly be explained by the fact that the majority of tree nurseries are family-run businesses. Boskoop in Holland, Europe's oldest tree nursery center, is the best example for the longevity and the continuing adherence to this structural model.

## BOSKOOP'S RICH TRADITION OF TREE PRODUCTION

The development of this tree-cultivation area owes much to the skillfulness of the Dutch in land management and, later, in the plant trade. This is reflected in the name Boskoop, a malapropism of the old Dutch term "Buckiscope," a Cope (koop) being a piece of land that has been drained, while a Buckis (bos) is the person who first reclaimed it.

After the ice caps melted following the last glacial period large deltas and moors formed in the region around Boskoop. The area is covered by a layer of peat made up of silt and organic material that is up to eighteen meters thick and provides an excellent foundation for tree cultivation. Around 1100 peasants constructed the first dikes in order to empolder their fields and to control the water level, both essential for tree cultivation. The region's lakes also originated at this time; they were created when the moors were drained in order to produce combustibles.

The tradition of tree production in Boskoop goes back seven hundred years. Fruit-tree cultivation was initiated in 1222 by the Abbey of Rijnsburg, who had acquired the land from King William I. The cultivation of fruit trees in nurseries officially began in 1466. Since that time one of the town's characteristic features is its long street built on a mound of earth. The land along either side of the street was divided into plots of some twenty hectares that are still drained by narrow canals and sport small old wooden houses.

In the course of the eighteenth century Boskoop became an important trading town: a wide assortment of plants was developed there and fruit trees and strawberry plants were transported in large wooden crates on the canals to the ports of Rotterdam, The Hague, Amsterdam and Hamburg.

Around 1900, when Boskoop's distribution areas had significantly expanded, the cultivation of ornamental plants began. At the time there were two kinds of nurserymen, those who stayed on the land and worked in production and the traveling plant salesmen, who sold products abroad and imported new plants. As Wim Hoogendoorn, a local nurseryman and formerly responsible for exports to Switzerland, explains during the tour of the Boskoop nursery museum, the first nurseryman traveled to Hamburg with a German-speaking waiter as his translator in order to negotiate the prices of his plant products on site.

Until the middle of the twentieth century nurseries in Boskoop chiefly produced and exported fruit trees, before adding strawberries, roses, ornamental trees and shrubs, as well as different types of street trees, including many Dawn Redwood trees *(Metasequoia glyptostroboides)*.

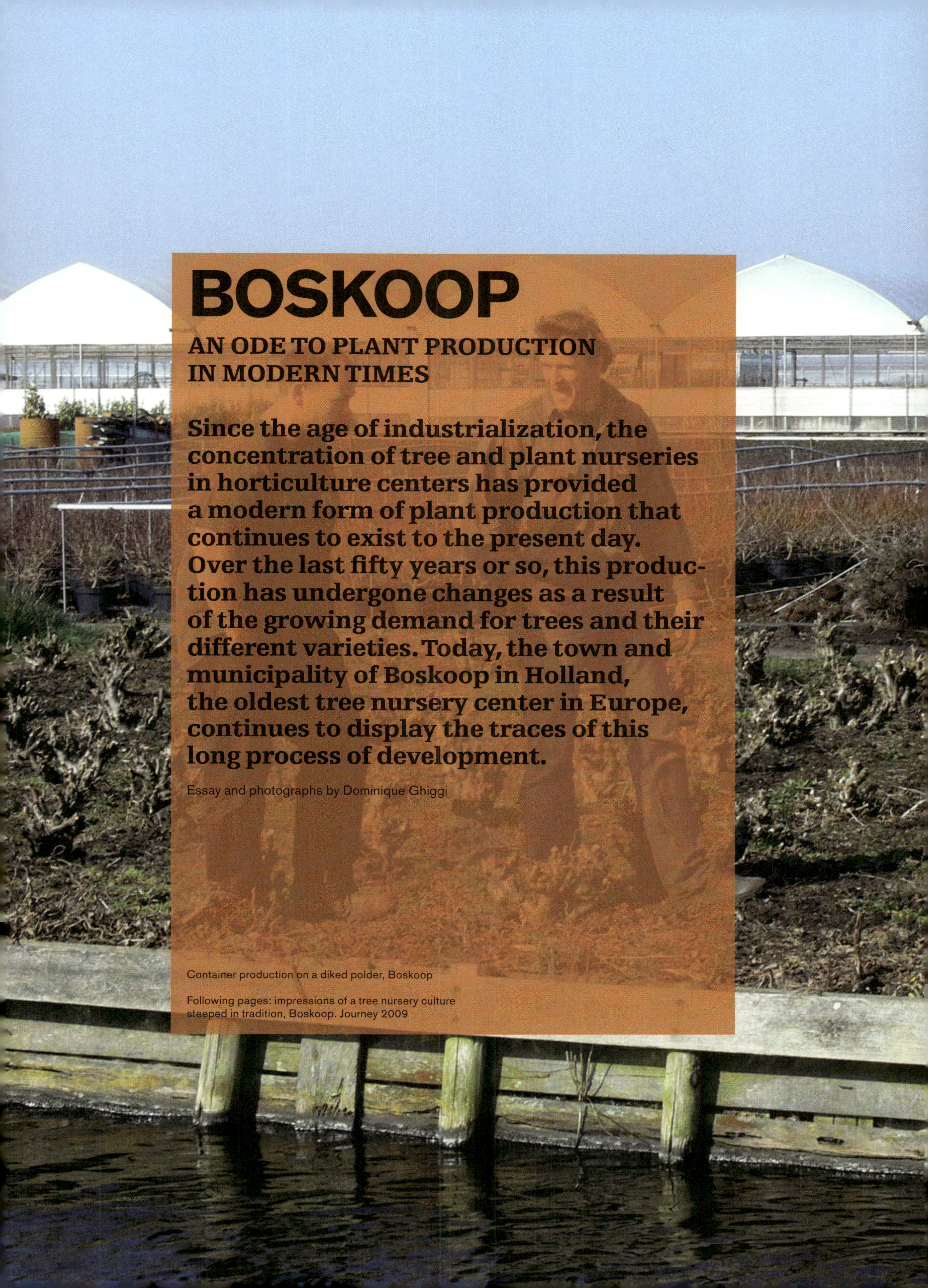

# BOSKOOP

## AN ODE TO PLANT PRODUCTION IN MODERN TIMES

**Since the age of industrialization, the concentration of tree and plant nurseries in horticulture centers has provided a modern form of plant production that continues to exist to the present day. Over the last fifty years or so, this production has undergone changes as a result of the growing demand for trees and their different varieties. Today, the town and municipality of Boskoop in Holland, the oldest tree nursery center in Europe, continues to display the traces of this long process of development.**

Essay and photographs by Dominique Ghiggi

Container production on a diked polder, Boskoop

Following pages: impressions of a tree nursery culture steeped in tradition, Boskoop. Journey 2009

The breeding of new varieties, or "new introductions," has been practiced over many generations in Boskoop and first became fashionable in the nineteenth century. Breeding was based above all on grafting, and one of the region's most successful examples remains the apple variety "Belle de Boskoop," first produced in 1850. Even today Boskoop nurseries continue to practice propagation methods that are rarely found elsewhere. The tree grower Harry van de Laar, who passed away ten years ago, was particularly adept in this field and used his garden to test new varieties for the trade. In the nineteenth century it was the "Royal Association for Boskoop Cultures" which officially examined the product range.

At the time tree nursery enterprises were generally divided into four areas of operation. The plants were propagated in greenhouses, while another area was used for the development of the seedlings. Special glasshouses were used to acclimatize the plants, and experiments with new cultivars were conducted in the garden area. Some nurseries also featured a small building known as a *speelhuis* in which negotiations were conducted between nurserymen and exporters—they were often concluded with a glass of schnapps. Although the *speelhuis* has disappeared, the traditional division of the production process can still be seen today.

## BOSKOOP TODAY

Boskoops's townscape is shaped by the many small family businesses, which form a dense patchwork of plots divided by a myriad of channels used to irrigate the plants. Water quality test results are published weekly in the local paper.

Of Boskoop's 16,000 inhabitants, some five thousand run tree nurseries. A majority of these are sole-proprietor enterprises with less than one hectare of land, whose main income is secured by the cooperation with one of the larger nurseries. There are also a number of large-scale enterprises that export most of their produce.

Since the market has begun to demand more plants and shrubs in containers, the larger companies in Boskoop have also switched to this form of production. Moreover, a growing number of small businesses have managed to extend and automatize their operations in order to cultivate product ranges for hardware stores and gardening centers. The short production process can be maintained with the help of seasonal workers, mainly from Poland. However, this means that while ever larger quantities are being produced, the range of plants is decreasing. This not only leads to a diminishment of the available assortment and a decline in expertise but also to the disappearance of many manual working methods.

Nevertheless, the majority of nurseries in Boskoop continue to cultivate in open soil. However, the constant removal of soil means that it is now more accurate to speak of a substrate that is created from a mixture of sand, peat and earth dug up in neighboring provinces. Due to their restricted size, these nurseries are unable to introduce the mechanization necessary for container production. There are still enough nurseries that rely on maintaining a wide range of plants and a specialized knowledge of the market. One example is the PlantenTuin Esveld, a tree nursery with an extensive product range that has been producing ornamental plants since 1865 and has introduced around 150 new cultivars into the European plant trade. With a staff of only nine people, the family-run business has remained small and is nevertheless renowned throughout the world for its specialized collections. The famous Esveld Aceretum, a collection of maples that is remarkable in both botanical and presentational terms, was started by the now-retired senior partner Dick van Gelderen. He took over the nursery from his deceased father-in-law, C. J. Esveld. Dick and his son Cor are the authors of the renowned and richly illustrated book *Maples for Gardens*. Of the 11,000 varieties offered by Esveld in their general catalogue, the nursery produces six thousand itself—evidence of the great passion and responsibility which the family feels for its own plants.

## A PASSION FOR CULTIVATING TREES

With approximately eight hundred tree nurseries on one thousand hectares, Boskoop remains Europe's densest tree nursery center, featuring the greatest number of individual businesses. More than half of the plants exported by the Netherlands still originate here, although the area's significance as a large trading center is in general

decline. In recent years a growing number of smaller enterprises run by aging owners without children to take over the business have been compelled to offer their land for sale to neighbors. However, they often cannot find buyers. Moreover, the high cost of maintaining roads that are constantly sinking into the moor below has left the municipality in debt. As a result, more and more fields are lying fallow—not even temporary alternative uses are being considered. They have become phantom islands sitting on layers of innumerable colored pebbles and fragments that bear witness to a long tradition.

Thanks to the care of its inhabitants, Boskoop remains a "protected tree cultivation area." With its high level of specialization and the cooperation between the many small family businesses, it still strives to counteract the anonymity that has become the hallmark of the international economy. Boskoop presents a vivid model of a large workshop, infused with passion—for more than five hundred years it has provided scientific and cultural enrichment in the form of knowledge, prosperity and the joy of undertaking new ventures.

# CLIMATE ZONES

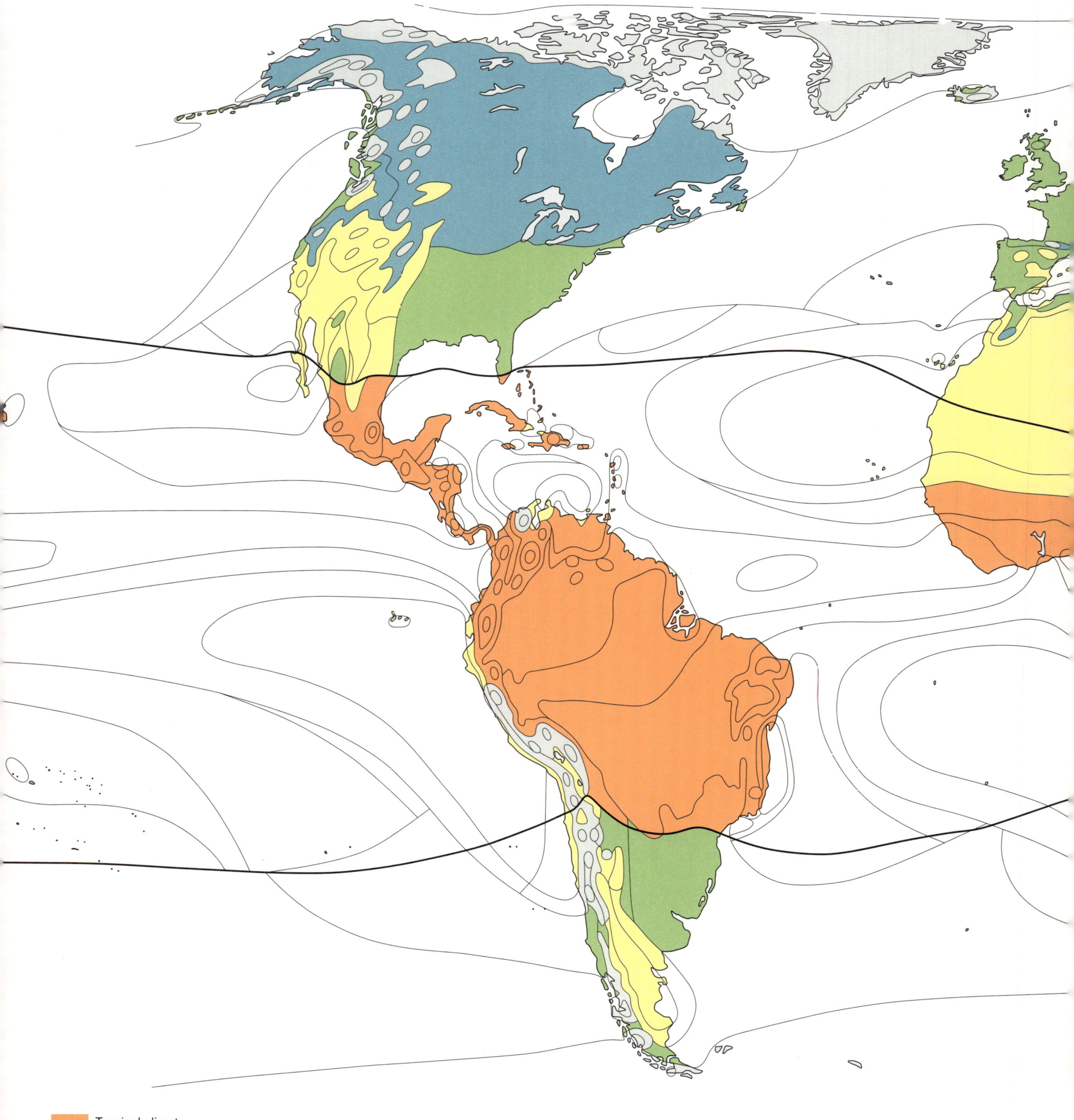

Tropical climate
Dry climate
Temperate climate
Snow forest climate
Polar climate and high-mountain climate
Boundary of the tropical belt (annual temperature amplitude = daily temperature fluctuations)

Illustration: based on "172.1 Klimazonen und Meeresströmungen" (climate zones and ocean currents), *Schweizer Weltatlas*, 2008 edition

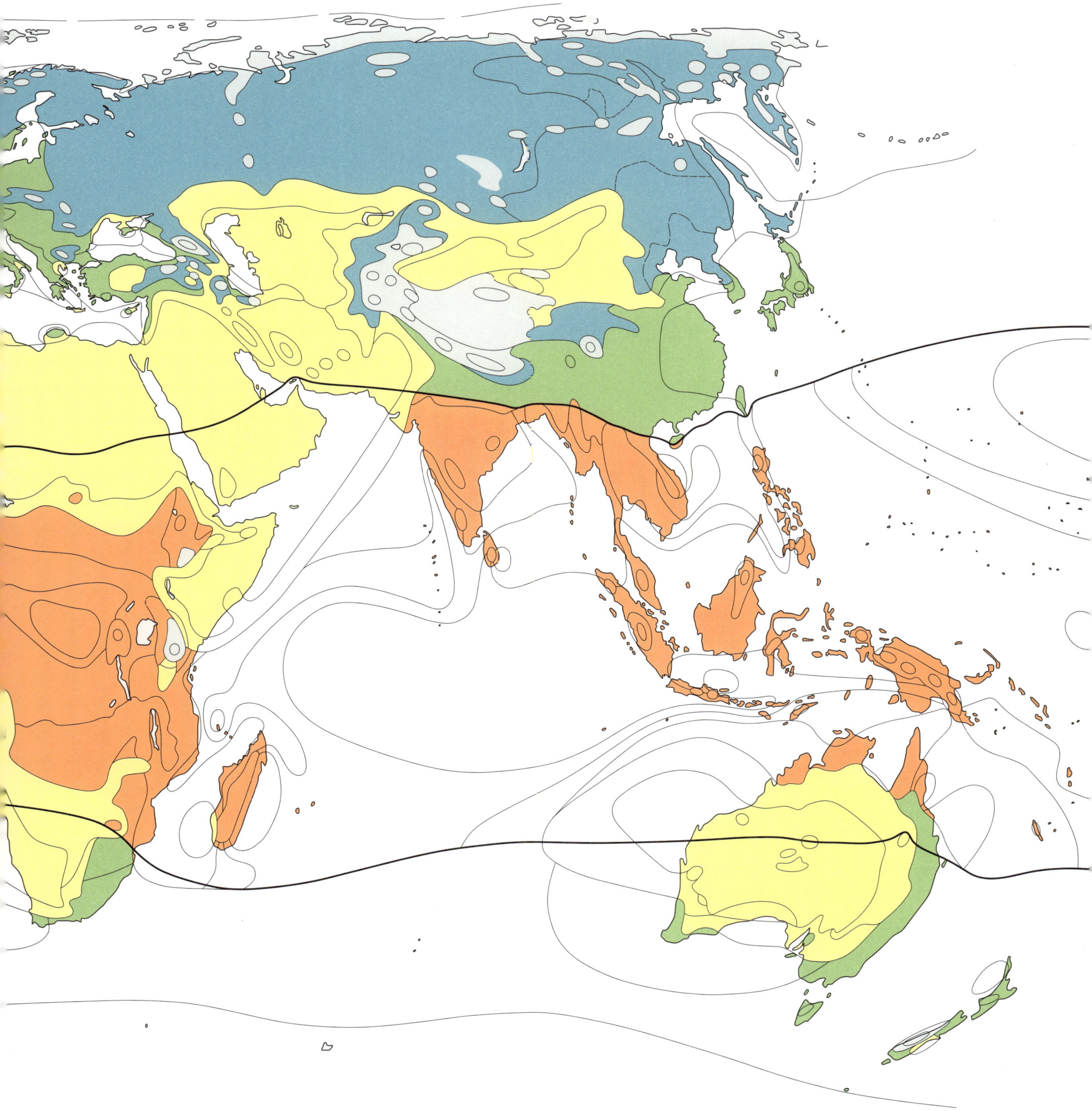

# POTENTIAL VEGETATION

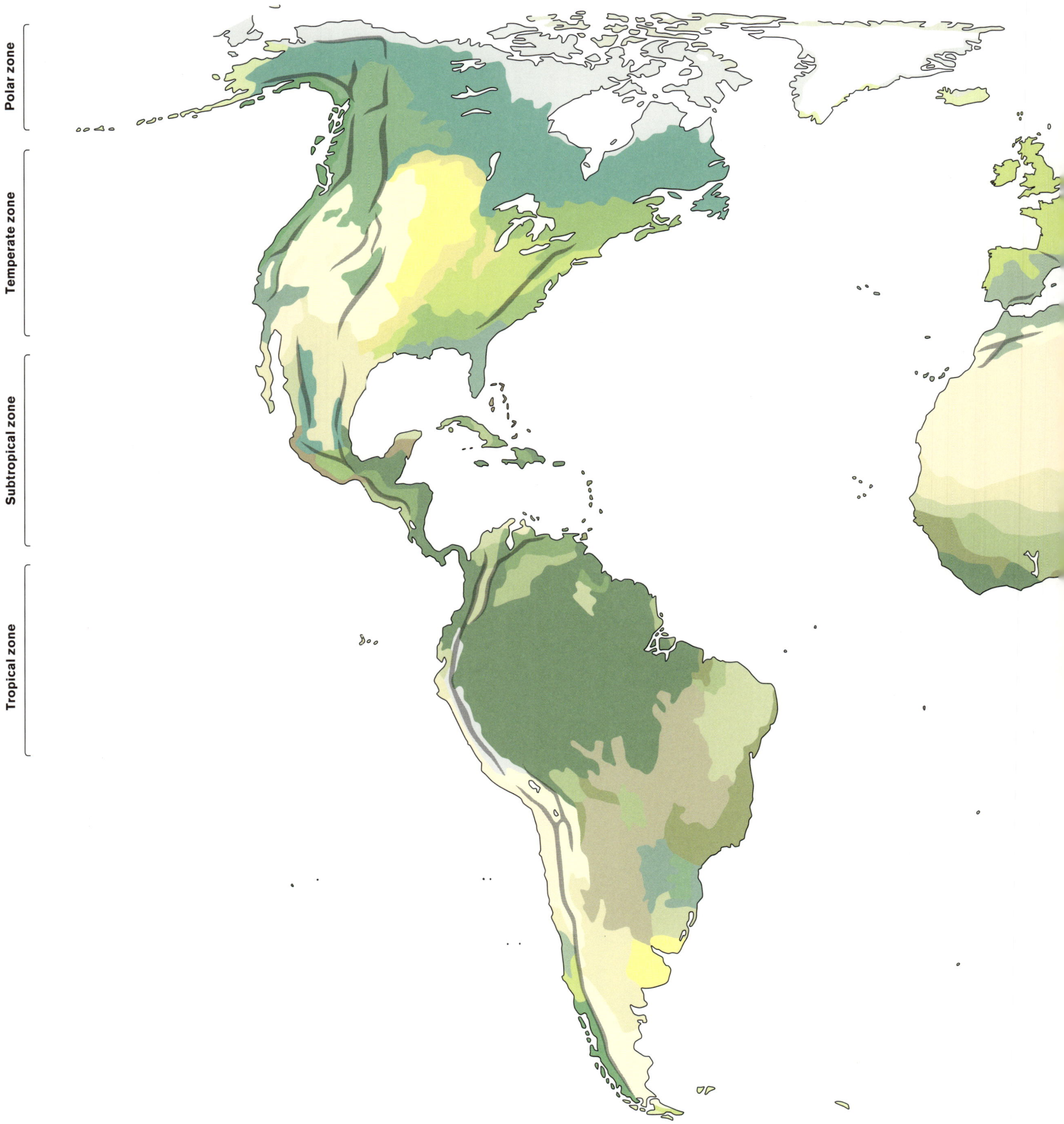


**Polar zone**

- Inland ice, glacier
- Cold desert
- Tundra, alpine tundra and grassland
- Subpolar meadows and deciduous plants

**Temperate zone**

- Evergreen coniferous forests
- Deciduous coniferous forests
- Temperate rainforests
- Mountain coniferous forests
- Broad-leaved and mixed forests
- Deciduous broad-leaved forests

**Subtropical zone**

- Sclerophyllous vegetation
- Subtropical rainforests
- Deciduous tree steppes
- Transitional and black-earth steppes (prairies)
- Dry steppes
- Semi-deserts and deserts

Image: based on "176.1 Potentielle Vegetation" (potential vegetation), *Schweizer Weltatlas*, 2008 edition

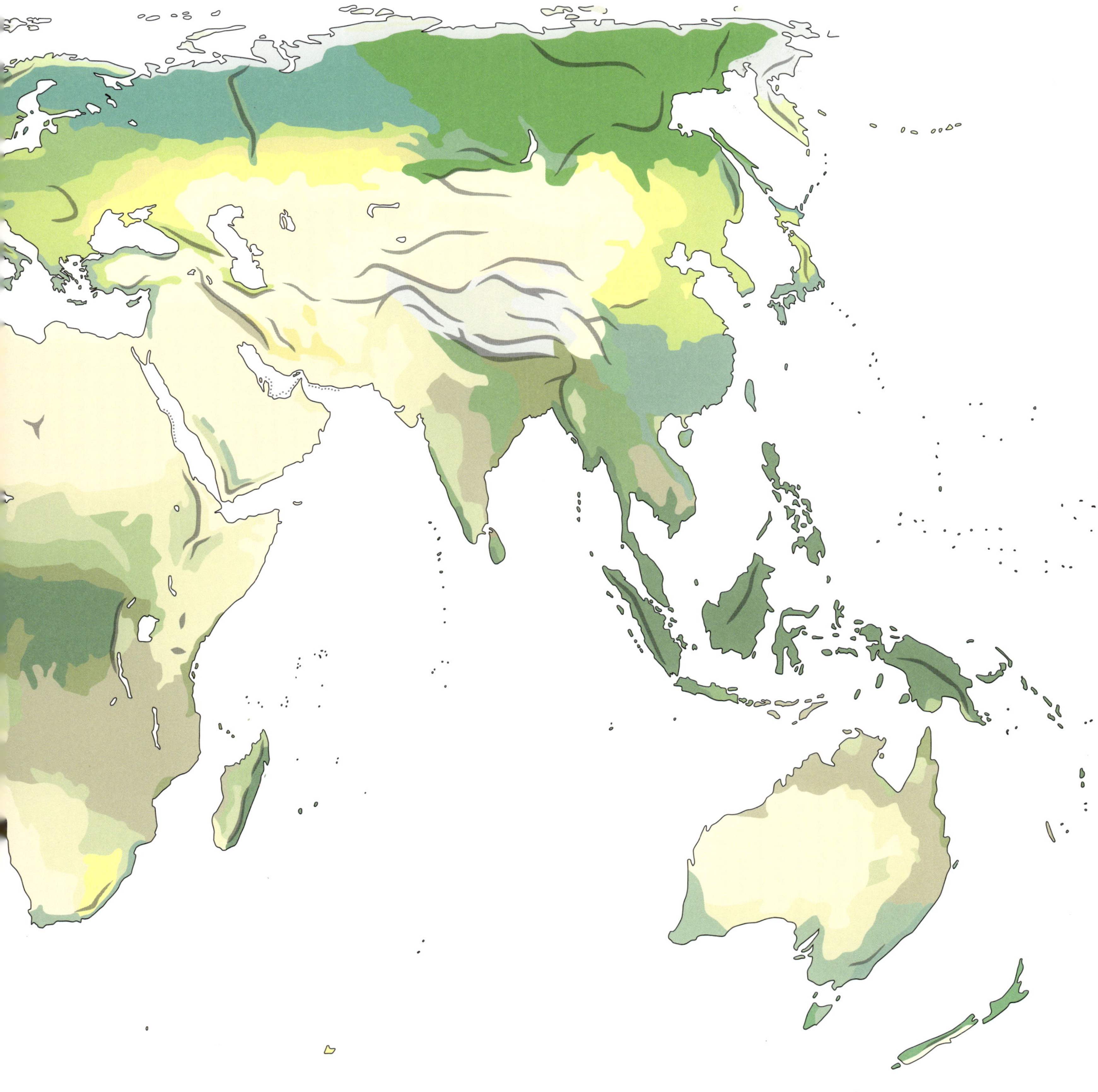

**Tropical zone**

- Thorn savannahs, formations of thorny scrub and succulents
- Dry savannahs
- Dry forests and cerrados
- Wet savannahs
- Monsoon forests
- Tropical semi-evergreen rainforests
- Tropical evergreen rainforests
- Mountain ranges

# SOILS

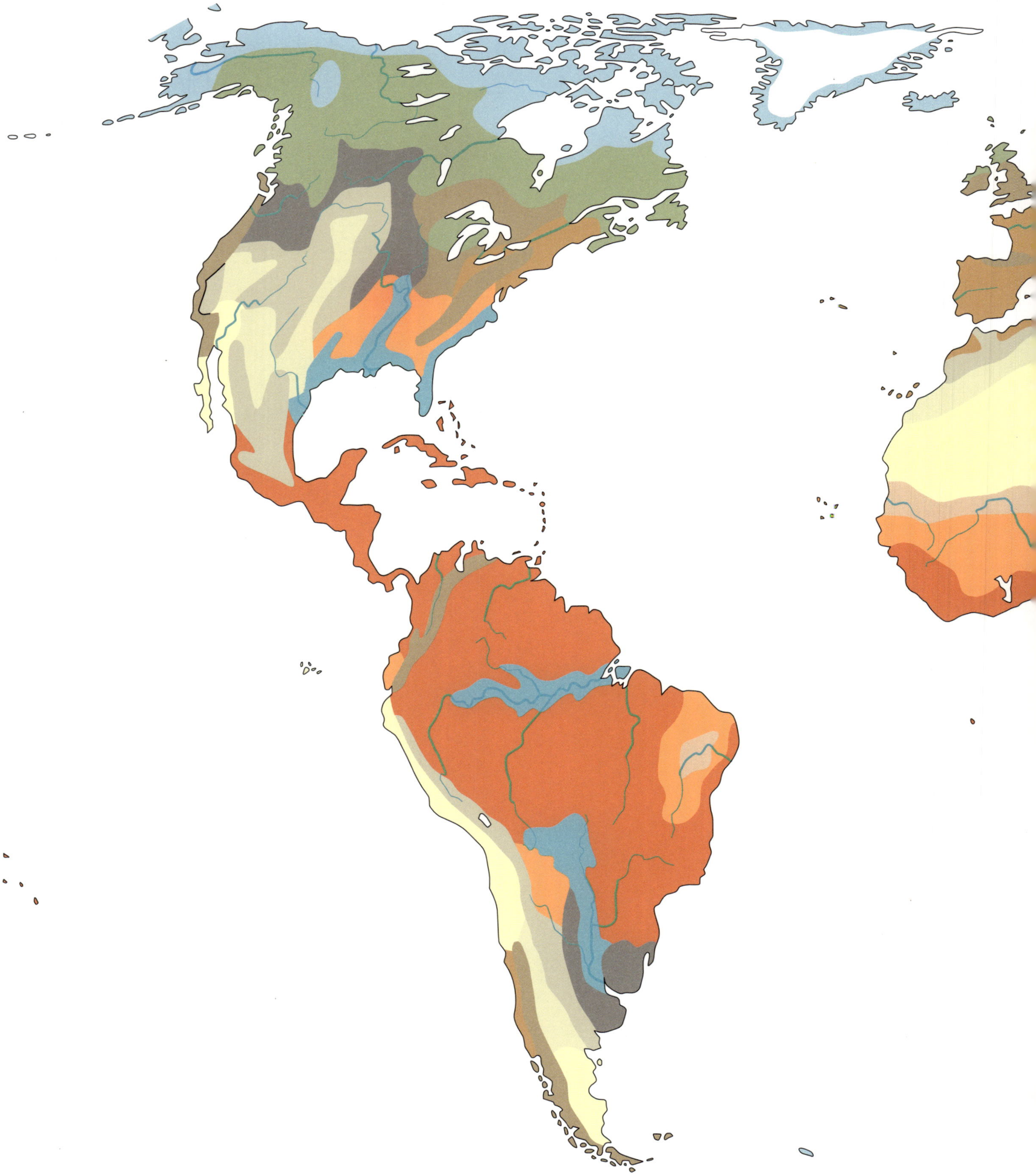

**Polar and subpolar zones**

- Arctic soils and tundra soils
- Taiga soils (podsols)

**Temperate zones**

- Mixed-forest soils (parabrown soils, pale leached soils)
- Broad-leaved forest soils, Mediterranean soils (brown soils, parabrown soils)
- Prairie soils (chernozems)
- Steppe soils (castanozems)

**Semi-deserts and deserts**

- Dry and shrub steppe soils (brown-gray soils)
- Desert soils

Illustration: based on "176.2 Böden" (soils), *Schweizer Weltatlas*, 2008 edition

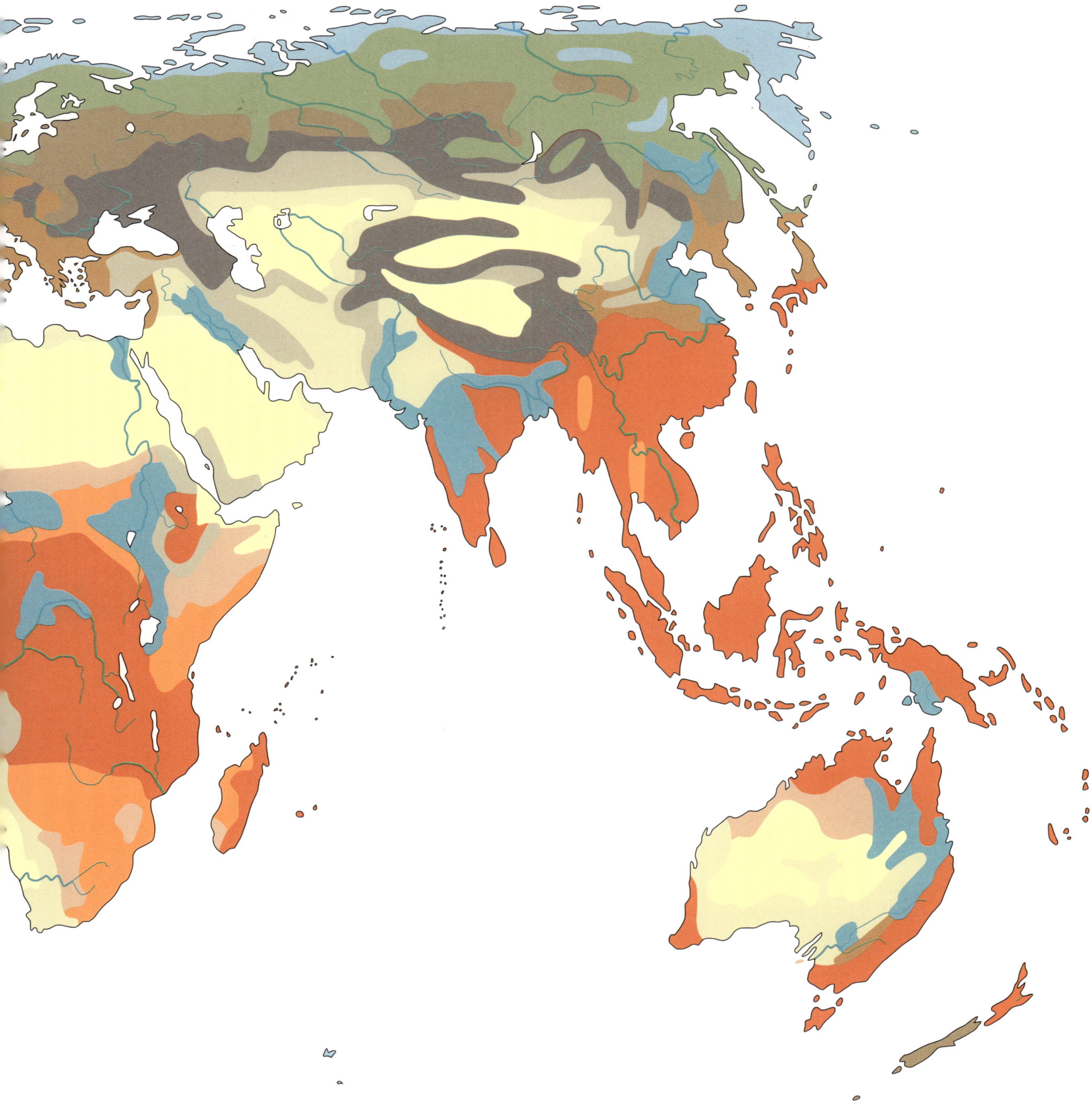

**Tropical and subtropical zones**

- Soils of the thorn savannahs (red-brown soils)
- Savannah and dry forest soils (fersiallitic soils)
- Rainforest and monsoon forest soils (lateritic soils)
- Wet soils and vertisols

# PLANT DOMESTICATION

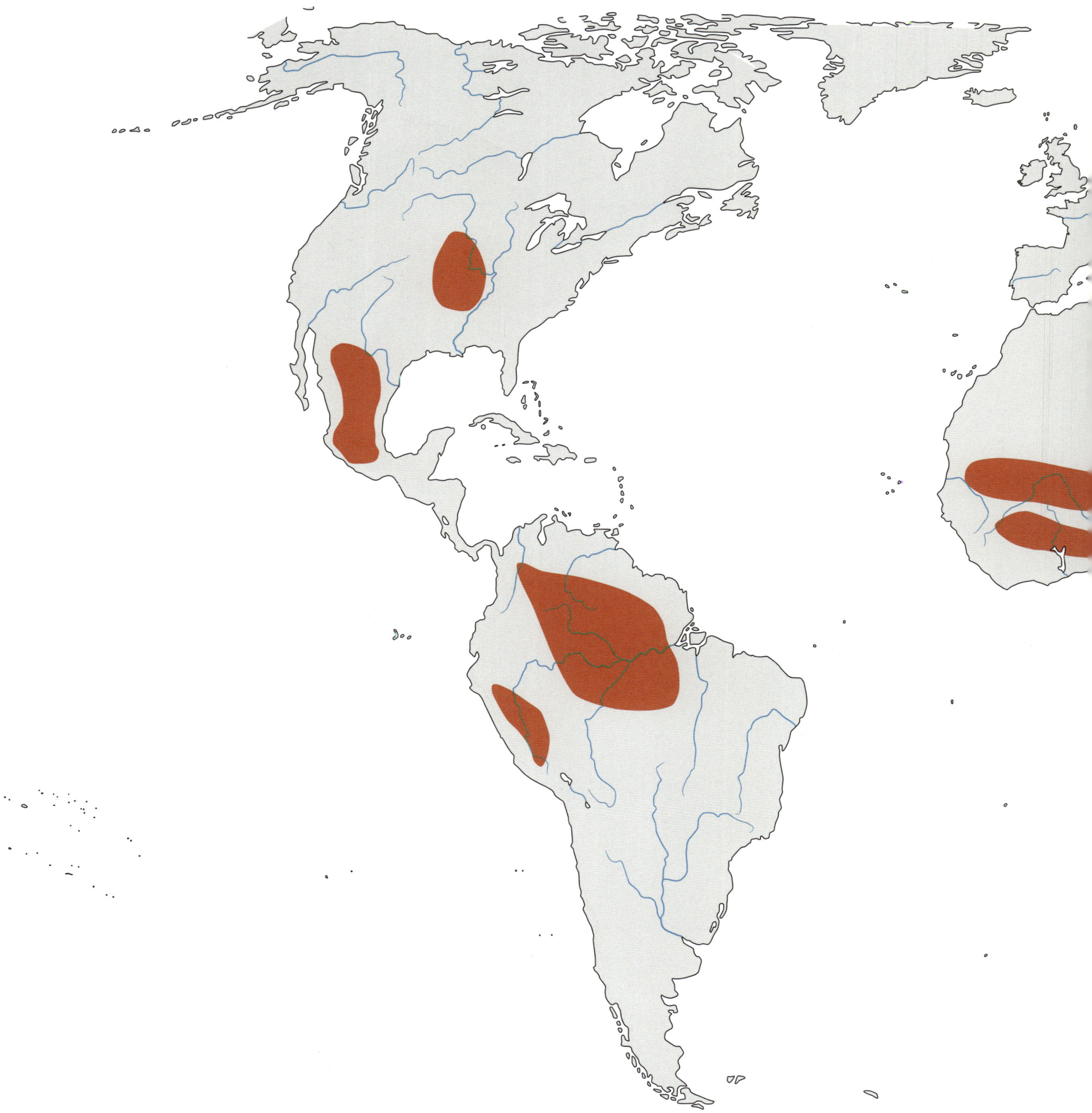

**CENTERS OF THE GENESIS OF PLANT DOMESTICATION**
Archeological finds provide an insight into the anatomical development of modern human beings over some 180,000 years. During this time human beings moved out from Africa to conquer the Old and subsequently the New World, in the process establishing an enormous range of settlement areas. Forms of plant cultivation were already practiced at an early stage, but it was only towards the conclusion of the last Ice Age, around 12,000 years ago at the end of the Pleistocene, that people began to cultivate grains. This new way of life marked the beginning of a complex process of transformation that constitutes a fundamental element of the history of humanity.

The areas in which agriculture originated can be found on nearly all continents. In Eurasia the so-called Fertile Crescent on the Euphrates and in the Jordan Valley as well as China constituted the most important centers of early plant domestication. In the New World, agriculture began in Central and South America. In Southeast Asia—above all in New Guinea—agriculture can also be traced back a long way. The African continent is the least researched in this respect, but the most recent finds also indicate that agriculture emerged there at around the same time as in other places. On the other hand, African agriculture developed differently as a result of the continent's specific climatic history, during which hot dry periods alternated with wet warm periods. New archeological research of areas that had previously been largely neglected shows that agriculture and forms of cultivation developed highly independently on the different continents.

Illustration: based on Detlef Gronenborn, "Letzte Jäger – erste Bauern" (last hunters—first farmers), *Archäologie in Deutschland*, 3/2006, 18–23

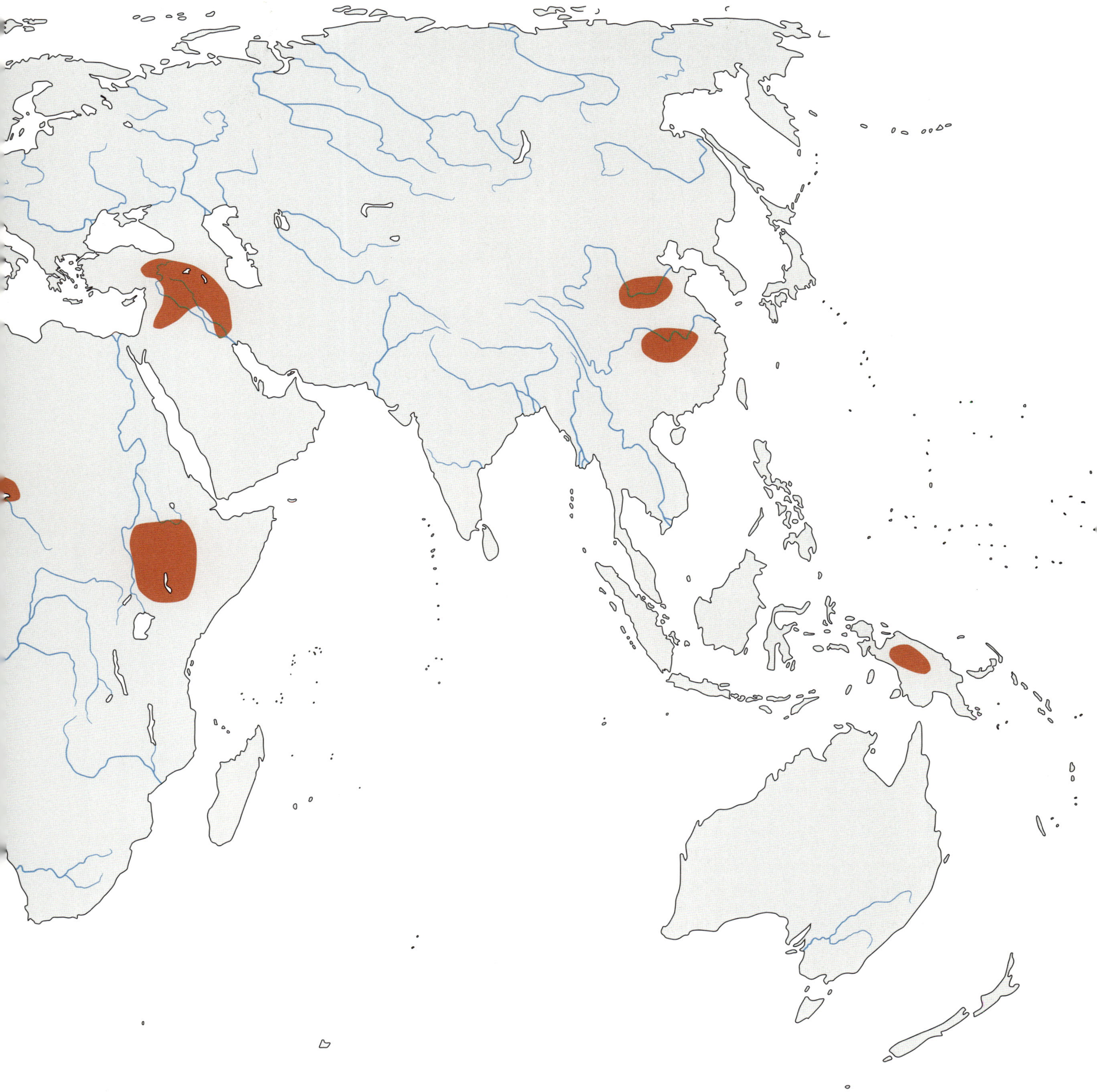

# LAND USE

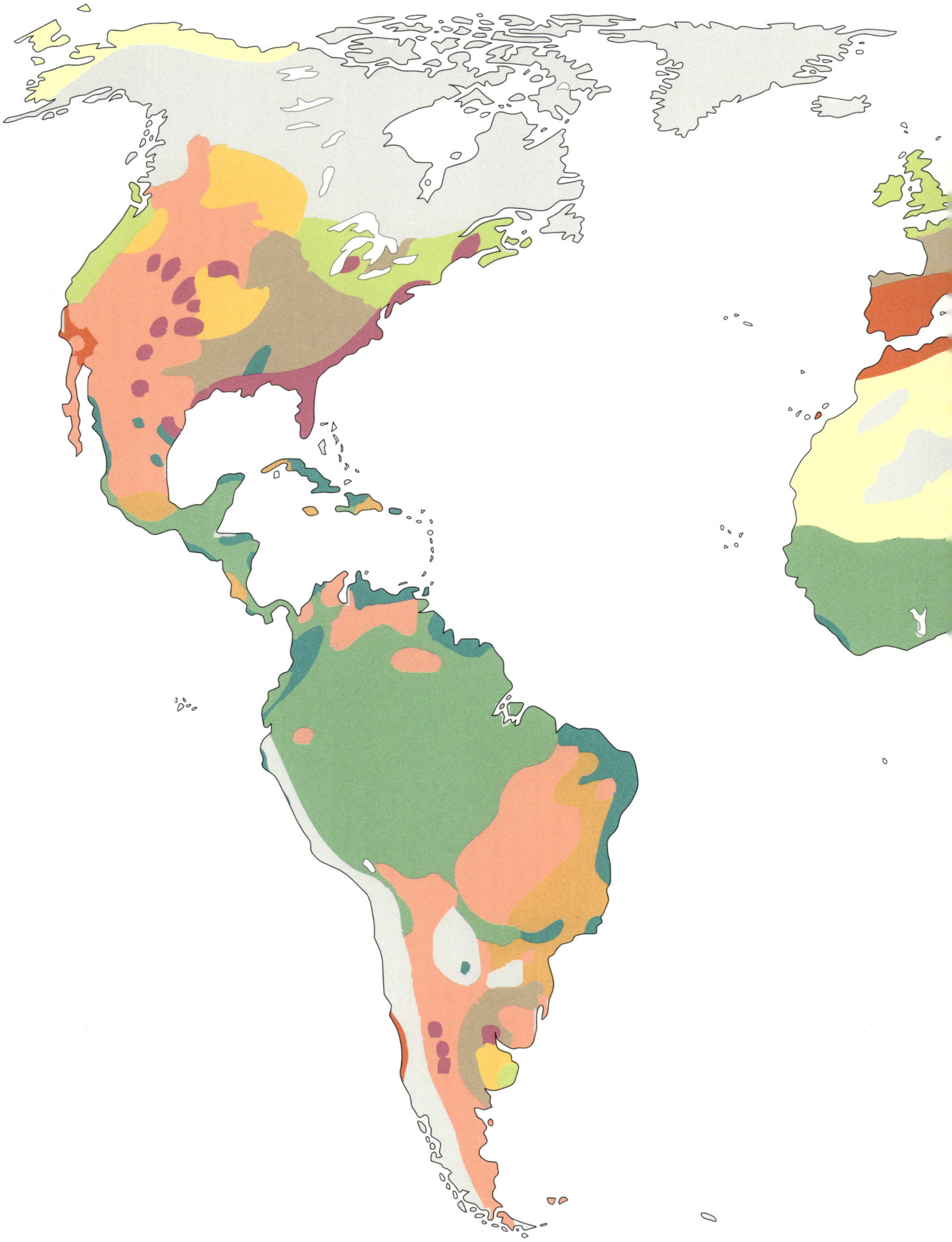

Market-oriented land cultivation and animal husbandry

Dairy farming

Market-oriented grain cultivation

Land cultivation and animal husbandry for self-sufficiency

Intensive land cultivation for self-sufficiency (rice predominant)

Intensive land cultivation for self-sufficiency (rice unimportant)

Mediterranean agriculture

Sedentary pasture economy

Nomadic pasture economy

Extensive land cultivation for self-sufficiency/ shifting cultivation

Plantations

Cultivation of specialized crops

Little or no agricultural use

Illustration: based on 178.1 "Landnutzung und marine Primärproduktion" (land use and marine primary production), *Schweizer Weltatlas*, 2008 edition

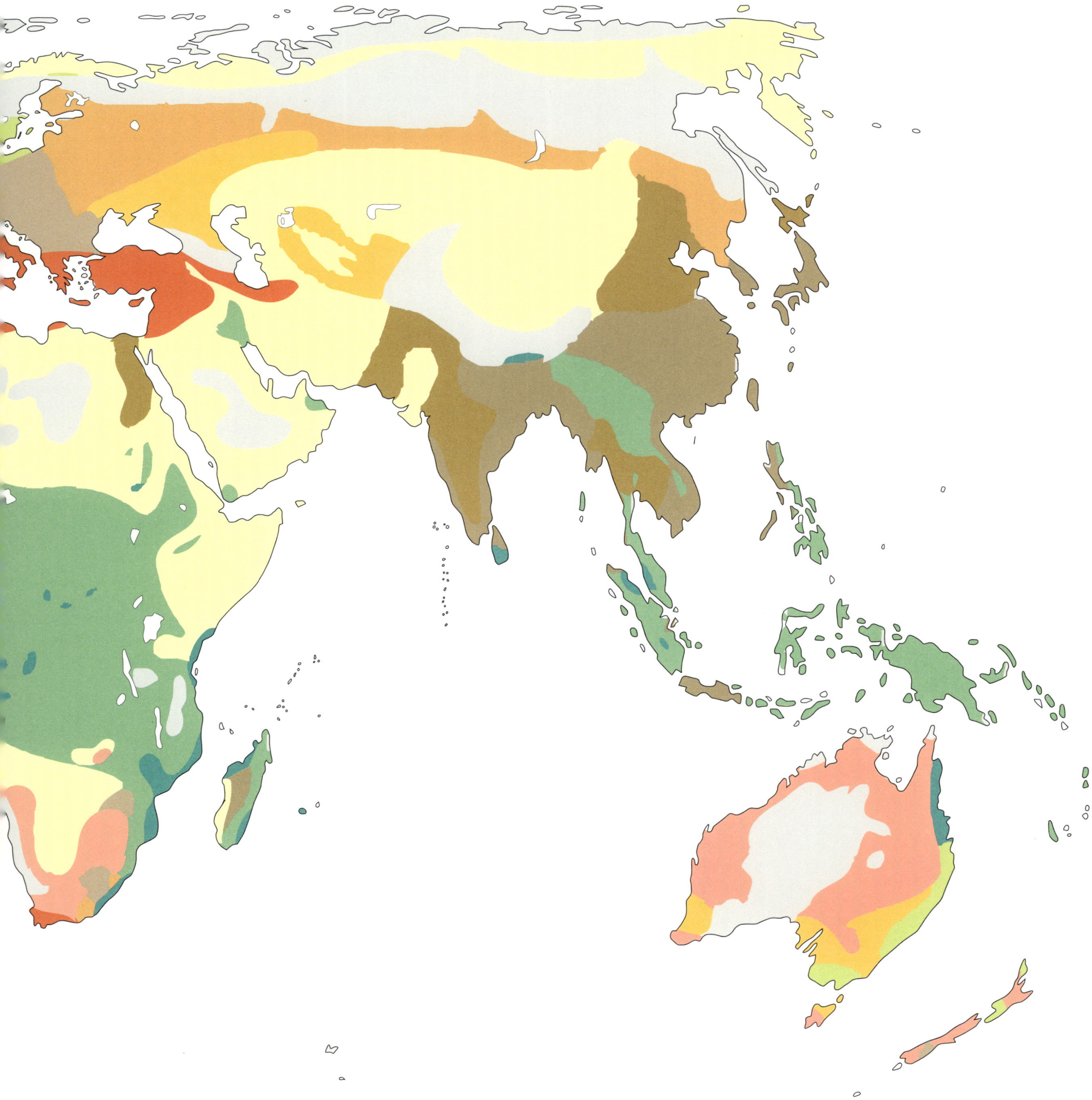

# DESERTIFICATION

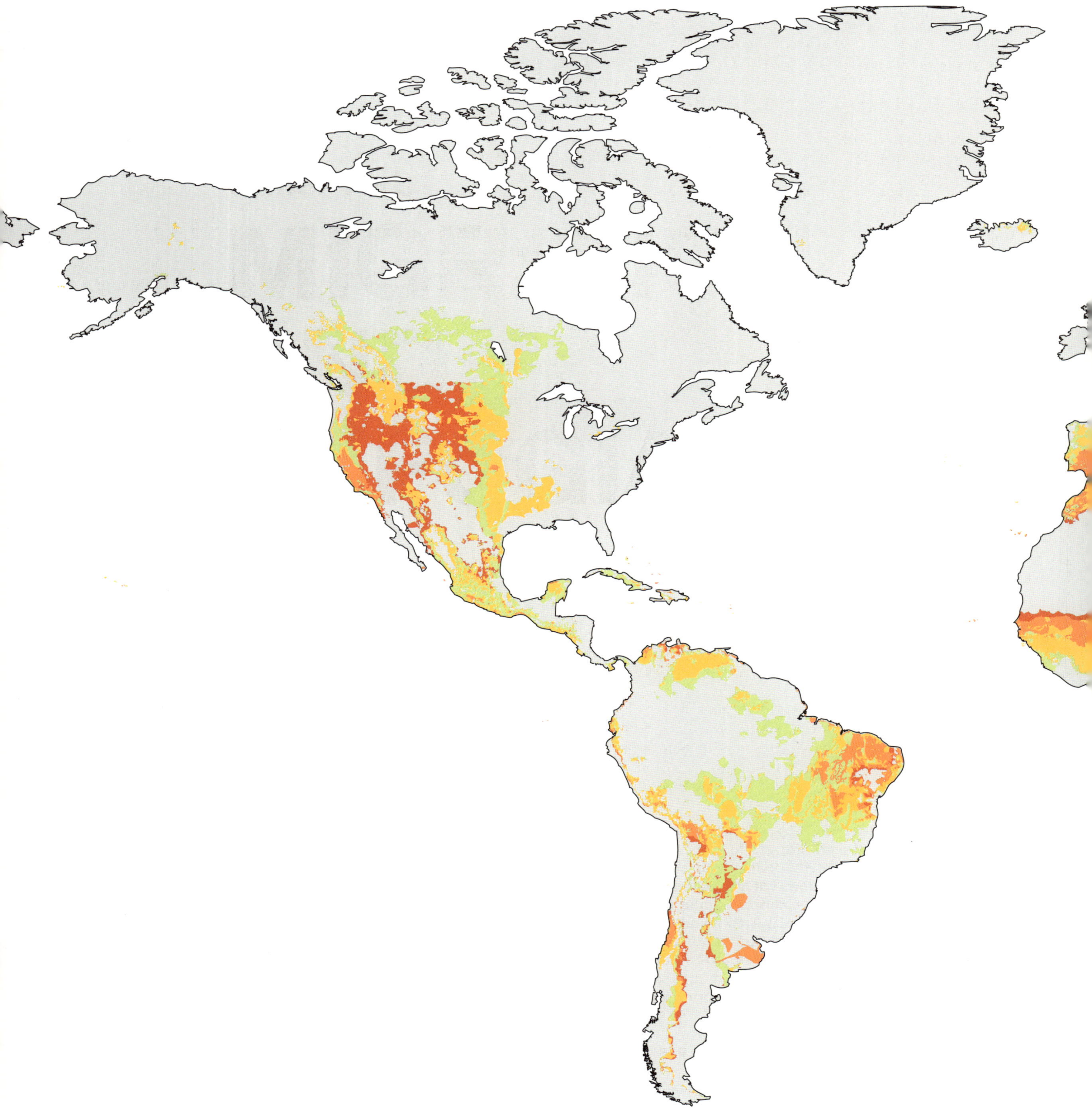

**World map showing degrees of vulnerability to desertification**



Illustration: based on Natural Resources Conservation Service of the United States Department of Agriculture

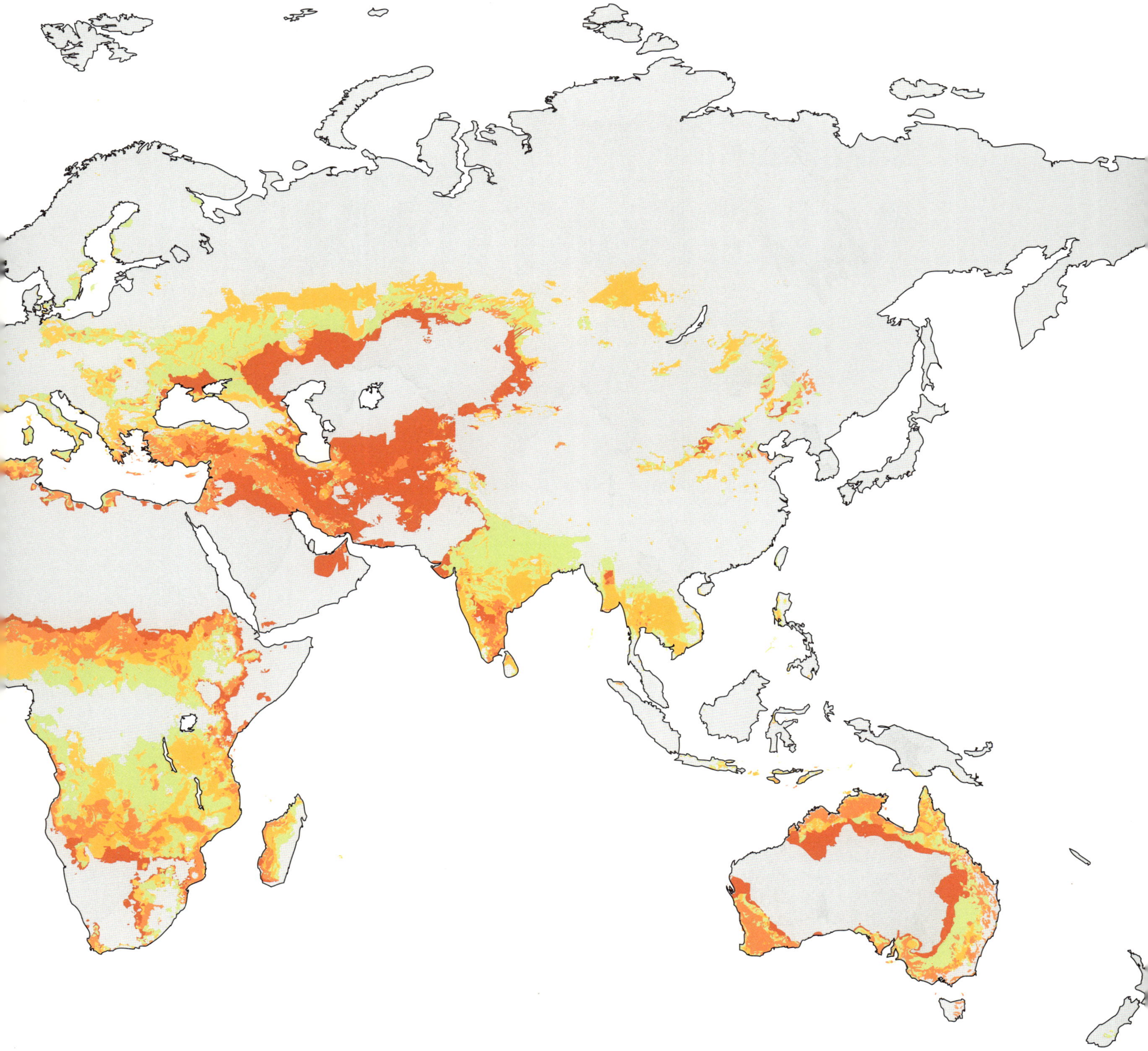

## Sahel Vert:

# MIGRATION AND REFUGIA

**Trees in the Sahel have long been part of what is today called "farming." In Africa the cultivation and tending of trees represents a traditional form of organic farming in which people, plants and trees complement and support one another. Particularly in light of ongoing desertification, trees here provide a vital resource for countering soil erosion and the overuse of the vegetation cover that is being indirectly aggravated year after year due to migration and the rural exodus to the cities. Agriculture is vital to Africa's future. Reforestation with local, mostly endangered tree species can help promote natural regeneration and thus the preservation of biodiversity. As part of a dynamic system that coordinates the collection and storage of seeds and the production and planting of trees, tree nurseries offer enormous potential for both small- and large-scale revitalization projects.**

Traditional granary in Teli, Dogonland, Mali
Photo: Jörg Müller

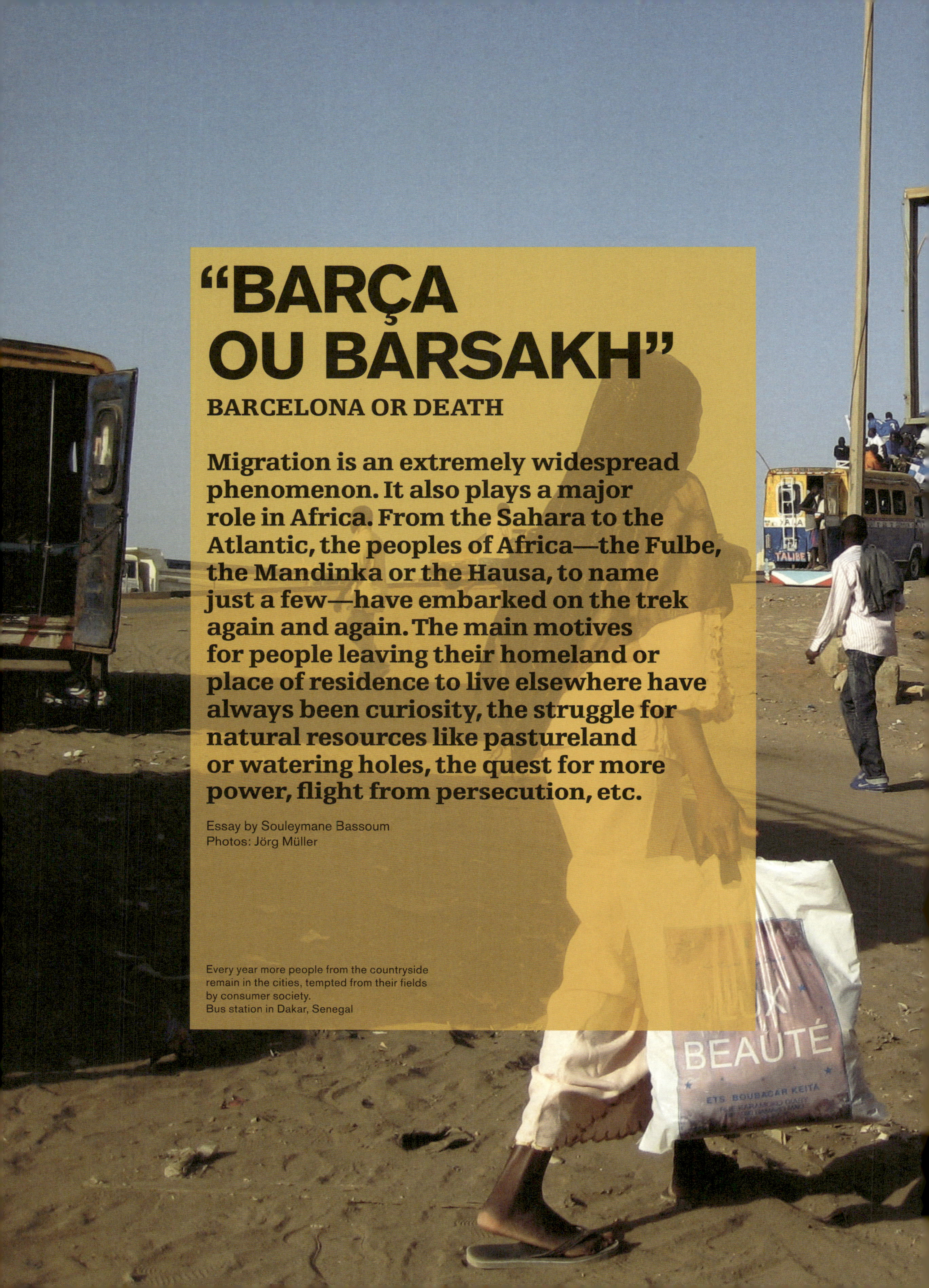


# "BARÇA OU BARSAKH"

## BARCELONA OR DEATH

**Migration is an extremely widespread phenomenon. It also plays a major role in Africa. From the Sahara to the Atlantic, the peoples of Africa—the Fulbe, the Mandinka or the Hausa, to name just a few—have embarked on the trek again and again. The main motives for people leaving their homeland or place of residence to live elsewhere have always been curiosity, the struggle for natural resources like pastureland or watering holes, the quest for more power, flight from persecution, etc.**

Essay by Souleymane Bassoum
Photos: Jörg Müller

Every year more people from the countryside remain in the cities, tempted from their fields by consumer society.
Bus station in Dakar, Senegal

In addition to migration movements that have internal causes, a leading one being persecution as a result of Islamization, which drove people farther and farther westwards, in West Africa there were also external causes for migration movements, such as the slave trade or colonization.

The peoples of West Africa in particular repeatedly embarked on the trek, voluntarily or involuntarily, in search of pastureland or simply in the hopes of finding better living conditions, and this fact created a regular tradition of migration. These movements, whether motivated by internal or external causes, enabled religions such as Christianity, Islam, or the jihad of El Hadj Umar Tall, to expand their spheres of influence; but they also facilitated the spread of devastating diseases that had previously been unknown in Africa—syphilis, for example, which was spread by Senegalese soldiers returning from World Wars I and II, as well as AIDS.

Migration also played a significant role for the flora of Africa. On a journey from which there is likely to be no return, people take with them what they cherish most. Regardless of the mercantile interests of the slave traders who introduced "cash crops" such as peanuts, coffee, cocoa and sugarcane from the Americas to Africa, sometimes it was simply botanical curiosity that prevailed.

The politics of marriage propagated by the wealthy African upper class also long contributed to the dissemination of plant species. One goal was the preservation of peace, which is why kings married their daughters off to their allies. And when they embarked on the journey to their new home, the royal daughters would always take with them seed grain or their favorite plants.

Other examples can be found in the animal kingdom. Migratory birds, for example, carry only a few lightweight seeds with them, but that is already enough to contribute significantly to today's biodiversity. Through pastoral nomadism, the camels of Mauritania introduced desert plants into areas used as forest pasture in east-central Senegal. Wild animals such as the jackal played a key role in the spread of the jujube *(Ziziphus mauritania)* and the desert date *(Balanites aegyptiaca)*. Ruminant cows and goats have established the ana tree *(Acacia albida)* in areas where it was previously not found.

## MONETIZED AGRICULTURE

Nowadays migration movements have mainly economic causes. Agriculture provides a livelihood for roughly seventy percent of the West African population. The structural measures of the World Bank and the IMF have led West African countries to increasingly turn to the production of globally marketable goods, which in rural areas are among the few sources of cash. The agriculture business, once geared to the production of countries' domestic food supply, has undergone a gradual and almost unnoticed shift towards a complex and monetized system. The frenzied quest for money, which constitutes the only means to pay for healthcare, education or coveted consumer goods, has ultimately meant that the production of globally marketable goods has become the only profitable means of income during the winter months. In practice this has led to the spread of monocultures, which in turn are responsible for soil depletion and the spread of nematodes, and ultimately cause diminished harvests. The fact that subsistence farming has been neglected for many years, resulting in a steady decrease in yields, has also contributed to the weakening of the rural environment. This is one cause of a new kind of migration, which is simply called rural exodus.

## RURAL EXODUS IN SENEGAL

In Senegal a close relationship has existed since colonial times between urban and rural areas: During the dry season, after the harvest was done, young people moved from the countryside to the cities, where they earned a living as so-called seasonal workers, for example as water vendors. Their only need was to buy themselves new clothes, and it would have been unthinkable for them not to return to the countryside for the next rainy season. Ultimately, however, consumer society in the cities proved to be too tempting, and some of them realized that, even during the rainy season, they could earn much more money in the cities than they could in the country. Eventually more and more people from the country chose to remain in the cities, many of them keeping their rural customs. They stuck together, supported each other, took on small, poorly paid jobs with which they could barely make ends meet, and hardly managed to send any money to their relatives in the country. Because of their precarious existence, they never really established a sense of belonging to the city, but at the same time they ended up losing their ties to the country. Since as a rule they did not have any vocational training, they were forced to join the masses of the urban unemployed, and were exposed to all the related problems, such as crime, prostitution and alcohol.

The number of these people with rural backgrounds increased steadily. They tried to form a new common identity on the fringes of the cities, occupying the urban zones that were classified as *non aedificandi,* meaning that they were off limits for development because they were situated in flood zones, for example. In 2006 the presidential election in Senegal was even postponed because the funds designated for the election were to be used to support the inhabitants of the Dakar outskirts who were affected by the floods. Fifty-two billion CFA francs (almost 80 million euros) went to a construction program, the so-called Jaxaay Plan, which was to help with the resettlement of 160,000 people from flooded residential areas. These people were living in squalid slums that were virtually devoid of basic social structures, as they tried to eek out a living by growing vegetables or breeding sheep on tiny parcels of land.

## CLIMATE CHANGE AND ANIMISM

In 1973, in the middle of the rainy season, precipitation unexpectedly ceased across much of West Africa. The millet crop was in the process of forming ears, while legumes such as cowpea, bambara peanut and others were in full bloom. The ground vegetation layer hadn't fully developed yet.

There was widespread distress and helplessness: For as long as anyone could remember, nothing like this had ever happened before. Religious leaders interpreted it as divine punishment for declining moral values. At first there was much praying in the mosques and churches. But as the rains still didn't return, there were heated discussions under the palaver tree about the practices and rituals of the ancestors. During this period it became clear to me that while ninety-four percent of the population of Senegal are Muslim and five percent Christian, one hundred percent are followers of animism. Apparently, animism is the faith that we in Senegal fall back on when we see no way out. But no matter how many sacrifices were performed, the rains simply wouldn't return. The more the end of the rainy period approached, the greater became the despair. The stockbreeders were the first to go looking for new pasturelands. On their treks, they lost over two thirds of their herds. Younger farmers left for the cities. An unprecedented exodus from the countryside began.

Those who remained in the villages—women, children and the elderly—survived on food aid. Many of the children born in this time were named after the kinds of grain that were being distributed. During this time we ate rice for the first time ever; twenty years later it had become the main staple food. Today, Senegal imports a whopping 600,000 tons of rice per year!

I later came to the realization that the events of 1973 were nothing less than the first harbinger of climate change. The drought returned in 1985, and then again in 1992. Climate change is evident both in the form of excess and shortage: too much heat, too much cold, flood and drought. Diseases such as malaria, which we used to have only in the winter months, now threaten us throughout the year. Allergic respiratory afflictions and eye and skin diseases are now commonplace.

In Dakar most of the people who fled the villages were stranded in neighborhoods like Khar Yall, Pikine, Thiaroye, Guédiawaye and Yeumbeul. At the time they settled there, there was terrible drought. They left their villages because they had lost all hope that the winter rains would ever return. As a result, they did not give much thought to the fact that they had settled in the dried-out swamplands around Dakar.

To their great misfortune, however, the rains came back in 2005. The water, which never forgets its old ways, flooded their quarters and they became environmental refugees. Some of the population of these areas was resettled; many others still live there, in squalid conditions, surrounded by putrid pools of water.

PLANT PRODUCTION IN THE CITIES
Mixture of markets stalls and living barracks in Kumasi, Ghana

Agriculture along the Niger in the city center of Bamako, Mali

## ENVIRONMENTAL REFUGEES

As long as food shortages, financial crises and climate problems continue, the flow of migrants and refugees will not dry up. Today, when entire populations are forced to leave their homes because the ecological basis for agricultural production has been permanently destroyed, we speak of environmental refugees. According to a 2009 report by the NGO Oxfam, by the middle of the century, six hundred million Africans will be threatened by drought and famine. This means that the number of environmental and war refugees will continue to increase in the coming years, unless African nations succeed in taking effective measures to cope with climate change.

In addition, the continuing poverty in the southern hemisphere, and in Africa in particular, where low levels of economic growth mean there are hardly any new jobs for young people, is driving increasing numbers of people to illegally enter the countries in the north. International migration gets considerable media attention, not least due to developments in the Canary Islands, where, since 2006 alone, 30,000 people have registered as immigrants wishing to enter Europe. The causes of this growing tide of people who are drawn from Africa to Europe can be found, on the one hand, in the demographic trend that has been evident in Africa over the past years, i.e., the large percentage of young people with respect to the total population, and on the other hand in the steadily increasing number of the immigrants' countries of origin. They come from the Spanish enclaves of Melilla and Ceuta, from Layoun in Morocco, Nouadhibou in Mauritania, Saint-Louis, Dakar and Casamance in Senegal. The common saying used by those in Senegal who want to emigrate is "Barça ou barsakh," or "Barcelona or death," and this clearly expresses just how determined they are to make it to Europe. By Continental or international standards, migration costs countless lives. Between 2006 and 2009, many hundreds of people from various regions in Sub-Saharan Africa have drowned at sea, either because their refugee boats sank or because smugglers simply threw them overboard. And many of those who make it to Europe are transported back to Africa under inhuman conditions.

Nonetheless, migration is not a completely negative phenomenon. There are also some positive effects that can be identified. "In terms of international financial exchange, the existence of emigrant communities abroad leads to a dynamic exchange of goods and capital between country of origin and country of entry. For many developing countries, the money transfers of their emigrants surpass the level of development aid. It is not uncommon for these transfers to amount to a substantial percentage of the gross national product, and for the emigrants' countries of origin, they constitute the second most important source of foreign currency after the export of goods." [1]

The migration movements we are speaking about here, regardless of whether they have internal or external causes or are voluntary or involuntary, actually represent strategies of adapting to changing living conditions. Such migration movements have considerable social impacts. The encounters between different societies, cultures, ethnic groups, even families themselves do not remain without consequence and can lead, for example, to changes in language or even in eating habits.

## MIGRATION OF SEED: SMALL-SCALE STRATEGIES

For the African countries, the migration movements have very negative effects at various levels. The continuing exodus from the countryside robs rural regions of their best workers. A large segment of the youth sees no future in agriculture; this is compounded by the fact that governments contribute less than ten percent of their budgets to this sector. Instead, West African countries devote their attention and energy to simply devising strategic concepts to fight poverty. In many countries agricultural policy consists of nothing more than the announcement of campaigns or the proclamation of catchwords. A typical example of this is Senegal's GOANA program, which stands for "Grande Offensive Agricole pour la Nourriture et l'Abondance" (Major Agricultural Offensive for Food and Abundance). Meanwhile, supply bottlenecks and their primary symptom, the rural exodus, reinforce each other and lead, in the long run, to low levels of agricultural production across Sub-Saharan Africa.

In spite of this, it is possible to develop strategies aimed at limiting and controlling the flow of refugees from Africa. A significant component of my vision of the future is the migration of seed to help preserve biodiversity. In the face of the great threat posed by genetically modified foods, the search for alternatives becomes crucial. In order to illustrate this vision of the future, I'd like to introduce the concept put forward by the nongovernmental organization Agrecol Afrique, whose mission it is to promote ecologically sound agricultural practices in Africa.

Working together with farmers, the organization develops strategies of self-reliant sustenance. In other words, the farmers learn, with us, to produce what is actually eaten. In order to bring diversity back into the available stock of seed, Agrecol Afrique organizes seed exchanges after each year's harvest. Participants from different villages come together and prepare food using their agricultural products. Every participant is free to try the food, or to take a gourdful of his or her seed of choice. Seed that was previously only grown in a certain ecological zone is thereby spread to other parts of the country—even if experts and agronomists maintain that it might not be suitable to different climactic conditions.

This dissemination of seed occurs according to the principle of free exchange. Sometimes a community might entrust a particularly valuable seed to experienced farmers, in the hopes that they will grow it well and spread it further. After an initial harvest, it is planted on the community's test fields so that everyone can become familiar with its characteristics. At the end of the winter season, the harvest is stored as the basis for a seedbank, so that the seed is then available to the community in the future as well. This ensures that knowledge and new developments relating to all aspects of storing seed are gathered, expanded, refined and passed on.

Agrecol Afrique's initiative constitutes a highly effective measure for adapting to climate change. Not only does it enable a strengthening of agro-biodiversity on a national level, it also promotes a better preservation of seed with the help of seedbanks. The rainy season now starts later and later, and it ends later as well. The seed that is available for research has not adapted to these changes. In light of this fact, it is of great advantage if long-forgotten types of seed come back into circulation on the markets.

Thus the diversity that once existed can return. Farmers have a greater variety of seed at their disposal, and with it a greater chance of achieving a high-yield harvest. They regain their self-sufficiency because they don't need anyone telling them what to plant.

## LARGE-SCALE STRATEGIES

On a larger scale as well, strategies must be developed in order to more effectively confront the phenomena of migration and rural exodus in Africa. Governments must step up their investments in agriculture and initiate an agricultural policy which actually improves the income levels and standard of living of the rural population. Other necessary measures are local reform and the development of regional centers, so that migration can be steered towards smaller cities as well and the uncontrolled growth in major cities can be prevented.

At the pan-African level, the NEPAD program "New Partnership for Africa's Development" is well equipped to advance regional integration and better utilize the specialized skills of people on the African continent. There should be fewer impediments to migration—more freedom of movement would benefit both the migrants' countries of destination as well as their countries of origin. An encouraging development is the example of the Economic Community of West African States (ECOWAS), with its common passport.

1 Jean-Pierre Guengant, "Migrations internationales et développement: les nouveaux paradigmes," *Revue Européenne des Migrations Internationales*, Vol. 12, 1996, pp. 105–119.

PLANT PRODUCTION FOR THE CITIES
Irrigated papaya monocultures in Sindia, Senegal

Selling oranges on the roadside in Rufisque, Senegal

*"Climate change is evident both in the form of excess and shortage."*

Animist high priest *(hogon)* in Dogonland, Mali

Spreading desert. View from the *Falaise de Bandiagara*, Dogonland, Mali

Organic farming supported by Agrécol Afrique in the farming village of Sessène, Senegal

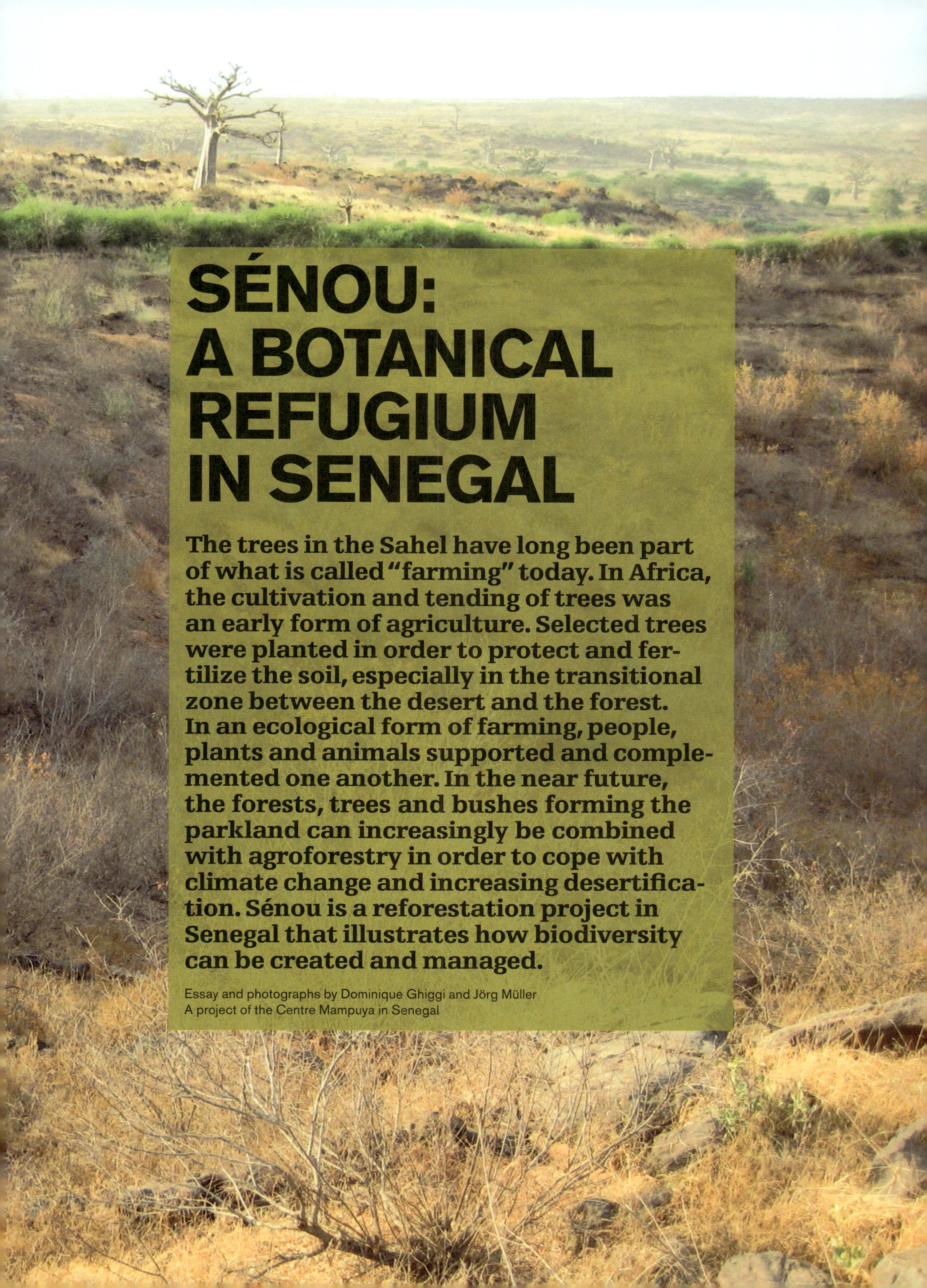

# SÉNOU: A BOTANICAL REFUGIUM IN SENEGAL

**The trees in the Sahel have long been part of what is called "farming" today. In Africa, the cultivation and tending of trees was an early form of agriculture. Selected trees were planted in order to protect and fertilize the soil, especially in the transitional zone between the desert and the forest. In an ecological form of farming, people, plants and animals supported and complemented one another. In the near future, the forests, trees and bushes forming the parkland can increasingly be combined with agroforestry in order to cope with climate change and increasing desertification. Sénou is a reforestation project in Senegal that illustrates how biodiversity can be created and managed.**

Essay and photographs by Dominique Ghiggi and Jörg Müller
A project of the Centre Mampuya in Senegal

### A TRANSITORY DRY ZONE

Senegal is a semitropical country located in a transitory dry zone on the West Coast of Africa. The subtropics are characterized by a dry season during winter and a rainy season during summer. Over the last few decades this zone has been subject to increasing desertification since some years have had no rainy season or seen only little rainfall. In the entire Sahel region, the phenomenon of advancing desertification is combined with a fragile ecological and socioeconomic context and has resulted in an urgent need to act on a local level.

The Centre Mampuya was founded in 2002 on the Sénou hills close to Toubab Dialaw, a former fishing village fifty kilometers to the east of the Senegalese capital of Dakar. The founders, Jacqueline Moesch Mampuya (Switzerland/Congo) and Urban Fraefel (Switzerland), have worked for eight years to build a foundation for the protection of natural resources. In cooperation with local partners and the rural population, the team fosters approaches to ecological revitalization, cultural exchange and social and economic development. The project was initially restricted to the main hill of Sénou. Anti-erosion measures were introduced in certain areas and this, thanks to considerable efforts, led to successful reforestation and soil regeneration. In 2008, when the grounds of the Centre Mampuya were expanded to include two adjacent hills, the Sénou landscape project was launched in cooperation with the authors of this text on a total area of about fifty hectares. Its objective was to ensure the continuity of the ecological project for the protection of the hill (initiated in 2002) and to promote reforestation. Furthermore, participants developed a new scenario that provides for the extensive reforestation of the area of the Centre Mampuya. This will also encourage the regeneration of nature in neighboring areas and thus secure the biodiversity of plants and animals in the entire region. The hills represent a botanical refugium, a kind of living repository of genetic material for both endangered and well-adapted tree species. The work focuses on a tree nursery already existing on the grounds and a planned seed bank.

### NOUNGOUMA

The Centre Mampuya stretches across the Noungouma hill formations on the Massif de N'Dias. Sénou is located seventy-one meters above sea level and constitutes the highest point in the formation and thus the most prominent feature of the local landscape. The Massif de N'Dias consists primarily of sandstone that is covered by a laterite crust and divided into manifold smaller hills. During the rainy season the fertile valley lines, or thalwegs, between the hills are transformed into dynamic riverbeds that are repeatedly flooded for several days each year. Once the floods recede, the farmers in the interior of the country begin using the water for their fields. One of these valleys is located in the low-lying area around the hills of Sénou, where for generations local farmers have practiced rain-fed agriculture centered on trees, millet, sorghum, fonio and cowpea. Since the sixties they have also planted peanuts. The soil on the hills mainly consists of layers of marl, lime and laterite, with a mosaiclike vegetation cover that changes from prairie to bush savannah to tree savannah. Alongside this bushy dry savannah, known as *brousse* in the local French vernacular, there is a bush landscape that was created by the clearing of trees and has been gradually increasing in size. Bushes and trees are a vital natural resource for Senegal's dry soils. They were neglected by the French colonial powers and even regarded as inferior scrubland. Then, in the seventies, a severe drought struck the Sahel and experts began to enquire what could be done about desertification and famines. The significance of the various trees in the middle of the bush finally started to be recognized. The flat country in the region of the Centre Mampuya features many such parklands, which represent a special form of agriculture in which different types of trees are scattered across the area in groups of twos or threes; the land is simultaneously used as pasture and for planting. The agroforestry that the reforestation project has proposed for the parkland incorporates a cross-generational timeframe and is capable of adapting to different physical and climatic factors. At the same time, it meets the needs of both humans and cattle. Trees are one of the most important elements in the parkland system since they can be used for many generations; most parkland trees are the

product of human breeding and cultivation work. Traditionally, decisions about whether, when and where a tree or shrub was to be cut down, dug up or planted anew, and when and what was to be planted among the trees, were the result of a collective planning process that also took other families into account. The choice of trees and shrubs and their desired long-term growth were always determined by local conditions and thus depended on geology and climate. These tasks required not only an exceptional ability for combining many different elements, but also an astonishing breadth of knowledge that came from direct observations and experiences and is at risk of disappearing today.

## UNCONTROLLED DEVELOPMENT

Land is in principle the property of the state in Senegal, though there have long been efforts to privatize land rights. Local authorities have administered the land since the nineties and have approved a variety of uses (e.g., buildings, fields and gardens). However, much of the land—including the hill formations—is unregulated and subject to free collective use. Today the traditional ownership structures that may have made sense in the past have become one of the leading causes of the overexploitation of nature and the decline in biodiversity. The population regards the large areas of the bush, which are currently not being used, as land that they are free to exploit as they please. Due to economic hardship, areas that were extensively used and traditionally administered by the collective are now being exploited with growing intensity. Grazing cattle degrades the land; trees and shrubs are harvested for food and medicinal purposes until they die out; and the scant supplies of wood are gathered to make fires. The extensive, once widespread forest agriculture has almost entirely disappeared along with the related practices of managing the landscape. Some years ago, rumors spread that the fertile land around the Sénou hills would not be planted any longer, sparking land speculation in the area of Noungouma. Today the only human beings who move through the fallow hedge-enclosed fields are herdsmen with their flocks. From atop Sénou, one can see how the fields that are still vacant in the interior of the country are slowly being transformed into a chaotic helter-skelter succession of half-developed plots closer to the sea. The speculation results from the proximity to both the capital and the sea and the plans announced years ago for a new airport to be built in the town of N'Dias, eight kilometers from the hills. Many farmers have already sold their fields to investors such as FIFA or to medium-sized hotel chains and private individuals. Initially only the fields in the lowlands were affected, but over the past few years the hilly areas have also been the target of speculation, although these areas were traditionally not settled in Senegal. The landowners, mostly farmers and fishermen, have sold their land in the hope of a better life or to pay off debts. They no longer want to live in precarious conditions, depending on the climate and soil and the growth of their crops. Their changing needs, which they hope to satisfy with a quick injection of cash or a steady job in the city, determine the new rhythm of life. The young people's fascination with the dynamics of urban life and the older generation's desperation are contributing to the surge of construction activity in the Noungouma region.

In 2002 the local team from the Centre Mampuya, supervised by Jacqueline Moesch Mampuya and Urbane Fraefel, began working to prevent the overuse of natural resources under deteriorating climatic conditions in an effort to protect the Sénou hills. But over the past few years the project has also had to cope with the uncontrolled development of the landscape. The protection of the existing resources through a viable landscape concept has become increasingly urgent, and there now is the prospect of establishing a regional protection zone extending from the Sénou hills to the lagoon.

Noungouma hill formations on the Massif de N'Dias

Previous double page:
Jacqueline Moesch Mampuya, founder of the Centre Mampuya, on the *cordon pierreux*. Ecological revitalization since 2002

## THE CONCEPT OF THE BOTANICAL REFUGIUM

The changes that the vegetation on the African continent has undergone for millions of years illustrate the climate's direct long-term impact on forest formation. The retreat of the tropical forest over the past 8000 years is a sign of the radical climate change that has taken place during this period. When climatic conditions worsened in low-lying areas, mountain regions repeatedly served as a suitable refuge for tropical and semitropical trees. As soon as conditions improved, the plant populations left their refuges and once again spread to the lower-lying areas.

Anthropogenic influences and climatic changes over the last decades have caused the forest vegetation in the Sahel and the area around the Centre Mampuya to recede more quickly. The vegetation that originally typified the open woodland *("forêt claire")* has virtually disappeared and has been replaced by shrub steppes and bush and tree savannahs. Aerial photographs reveal that the forested areas have shrunk considerably, particularly over the last fifty years. The soil's stability and water capacity have also noticeably declined during this period. This decline has resulted in increased erosion, which causes visible damage to the soil, especially during the rainy season. The vegetative soil layer has eroded, even on slight slopes, and bare laterite soil predominates in exposed areas. Moreover, a large number of the tree and shrub species that the older population knows from earlier years have disappeared since overfarming has made it impossible for these species to reproduce. Climate trends raise fundamental issues for the revitalization project. The project's most important principles are the economical use of available water supplies and a focus on plant species that have a high level of genetic variability and are well adapted to the location.

Similar to the central role that mountain regions have played for forest vegetation on the African continent over the last millions of years, the Sénou hills serve as a refugium—though on a much smaller scale—for the tree flora that has disappeared from the region of the *forêt claire*. The refugium concept draws on the fundamental view that the landscape is an ecosystem that changes over time, one in which plants continually adapt in a dynamic process. In order to ensure that the trees are capable of adapting to different locations both inside and outside the Centre Mampuya—even under changing climatic conditions—the team must restore genetic diversity in a protected area that is inaccessible to people and animals that are not part of the project. A total of two pools of species are planned. One consists of several gardens around the existing buildings of the Centre Mampuya. The local tree species planted in these gardens are highly demanding during the first few years and must be watered daily during the dry season. However, after a few years, they can spread and spontaneously regenerate in the neighboring gallery forests along the Ndoungoumou River up to the lagoon. The second species pool is located in the area of the neighboring hills, which have been severely degraded by deforestation and goat grazing. In a testing ground located there, the seeds of less demanding indigenous plant species will be sown shortly before the rainy season ("direct seeding"). This area was selected primarily because of its heterogeneous relief structure. These seedlings will not be watered, encouraging a process of natural selection that will later provide important insights into the adaptability of different tree species to specific locations. A key prerequisite for spontaneous regeneration is the construction of a fence to protect the entire terrain. Over the long term, this will also be important for forming a *forêt claire* that can be used extensively as healthy parkland. In addition to wild monkeys, jackals, lizards, goannas and a large number of birds and insects, the animals in the area will include a horse, a few cows, sheep, geese and tortoises. Their stocks will be monitored and are intended to ensure the fertilization of the soil, the spread and growth of trees, as well as the formation of parkland.

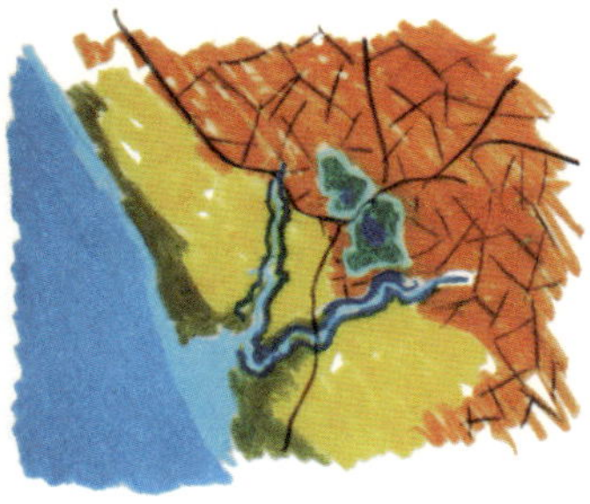

1

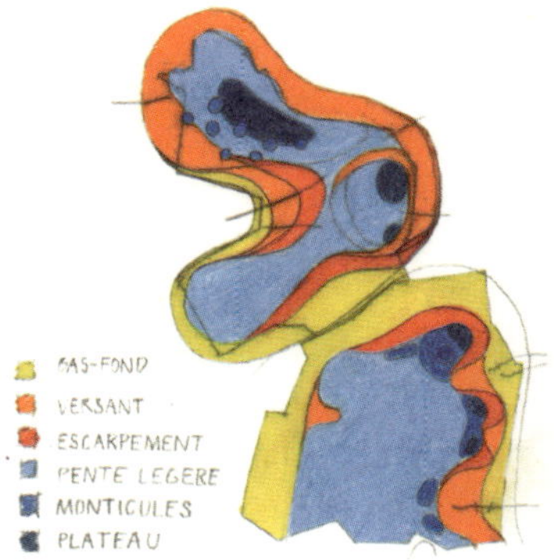


2

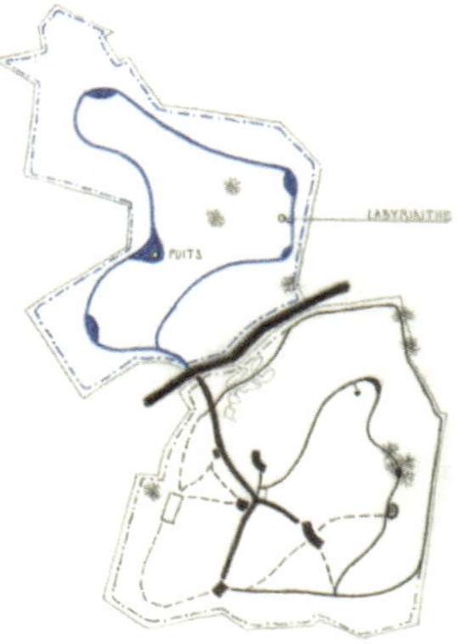

3

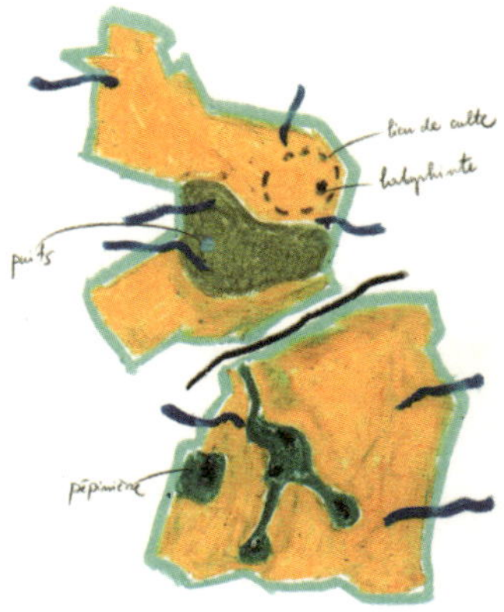

4

5

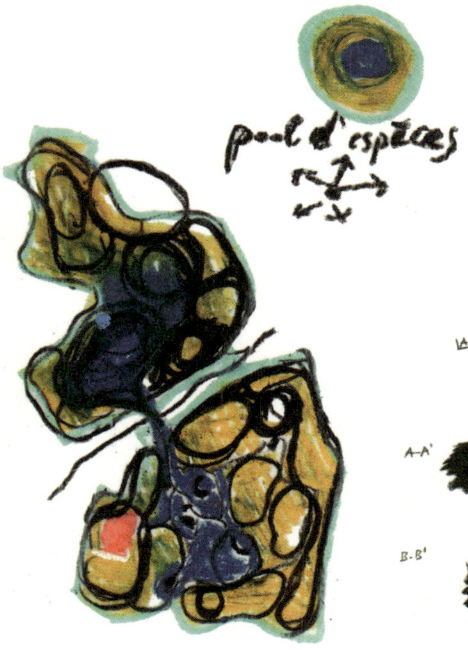


6

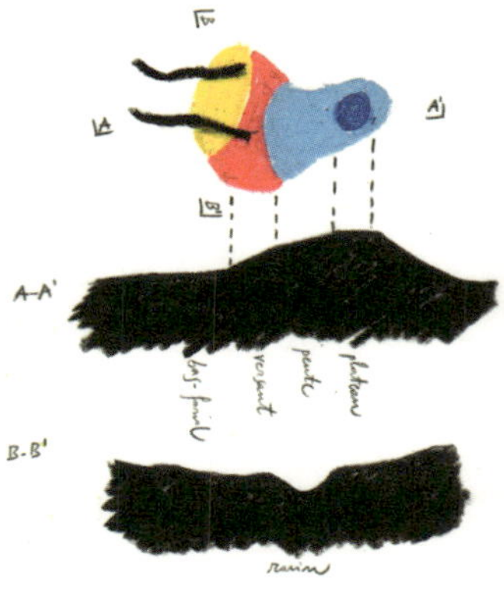


7

DESIGN SKETCHES
1 Botanical refugium concept for the entire region
2 Topography
3 Access paths
4 Revitalization model. Orange: spontaneous regeneration; khaki green: experimental area for direct seeding; dark green: tree nursery and irrigated areas around existing buildings
5 Location of the Centre Mampuya near Toubab Dialaw, Senegal
6 Formation of a species pool *(pool d'espèces)* inside the fenced perimeter
7 Experimental area for direct seeding on a relief
Sketches by Dominique Ghiggi and Jörg Müller

## REVITALIZATION MODEL

Given the decline in the price of agricultural products and the sharply rising food prices, the rural population in the interior of the country has gradually changed its way of thinking. Many families would like to regain security of supply and greater economic independence by using traditional natural resources as well as existing and new expertise. There are also signs that attitudes toward the use of extensive land areas could slowly change again, though the authorities and the population are still little aware of the potential offered by the vast bush and forest areas.

From the perspective of interested population groups in the surrounding villages, the botanical refugium is a revitalization model that, through agroforestry, fosters self-sufficiency and supports the marketing of trees suited to the area. Reforestation work has been supported by groups of women who have promoted the planting of trees in their villages in order to earn crucial income from harvests. Since the hydrologic and topographic conditions on their land are similar to those in the Sénou hills, the revitalization model is able to provide them with information on which plant species grow without irrigation in the relieflike test area and can hence be used economically. Plans have been forged within the scope of the first partner project to support efforts to fence in a revitalization area in the village of Ten Toubab.

## TREE NURSERIES FOR THE PRESERVATION, PRODUCTION AND SPREADING OF TREES

In 2002 a small tree nursery *(pépinière)* was set up on the grounds of the Centre Mampuya in order to produce forest and ornamental plants. In terms of appearance, it resembles a tropical allotment garden, but it has in fact been subdivided into various small plots in the traditional African style. This *pépinière,* which covers around one thousand square meters, is characterized by several beds laid out with stones and by scattered shady trees. Depending on their requirements, the individual botanical species—primarily wild, endangered and well-adapted trees—are grouped together in the shade or partial shade of a large tree; in dense or relatively open stands; or in a specific combinations of trees. The shade of the existing tall trees is controlled by pruning the crowns and the various branch levels. Each tree is labeled and documented in a catalogue. Since most are transplanted to the area when they are still young, they are not lined out in the ground, but in reusable pots.

Since they play an important role in the preservation, production and dissemination of local biodiversity, the grounds of the tree nursery have been expanded considerably during the last two years and further developments have been added. Today there are four functional areas, which stretch from the center of the tree nursery far into the field. The first functional area is devoted to the production of a wide assortment of local tree species in the central nursery. These species are propagated by conventional methods such as sowing, grafting and the use of cuttings. The second area collects seeds and cuttings in the area of the Centre Mampuya and the entire region. The third is concerned with the storage of seeds in a seed bank (planning for this area began in 2010). Finally, the fourth area experiments with direct sowing in topographically heterogeneous testing grounds in the area of the Centre Mampuya.

Taken together, these areas form a dynamic and coherent system whose processes are regulated by people, animals and the rhythms of nature. Something is planted and harvested every day, and during the dry season, the young, lined-out plants in the *pépinière* must also be watered daily to keep them alive.

Tracks left by the herds of goats moving through the surrounding area. Intensive grazing by goats is increasingly destroying the soil.

A group of women from the neighboring village of Dagga dedicated to planting extensively used trees

Deforestation has radically reduced the soil quality in this region

Development of a tree savannah through spontaneous regeneration in the Parc de Bandia in Sindia, not far from the Centre Mampuya

1 Sahel dry zones
Senegal is a subtropical country located on the west coast of Africa between the desert and the tropics in a transitory dry zone. Over recent decades this zone has been subject to increasing desert formation due to the fact that in some years the wet season does not come at all or, when it does, provides insufficient rain.
Illustration: Dominique Ghiggi

2 The spatial structure of the African rain and mountain forest approximately 72,000 BP, 20,000 BP, 8000 BP and today
Changes in the vegetation over millions of years illustrate the long-term influence of climate on the region. The retreat of the tropical rainforest over the last eight thousand years points to a significant change in the climate.
The diagram illustrates the role of mountain regions as a refugium for tropical plant species that have retreated from dry, endangered zones over the course of time.
Illustration: based on A. C. Hamilton, "The Significance of Patterns of Distribution Shown by Forest Plants and Animals in Tropical Africa for the Reconstruction of Upper Pleistocene Palaeoenvironment: A Review," *Palaeoecology of Africa*, 9, 1976, 63–97

3 Main vegetation formations in western tropical Africa
The open Sudanese forest *(forêt claire)* represents the normal, natural vegetation of this region. Anthropogenic influence in the form of clearing, grazing and agriculture as well as changes to the climate over the past decades have accelerated the phenomenon of receding vegetation that has been continuing for eight thousand years, resulting in the replacement of Sudanese forests by shrubland and bush savannah.
Illustration: based on Paul Ndiaye, *Atlas du Sénégal*, Édition Jeune Afrique, Paris, 2000

4–19 Typical parkland trees that grow spontaneously and are planted in the area of the Centre Mampuya. Their leaves, bark, roots, seeds, blossoms and fruit are used in medicine, food, agriculture and industry.
Source: Al Imfeld, Elefanten in der Sahara, Zurich: Rotpunktverlag, 2009

4–5 *Acacia albida*, mostly referred to as *Faidherbia albida* today (family: Mimosaceae)
This acacia species, called the ana tree, was valued by the population and favored by cattle for several reasons. Its fruit is rich in protein, its leaves are an excellent substitute fodder for cattle, and its shade protects the soil (the tree is a resting place for cattle, which leave behind dung). Finally, its rhizome—the rootlike shoot system—adds nitrogen to the soil. Together with *Acacia senegal* and *Acacia nilota*, ana trees keep the ground fertile and serve as a windbreak. They are also considered sacred.

6–7 *Adansonia digitata* (family: Bombacaceae)
The baobab, also known as the monkey-bread tree, occurs primarily in the parklands of Senegal and Nigeria. As one of the most important economic trees in the Sahel, it testifies to the presence of human beings. Large hollowed-out baobabs were used, for example, to store water

8 *Balanites aegyptiaca* (family: Balanitaceae)
The desert date has thorny branches; the pulp is edible.

9 *Combretum micranthum/glutinosum/nioroense* (family: Combretaceae)
The leaves of the combretum shrub attract insects.

10 *Cordyla pinnata* (family: Caesalpiniaceae)
The bush mango occurs in the Sahel and West Africa and is valued for its fruit, leaves, bark and roots. The fruit is an important medicine for stomach ailments.

11 *Diospyros mespiliformis* (family: Ebenaceae)
The African ebony occurs throughout the Sahel and in the African savannahs. It is between fifteen and fifty meters high and an evergreen. The fruit—jackalberries—is used to brew beer and produce African wine, the wood to carve masks and statues.

12 *Euphorbia balsamifera* (family: Euphorbiaceae)
The balsam spurge grows in very dry sandy areas. The bush is regarded as a quick-growing weed, which is nevertheless left in the ground to protect the soil from excessive amounts of sunlight. The tree is popular for fencing in residential areas and pastureland and is also highly valued as animal fodder since cattle will eat its leaves either fresh or dried. The white milk is toxic but has diverse medical uses.

13–14 *Jatropha curcas* (family: Euphorbiaceae)
The Barbados nut, also known as the purging nut or nux vomica, is a very robust bush that can grow deep in the desert. It is used as a protective hedge, mostly in combination with other plants, and is also important for preventing soil erosion. The fruit is toxic, containing curcin. The juice is used for lamp oil and the crushed nuts as fertilizer.

15 *Piliostigma reticulatum* (family: Caesalpiniaceae)
This evergreen bush grows in the wild and is not cleared from fields because of its leguminous (nitrogen-fixing) quality. The fruits are rich in crude proteins, carbohydrates and minerals, and the seeds have an analgesic effect on burns.

16 *Parkia biglobosa* (family: Mimosaceae)
The carob tree is popular among the poor as a source of simple food. It is well suited for reforestation programs on steep slopes.

17 *Sclerocarya birrea* (family: Anacardiaceae)
The marula tree has several names depending on its size and shape, location, and the use of its fruit. It flourishes in the open savannah or on steppes and can grow to a height of fifteen meters. Its bark is silvery gray. Even if there is little rainfall, the tree produces a substantial crop of golden plum-sized fruit that are a staple in certain parts of West Africa. The seeds are very rich in protein and are added to porridge and sauces, to maintain people's health. The pressed seeds are used to produce a body care oil. The bark was once an important malaria medicine, as well as a remedy used to treat malaria attacks. The leaves were chewed like chewing gum and also used against constipation

18 *Tamarindus indica* (family: Caesalpiniaceae)
The tamarind is a pan-tropical tree—it is found everywhere in the tropics. It grows to heights of six to twenty meters and is an evergreen. The fruit is sour, rich in tartaric acid and vitamin C, and used for seasoning.

19 *Ziziphus mauritania* (family: Rhamnaceae)
The jujube originally comes from Central Asia. The tree is thorny and grows on the edge of fields and paths. It offers protection from stray animals and bears fruit that is edible for both animals and people.

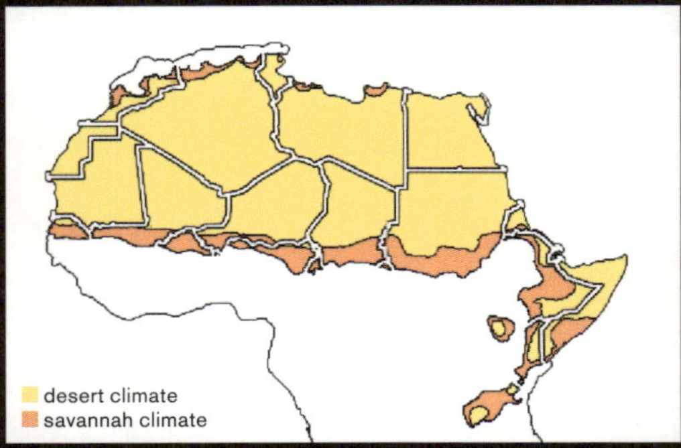


1

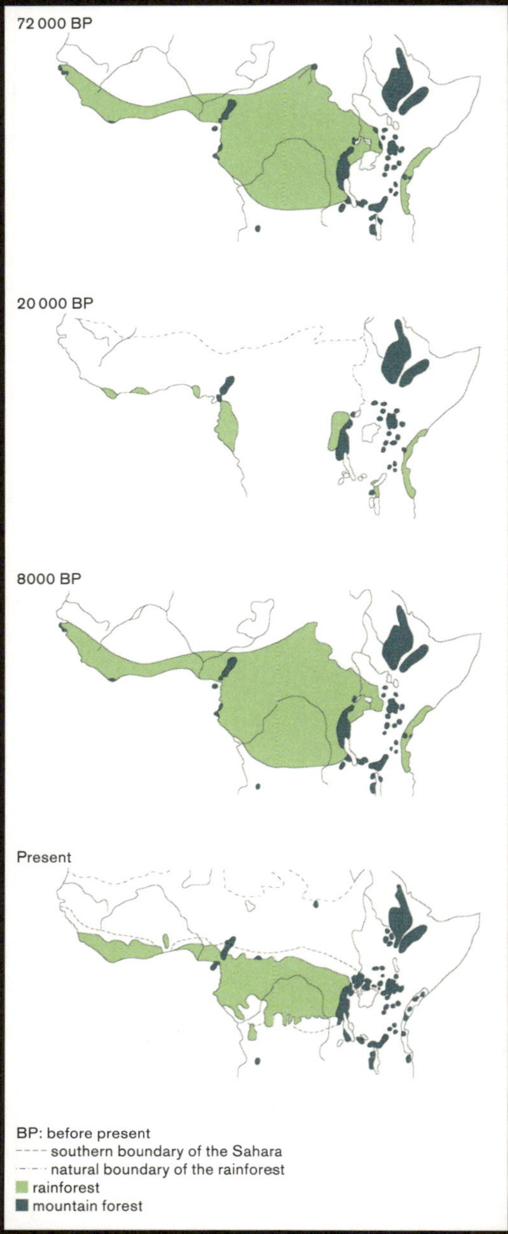


2

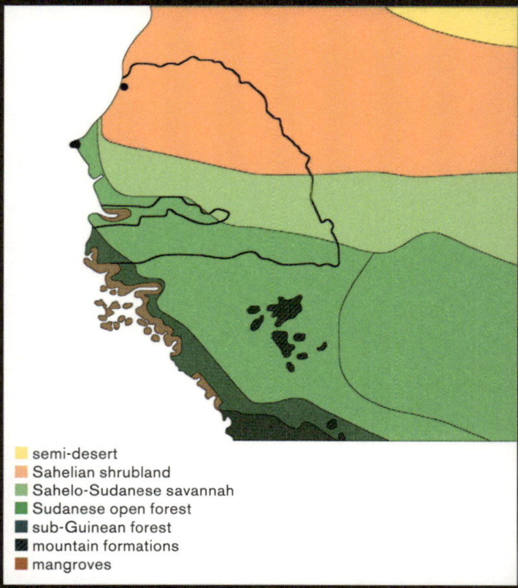


3

4
5
6
7
8
9
10
11
12
13
14
15
16
17
18
19

## SEED BANK

By collecting and storing the seeds of adapted and endangered wild plants, nursery staff are able to carry out extensive and targeted ecological reforestation, suited to the conditions of the site. It is extremely important to collect seeds of different origins for each tree species in order to guarantee natural adaptability through spontaneous regeneration. The best seeds in the project are used to produce cuttings or are directly sown in the area. Seeds are also supplied to local farmers.

Although there are traditional seed preservation customs in the area, the long-term storage of seeds is a pioneering undertaking in Senegal and exemplary for the entire Sahel region. There are plans to build a concrete warehouse that can hold a total of twenty tons of seeds. Grain seeds will be stored in a room in which temperatures range between 18°C and 28°C. The seeds of wild tree species, on the other hand, require cool storage. The last time seeds were inventoried in Senegal was in 1998. Already at the time, it was discovered that the biodiversity of local seeds had heavily declined. In earlier times it was primarily wars, droughts and socioeconomic crises that caused large losses; today these losses have been increased by migration from the land and the globalization of the seed market through international companies. For example, African rice *(Oryza glaberrima)* was displaced by Asian rice *(Oryza sativa)* when the latter was introduced into Africa—first by the Arabs in medieval times, later by colonial rulers and from around 1970 by state and private importers. Today rice is a staple food in Senegal. To compensate for the loss of seeds from local trees and grains, an effort must be made to gather these seeds again and to store them in special warehouses. In addition, seeds must be collected and exchanged by rural farmers, e.g., at local seed markets *("foires de semences")* and other venues. The great advantage of trees over grains is that, once they have been planted, they provide benefits over generations. This is why they should be cultivated in large numbers and planted directly in the fields.

The Centre Mampuya's tree nursery covers approximately one thousand square meters. Following African tradition, the garden is subdivided into a number of smaller areas. Conventional techniques such as sowing, grafting and root cuttings are used here to grow different local and endangered tree species.

The terrain revitalized between 2002 and 2010 through planting and spontaneous regeneration within the fenced compound of the Centre Mampuya

# THE SVALBARD GLOBAL SEED VAULT

## A BIOLOGICAL SAFE DEPOSIT BOX IN THE ARCTIC

**There are some 1400 gene banks around the world that preserve plant seeds. All of them can send material to an island in the Arctic. The seed bank there is unique, above all due to its location. Samples stored in the Svalbard Global Seed Vault are about as far away as they can possibly be from the world's trials and tribulations—a mere thousand kilometers from the North Pole, at a latitude of seventy-eight degrees, thirteen minutes north.**

Travelogue by Christoph Seidler
Photographs by Mari Tefre/Global Crop Diversity Trust

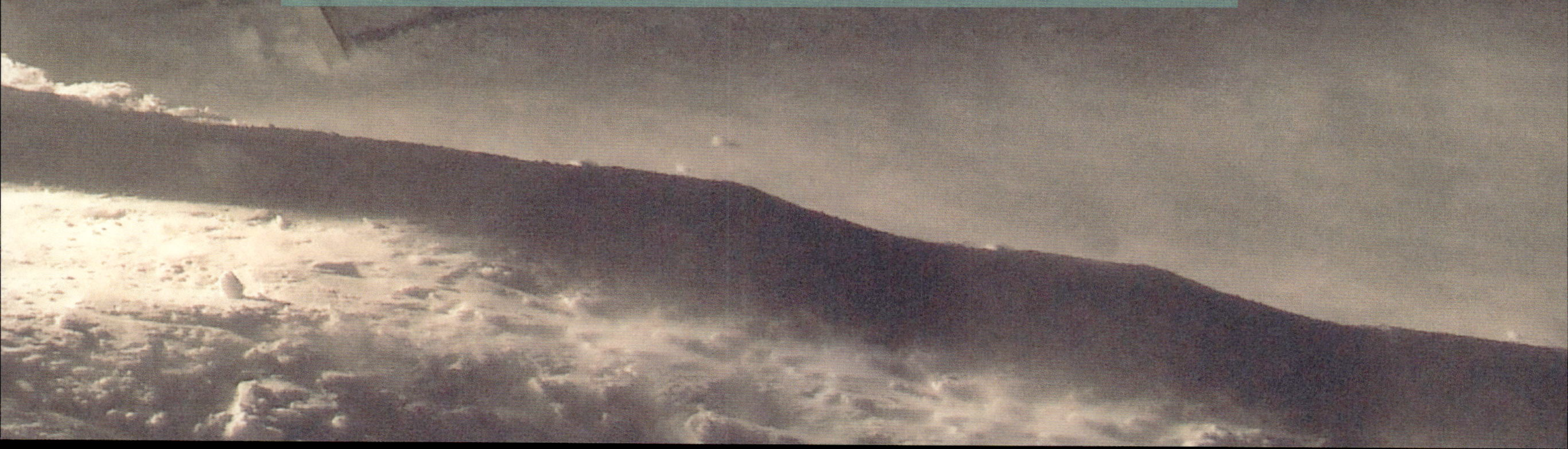

Entrance to the Svalbard Global Seed Vault on Spitzbergen. Art project: Dyveke Sanne

Svalbard, Spitsbergen. The taxi driver is a bit puzzled as to why I ask him to stop here. The cutting wind is icy; dark shreds of clouds are scudding overhead. The surroundings look anything but inviting. However, with the meter still cheerfully ticking away, he does not ask any questions. He keeps the motor running while he waits in the warm car. One can hear the radio even through the closed doors. As the driver has explained on our short trip from the town center, there is not really much to see out here. We have driven uphill from the airport in Longyearbyen, the largest settlement on the Arctic island of Spitsbergen. Its runway is used by passenger jets arriving from the Norwegian mainland as well as small propeller-driven aircraft for local transport. These carry miners working at the nearby Svea Nord coal mine or polar scientists from the research stations further north in Ny-Ålesund. On the other side of the Adventfjorden, the tips of snow-covered mountains rising above the deserted mining settlement of Hiorthamn peek out of the clouds every now and then.

The global seed vault is only a few steps away, 130 meters above sea level. The entrance rises from the dark sandstone half way up the Platåberget like a fang of some ancient predator. There is no reception building, no sign, nothing. On the concrete wall, next to a blue and green logo, unpretentious metal letters spell out "Svalbard Global Seed Vault." A cooling unit whirs nearby in a shipping container. I attempt to shake the stainless steel door in front of the tunnel leading into the mountain; it doesn't budge, not even a millimeter. It is firmly secured by two powerful locks.

Behind the door, deep in the Arctic permafrost, lie hundreds of thousands of samples of cultivated plants, above all grain varieties. Should a species become extinct, be it from natural catastrophes, nuclear war or plant epidemics, Spitsbergen would subsequently provide the stock for its reestablishment. The scientists running the vault place particular emphasis on agricultural plants from the developing world. Genetically modified species are taboo. Moreover, not all agricultural crop seeds can be preserved at low temperatures. Gene bank managers are having particular problems, for example, with potato, sweet potato, apple, banana, breadfruit, yam and cassava.

According to the official documents, the distance from the main entrance to the back wall of the seed chambers— there are three of them—is just under 146 meters, with two additional security door systems along the way. Each chamber is as big as a gym: ten meters wide, six meters high and twenty-seven meters long. They contain long rows of steel shelving. Yet standing out here in the snow I can see none of this—which is somewhat disappointing for someone having traveled thousands of kilometers into the high Arctic to see humanity's biological safe-deposit box. Indeed, it is even dangerous to be out here without a gun. On Spitsbergen there are in fact more polar bears than people. The chance of actually encountering the planet's largest land-based predator here—comparatively close to the civilization of the island's capital—may be rather small. The theoretical possibility, however, is disturbing enough in itself.

And the taxi's meter keeps on ticking.

There are only three keys that provide access to this sanctum. One is kept in Sweden at the Nordic Genetic Resource Center in Alnarp, one in the office of Spitsbergen's governor, and a third in the Longyearbyen branch of the Norwegian state building authority, Statsbygg. The Arctic seed vault is not permanently staffed. It is only opened when new plastic containers with seed samples are brought up the dirt road from the airport. No exceptions are made for curious visitors like me.

There are some 1400 gene banks around the world that are currently used to preserve plant seeds. All of them can send material to Svalbard. The seed bank here is unique, above all due to its location. Samples stored in the Arctic are about as far away as they can possibly be from the world's trials and tribulations—a mere thousand kilometers from the North Pole, at a latitude of seventy-eight degrees, thirteen minutes north. The initiators of the project hope that this location will prove remote enough to protect the seeds from catastrophes, mismanagement and theft.

Additional protection for the seed vault is provided by the Arctic permafrost surrounding the facility. The sandstone bedrock here has a more or less constant temperature of minus three degrees. Still, only a few months after the official opening of the structure

in February 2008, the heat of the summer sun destabilized the upper soil layer, and as a result the building firm commissioned with the project had to make extensive improvements. Deep within the mountain, however, it is anticipated that temperatures will remain below zero for the foreseeable future, even though climate change causes the Arctic to heat up more than any other part of the planet.

A safety net, an insurance policy, a modern Noah's Ark—the media have found numerous analogies for the Global Seed Vault. A long way from here in temperate Rome sits a man who probably knows more about this building than anyone else. A phone call to Cary Fowler might not open that well-secured door, but he can provide a great deal of information about the amazing facility. Fowler, an American, is head of the Global Crop Diversity Trust, the international organization responsible for running the gene bank. His commitment to preserving the genetic resources vital to agriculture in the developing world was already recognized over twenty years ago when he was awarded the Alternative Nobel Prize. His vision for the Arctic project has now come to fruition.

"There are currently 526,000 samples in the Global Seed Vault, each comprising an average of five hundred seeds," says Fowler. That sounds like a lot. Is the emergency repository already full, so soon after its official inauguration? Fowler laughs and dismisses such concerns. Each of the three chambers, he says, can hold one-and-a-half million seed samples. And at the moment not even half of the first chamber has been filled: "Space is never going to be a problem for us." The facility, whose interior is cooled to a temperature of around minus twenty degrees, has deliberately been designed larger than is requisite. "We have created more storage capacity than we think we will ever need," says Fowler.

One might suspect that there are other reasons for the considerable size of the project. The building is owned by the Norwegian state, which is doing its utmost to strengthen Spitsbergen's profile as a science center. In Longyearbyen an ultramodern university center for 350 students and scientists has been constructed. Looking like a huge UFO that has landed a few meters above the fjord, it also includes a small research park containing the branch facilities

*"A safety net,
an insurance policy,
a modern Noah's Ark."*

October night in Longyearbyen

Entrance to the Svalbard Global Seed Vault

Seeds for Nigerian agricultural crops are sorted and packed for Svalbard
Photo: International Innovative Technologies Association (IITA), Nigeria

Containers full of seeds arriving in Svalbard

Transferring the seed boxes to the Seed Vault

Seed boxes stored on shelving

Cooling system required to preserve the seeds in the Seed Vault

*"Everyone hopes that they will never actually have to use their insurance policy."*

of a number of other research institutions. In addition Norway is encouraging international research teams to make use of the Ny-Ålesund stations, which are located a half-hour by plane to the north. Norway is intent on demonstrating its control over the archipelago, which was placed under the country's sovereignty by treaty in 1920. Nevertheless, citizens of the forty or so signatory states are permitted to settle and engage in economic activity on Spitsbergen.

Projects such as the seed vault, which cost nine million dollars to build, are thought to sustain Norway's leading role in this icy region. Every year the government in Oslo provides 100,000 dollars to cover the operating costs of the vault. One hundred and fifty thousand dollars are contributed annually by the Global Crop Diversity Trust, which is supported by numerous governments and by the Bill & Melinda Gates Foundation. Further financial support comes from the seed producers Monsanto, Syngenta and DuPont Pioneer Hi-Bred.

A number of observers have expressed concerns that the mountain refuge could become a genetic self-service store for multinational companies. In such a scenario, the industry would gain access to the world's genetic resources at a bargain price in return for the financial aid it is providing. Cary Fowler strongly denies this. He goes on to explain how the seed vault functions: "Only those who have submitted samples are granted access, and only to their own material." Any gene bank in the world that decides to send seeds to Spitsbergen signs an agreement explicitly stating that Norway, although it owns the seed vault, cannot claim ownership of its exotic contents. And neither can multinational seed producers.

The genetic resources remain the property of the gene bank that has sent them to the Arctic. Fowler promises that the plastic containers brought to Spitsbergen will not be opened, let alone the airtight silver bags they contain. In principle such regulations make sense because they protect developing countries from biopiracy, that is, the unauthorized use and sale of their genetic resources by others. Strictly speaking, this is the precondition for any state to participate in such projects. And the seed vault can only fulfill its function with global support.

On the other hand, these rigid regulations regarding ownership might prove to be problematic one day. If genetic resources are not readily available, food experts will find it difficult to respond to climate change. In a world with an ever-warming climate, it is crucial to determine whether it would be better to replace certain agricultural crops from one country with others that have shown themselves more resilient to the rising temperatures in other places. This kind of work is not made any easier by the strict regulations for the Svalbard Global Seed Vault.

Use of the seed bank is free of charge for the thirty gene banks currently involved. However, each country is required to organize the transport of the material to Spitsbergen on its own—and to pay for it. But Fowler promises: "No developing country will be excluded from the project on financial grounds." He points out that his organization provides money for the duplication of seeds. This is essential for some countries as it presents the only way for them to send samples to the Arctic without endangering the stocks of their domestic gene banks. In addition the Global Crop Diversity Trust has already provided developing countries with hundreds of thousands of seed envelopes and suitable plastic containers. It has further coordinated and financed the transport of seeds to the Arctic.

Admittedly the Svalbard Global Seed Vault is no sheet anchor for the biodiversity of the world's plants. Indeed it cannot be, because its function is limited to the storage of agricultural seeds. Fowler says this is solely due to practical reasons and that in principle he has no objections against expanding the scope of the project. However, most of the world's gene banks also limit their stocks to agricultural plants. The lack of experience with the storage of wild plants means that many key data are simply not available: How long can the seeds of a particular species be stored at low temperatures before their germination capacity is reduced below a viable level? How can new plants be cultivated from the remaining seeds to provide fresh seed stock? And so on.

A lack of comprehensive information in this area means that even in the future it is unlikely that the seed vault will be stocked with the genetic material of wild plants. "I'm not saying that it's a bad idea or that we are against it," says Fowler, "but it would make the

management of the facility more complicated and dramatically increase its operating costs." Nevertheless, there is one small exception. Researchers from the UNIS university center in Longyearbyen use the seed vault to store seeds from a number of wild plants found on the island of Spitsbergen. In this case, practical issues such as finding replacement stocks when necessary can easily be dealt with.

It is time to say goodbye to Cary Fowler and to trudge back through the freezing cold to my taxi. Back to central Longyearbyen, please. In the town's modern museum, several displays are devoted to the seed vault. A series of images allows visitors to follow the route of a delivery from Nigeria where the seeds are first packed to their storage in the Arctic mountain. One can only hope that the plastic containers sent from there will never actually have to be sent back, and if so then only for the sake of routinely renewing its contents. Or as Fowler puts it, "Everyone hopes that they will never actually have to use their insurance policy."

# ARUSHA: URBAN AGRICULTURE

**At first glance urban agriculture may seem like a contradiction in terms. For a long time agriculture was confined to the countryside but today cities are increasingly providing their own food. In Tanzania in East Africa the response to rapid urbanization has been a diverse urban agricultural sector. People are using a wide range of niches within the urban network to raise plants. The northern city of Arusha provides a showcase for several aspects of urban agriculture on the African continent.**

Essay and photographs by Tomas Caspary

Terraces on the edge of the River Themi in the inner district of Fire Brigade, near Range Road in Arusha, Tanzania

A closer look reveals agriculture is actually a widespread phenomenon within urban space—particularly where urban agglomerations have developed spontaneously and land that was previously used for purely agricultural purposes has been used in construction or sold in small lots to people wanting to build. Throughout the world there are 800 million people engaging in urban agriculture—whether in public space, market gardens, private gardens or urban niches such as roadsides, roof terraces and courtyards—and in doing so they are contributing to the food requirements of the urban population. Scarce and costly patches of soil in urban environments are being intensively cultivated, and in part fertilized with refuse, in order to grow a wide range of plants and keep small animals.

Arusha lies in northern Tanzania, somewhat south of the equator. The city is a rapidly growing center of between 200,000 and 300,000 inhabitants, depending on how the city boundaries are defined. The city's name derives from the Arush, a sedentary Maasai people, who traditionally lived for the most part on bananas, beans, small amounts of corn, millet and the milk and meat of their cattle.

Arusha is located at the southern foot of Mount Meru, which, at 4562 meters, is Tanzania's second-highest mountain after Kilimanjaro, situated one hundred kilometers to the northeast. The city sits between 1300 and 1500 meters above sea level and has a temperate climate. It is never colder than 8 °C and rarely hotter than 30 °C. A warm, dry season at the beginning of the year is followed by a long and a short rainy season between April and November.

The slopes of the volcanically formed mountain are extremely fertile and densely settled. Small farmers plant bananas as a staple food and coffee as a cash crop. Further below, on former bush land and in the Maasai Steppe, farmers try their luck every year with corn and beans. However, a successful harvest is never guaranteed. While the slopes of the mountain record an annual rainfall of 1200 millimeters, the lower areas in the west and south record barely more than 600 millimeters in good years and on average only around 300 millimeters.

## COLONIAL PERIOD

During the period of colonial rule, Arusha was not only an administrative center but also a residential area for European settlers, whose farms stretched mainly to the south and west. Arusha then was a very modest city, with a small town center geared to the needs of the farmer-settlers, offering hotels, banks, churches, workshops, shops, a post office and an English boarding school.

At that time the city's growth was guided by a development plan that provided for clearly defined public and private space. The residential quarter for colonial officials was located in the east of the city and featured bungalows surrounded by English lawns with rose borders and large trees as well as small vegetable gardens behind the houses, close to the accommodations used by employees. As a rule the wind blows from the east and one consideration informing the decision by colonial town planners to locate the quarter in the east was to prevent dangerous miasmas, including malaria, from being blown there from the more densely populated districts in the west. The area around the central marketplace in the western part of the city was dominated by small businesses run by Indians, while more outlying areas contained housing for indigenous officials of lower rank.

## UJAMAA SOCIALISM

Following independence in 1961, Ujamaa socialism became the foundation of state ideology, which had a strong focus on rural development. As a result, for a long time Arusha remained a peaceful little town. A lot of private housing was socialized and new groups of civil servants moved into the dwellings previously occupied by their English predecessors. These new officials came predominantly from the countryside and had fundamentally different ideas about how a garden should be used. Moreover the scarcity of food during the period of Ujamaa socialism contributed to the practice of replacing flower gardens and lawns with corn, banana trees and vegetables, and turning garages into cowsheds and chicken coops. Cars were a rare commodity.

## ECONOMIC LIBERALIZATION

The economic liberalization that began in 1990 and the resulting growth of the safari industry meant that the city changed rapidly. Arusha became the departure point for many tours into the Serengeti, Tarangire, Arusha and Manyara national parks and to the

1

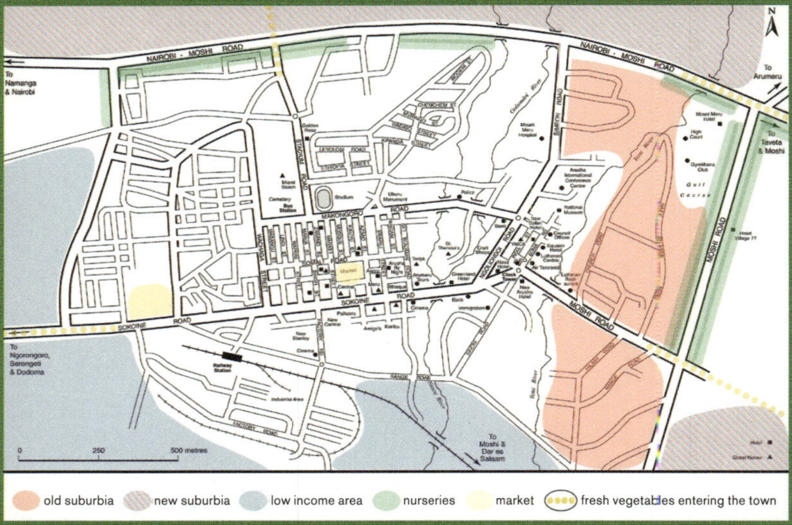


2

1 Backyard garden in the district of Esso

2 CITY MAP OF ARUSHA
The rapid urbanization of a small administrative center and its transformation into a complex urban conglomerate has created manifold logistical bottlenecks. The growing urban middle class expects fresh vegetables, flowers and seedlings for their gardens. The even more rapidly growing group of the urban poor is maintaining its rural eating habits and methods of food preparation. The best areas for agriculture in the urban environment are being destroyed by building development. The narrow streets leading to the inner-city markets are clogged with minibuses and trucks delivering fresh food.
Illustration: Arusha Node Marie

Ngorongoro Crater. The city also became the administrative headquarters of the East African Community, and a UN tribunal set up to investigate the genocide in Rwanda was established there as well. In addition Arusha came to be regarded as the center of trade for tanzanite gemstones. However, apart from a brewery and a few textile-processing enterprises, industries found it difficult to survive in the city. This situation changed at the end of the nineties with the establishment of the flower industry, which is now based in extensive greenhouses. The international airport located some fifty kilometers to the east provides daily flights to Amsterdam that link local producers to the Dutch market.

In the course of the nineties' economic liberalization, new inhabitants settled in Arusha's suburbs, which still exhibited a colonial character. Newly wealthy Tanzanians, former house owners who were given back their previously socialized dwellings, and new expatriates transformed their gardens back into domestic ornaments. On the other hand, domestic employees and security guards continued to use less clearly defined areas such as access zones and backyards to grow corn, bananas, pumpkins and spinach.

## URBANIZATION

The money generated by the overall economic upswing triggered a building boom. In the city center today, many of the buildings from the colonial period have given way to new high-rise office buildings, while in the suburbs the new middle class is building bungalows protected by high walls. On the fertile mountain slopes to the north high-quality agricultural land is being taken up by houses for the wealthy, and new suburbs are emerging on the poor-quality land to the south and west. The outskirts of these suburbs are dotted with the shacks built by new arrivals from poor rural areas, fleeing increasingly regular droughts and seeking a better life in the city.

As there is no effective town planning, the city is developing spontaneously on surrounding, fertile agricultural land. It is common to see modern houses built alongside old straw-roofed farmers' huts and still surrounded by field crops such as banana trees, cassava, corn and beans. Poor and low-earning city dwellers usually maintain small vegetable gardens since, unable to afford refrigeration, they need to collect fresh fruit and vegetables daily. Those who live on their own land use the area around their houses to grow vegetables, while others grow tomatoes, different types of spinach and cabbages along the roadsides and the banks of streams. This fresh produce is then sold to city dwellers as they head home in the evenings. In the neighborhoods on the outskirts of the city where water can be channeled from streams via irrigation ditches, so-called patchwork gardens can be found in which residents grow tomatoes, amaranth and cabbage. In cases where residents have become wealthier or older owners from an agricultural tradition have died out, gardens tend to feature ornamental rather than agricultural plants. Inventive small businesspeople are taking advantage of the newly emergent demand for ornamental plants by setting up small, informal nurseries along the roads leading to the old and new suburban areas.

However, in the absence of town-planning measures, the many small gardens and plant nurseries dotting the cityscape will eventually disappear due to the decreasing availability and increasing expense of building land. The flower gardens in the formerly colonial suburbs are becoming casualties of increased building density rather than being maintained as the city's green lung. And while the plant nurseries and small patchwork gardens are being forced into the dry, barren steppe, the volume of traffic in the city is growing. As a result air pollution and traffic jams are increasing while the plants that could filter the polluted air are disappearing. Today urban agriculture contributes in many ways to maintaining a functioning and healthy city and should be promoted for this reason.

3

4

5

3 Corn fields in the former colonial quarter

4–5 Banana plantations and organic millet cultivation in a settlement for single mothers in Kisongo. The settlement project was initiated by the nongovernmental organization DESWOS (German foundation for subsidized housing and settlement, Cologne) and financed by the German Ministry of Economic Cooperation. However, the women must repay part of the building costs. Today sixty-five houses have been built and another seventy-two are to be added.

**PATCHWORK GARDENS**
Until only a few years ago the only inhabitants of the former village of Olasiti in the southern part of Arusha were Arush. Their round, grass-roofed huts lay in the midst of banana groves. Irrigation ditches crisscrossed their gardens. However, around ten years ago many of the gardens were sold to outsiders, who have now built bungalows behind high concrete walls. Some families used the proceeds of these sales to purchase larger fields to the south of the city. This is an area with a much lower rainfall and no streams to feed irrigation ditches. Only a small number of more farsighted people declined to sell their land and are now using it to grow onions, beans, corn and different types of vegetables for the nearby markets.

A group of mainly women gardeners who were interested in organic cultivation methods decided to establish an organic farming organization and were given funding for the project by a safari company. The gardeners took this opportunity to learn about the use of ridge beds, the intercropping of different vegetables and wild herbs, herbal insecticides, crop rotation and organic composting. These gardeners favor leek and celery, which they intersperse with lettuce, red cabbage, fennel and different types of spinach. Their customers are above all Europeans, who particularly appreciate organically grown vegetables. However, organic vegetables are also selling well at local markets. The organic farming group is made up of twenty-two families, four of whom are Arush.

Each family requires a vegetable garden of some four hundred square meters. In 2009 such a plot of land cost ten to fifteen million Tanzanian shillings (around 5000–8000 Euros or 6500–9800 USD). Given that an unskilled laborer earns around 30 Euros (40 USD) a month and a small businessperson 300 Euros (about 400 USD), this is a great deal of money.

**TREE NURSERIES**
Tree nurseries in Arusha were initially developed on an informal basis on the banks of streams and runnels in response to the growing demand for ornamental plants above all. When water was made available from the city network, this business idea was taken up by an increasing number of residents. This reliable water supply thus led to the establishment of many tree nurseries along arterial roads in the old colonial suburbs. Arusha's city council appears to be supporting this development, at least in the sense that it is not prohibiting the use of public space by gardening enterprises. Gardeners are returning the favor by providing plants for public gardens and schools.

The plant and tree nurseries are mostly family businesses, although there are a number of enterprises that also employ outside help. The people working in the nurseries do not have any horticultural training but have acquired their knowledge on site and from one another. The nurseries are around ten meters deep and thirty to fifty meters long. Saplings, seedling and seeds are usually acquired from Dar es Salaam and Nairobi and then propagated locally. Some gardeners also gather plants from the mountain forests on Mount Meru, Kilimanjaro, or from the Amani nature reserve in the Usambara Mountains. The result is a diverse range of foreign and indigenous plants. Beetles, fungi and theft are problems, but the most damage is done by termites. Indigenous trees on offer include *Olea capensis* (small ironwood), *Rauvolfia caffra* (quinine tree), *Tamarindus indica* (tamarind), *Cordia africana* and *Croton megalocarpus*. Imported trees and plants include *Grevillea spp.*, *Eucalyptus sp.* (eucalyptus tree), *Cedrela odorata* (Spanish cedar), *Acrocarpus fraxinifolius* and a wide assortment of flowers, climbers and bamboos.

6

7

8

6 Plant nurseries along Moshi Road, opposite Hotel Village 77 in Old Colonial Residential

7–8 Plant nurseries along the arterial road leading to the national park in the district of Burka. Burka is a large coffee plantation that belongs to a Swiss consortium.

9 Transporting ornamental plants in a tree nursery along the Moshi Road

# Better City:
# URBAN DEVELOPMENT AND THE FUTURE

**In the modern city, life in the urban jungle is accompanied by significant planting programs—for example in Shanghai, where tens of thousands of trees were planted on the site of Expo 2010 prior to the opening of the World Exhibition. Ongoing urbanization in the twenty-first century means that ecological questions will continue to decisively influence economic and social development in the context of urban planning. Old concepts such as the green belt and the garden city remain relevant and are supplemented by new forms of urban agriculture and the integration of green areas into cities. On the basis of studies and projects, the question is raised of whether future urban planning should move the production of plants into the cities—a measure that would allow for the expedient temporary use of areas earmarked for large-scale urban development projects.**

Construction site in the district of Pudong in eastern Shanghai.
Photo: Christine Zimmerli

百年大计 安全质量第一
"豪浦服饰城"闪亮登场
汇聚服饰精品进场
豪浦欢迎东南西北
HYUNDAI
上海豪浦服饰

Today Shanghai is one of the largest metropolises in Asia. The city, which was originally built on swamplands and carries the word "sea" (*hai*) in its name, has experienced rapid growth during the last few decades. And it has big plans for the future, too: over the next decades it aims to become a modern international metropolis. The buzzwords are ecological city, healthy city and digital city. It is only during the last few years that environment protection and ecological awareness have become important issues for the general public. New words have entered the language, including "white pollution," which refers to the omnipresent plastic bags and Styrofoam boxes. These materials are used to package take-out food that is sold at street stands and restaurants throughout the country. In 2008 a fee was introduced for plastic bags at department stores and supermarkets. The themes of ecology and sustainability also figure prominently in reports about Expo 2010. Air quality readings are published and noise measurement stations have recently gone up on popular streets in the city center. They are equipped with monitors that show the decibels measured. This new environmental consciousness should be welcomed, even if it often comes across as a bit superficial. "Green" projects a modern, advanced and Western image, which is precisely why new cities and green areas are often given this label. However, it is not always clear whether the word has the same meaning as in the West. Sometimes it seems as if foreign concepts are adopted for image reasons alone and the new ideas are not fully developed. In terms of urban planning, Shanghai is also taking its cue from Western models. The creation of new satellite towns and a greenbelt around the city are part of the basic strategy that the Chinese have adventurously and pragmatically embraced.

## CONTRASTS

Photographs of Shanghai often feature the breathtaking skyline of Pudong, a district in the east. With its skyscrapers and cool, lifeless atmosphere, the area is sometimes reminiscent of a science-fiction film. However, there are other places in the city that transport visitors back to earlier days. The residential quarters with their tree-lined lanes bustle with life and many scenes exude an almost villagelike charm. In some parts of town such as the former French Concession, people spend most of the time outdoors, be it working, playing, reading or eating. The elderly walk down the street in their pajamas or sit reading the newspaper on a chair on the sidewalk. Bicycle vendors make their rounds, selling fruit, rice and even chickens, which are plucked and prepared on the spot. Knives are sharpened, electrical appliances are repaired and junk is collected. But at night the city rests and becomes astonishingly quiet. The days in Shanghai begin and end early. The city's rhythm seems to adapt to that of the sun, which sets no later than seven in the summer. Quiet reigns after midnight; streets that were heavily congested during the day are empty. In many places the sleeping city resembles a huge village. The crime rate is low and one feels surprisingly safe.

Shanghai and the surrounding provinces are among the richest regions in the country. For this reason the city cannot be seen as representative of China as a whole. The quest for wealth and riches is evident everywhere in Shanghai, and today large parts of the population are materially better off than they were ten or twenty years ago. People who have money enjoy flaunting it. Anyone familiar with other parts of the country can see that the gap between rich and poor is continuing to widen. The many migrant workers from rural areas who flood into the city each day, often working on construction sites or in the service industry, make this discrepancy especially clear.

One must not forget that thirty years ago China faced an entirely different reality. Through the policy of reform and opening, rapid economic and social changes began in the early eighties that affected all levels of society. Many of the developments seem to have taken place in fast motion. In recent years, the Chinese have increasingly perceived and discussed phenomena that were previously associated with Western society. The catchwords include work-life balance, burnout syndrome and depression. With the coming of age of the generation of Chinese that grew up under the government's one-child policy, issues such as the decline of values, disorientation and excessive consumerism have gained greater relevance.

## URBAN GROWTH AND MIGRATION

Shanghai impressively embodies the global phenomenon of urbanization. During the last few decades it has grown much more quickly than other large cities in China, but efforts to expand the infrastructure have not kept up with this rapid growth. In the period around

# BETTER CITY, BETTER LIFE

**The World Expo's grinning blue mascot can be seen everywhere in Shanghai. It adorns the signs and posters announcing the major event, which sport headlines like "A smiling city and content people: loving Shanghai begins with me." Or "For a better city, a better life and deeper friendship." The theme of the world exposition, which opened in May 2010, is "Better City, Better Life," and Shanghai was spruced up on a grand scale in the run-up to the event. Construction sites dotted the city, new subway lines were built, streets were modernized and façades were refurbished. The city has put on a green face, carrying out greening and forestation projects at a rapid pace.**

Essay and photographs by Christine Zimmerli

View from the Shanghai World Financial Center, which was opened in 2008 and is currently the world's third tallest building

# Of merchants, colonial masters and urban development

According to the currently prevailing view, Shanghai was founded during the Southern Song Dynasty (1127–1279). In the following centuries, the city established itself as a commercial and cultural center and a flourishing trade developed in tea and textiles. Located on the Yangtze Delta, the Shanghai region was extremely fertile and known as the "Garden of China." Temples were set amidst green parks while prosperous merchants, scholars and officials built private gardens, many of which have come down to us today. International contacts led to the importation of plants from abroad, including the *Magnolia grandiflora*, *Cedrus deodara* (Himalayan cedar), *Pinus thunbergii* and the pomegranate. From the sixteenth to the nineteenth century, Shanghai was surrounded by a circular wall. This rounded form clearly distinguished Shanghai from other Chinese cities, which traditionally exhibited a square-shaped structure. Shanghai grew organically and today one can still find streets that are not continuous.

In the aftermath of the Opium War (1840–1843) China was forced by Great Britain to open five of its ports, including Shanghai, to foreign trade. The following years brought an influx of merchants from Europe and America and with them Western cultural influences. Over the next decades and up until the thirties the city experienced a building boom that produced new districts featuring Western architectural styles. This period also saw the construction of Shanghai's typical lane houses (*lilong*). In the nineteenth century the foreign immigrants demanded and received extraterritorial status, creating foreign concessions that were not subject to local Chinese jurisdiction. Concession areas were separate political sectors with their own laws, administration and police. This demarcation also led to differences in the way urban space was used, and these have left traces that are still recognizable today.

Many foreigners in Shanghai led lifestyles similar to what they had known in their homelands, with the result that two separate social worlds existed side by side. The English and the French built parks based on Western models, which they considered indispensable to the city as sites of rest and recreation. In the process they also introduced Western plants and horticultural methods. The pioneers in this regard were the British, who initially constructed green areas above all for sporting activities such as horse racing, football and rugby. The classical Chinese gardens maintained privately by a small number of prosperous residents were designed around concepts of aesthetic contemplation and the reflection of moods in nature, and it was the Shanghai concession parks that first introduced the idea of public green areas as sites of sport and entertainment.

For a long time, however, the concession parks were only open to a small minority of Western foreigners along with "adequately clothed" Indians and Japanese. Chinese were refused entry. For the local population such parks were therefore a bone of contention and a symbol of colonialism. It was not until the beginning of the twentieth century that this segregation was gradually eased and finally abandoned.

Shanghai in the thirties. The city was divided into the area containing the foreign concessions and the old Chinese town, which was surrounded by a wall until the beginning of the twentieth century.
Illustration: www.reisenett.no

# Movement in the city

Early in the morning, when the city is still half asleep, Shanghai's parks are full of activity. Older people in particular come to the parks to do gymnastics, dance in groups, or play other types of sport. Parks are a site of entertainment and it is often very noisy there. Everyone pursues their particular hobby, whether it is playing music, singing, kite-flying, playing cards, talking, reading or physical exercise, accompanied by music from radios or portable cassette players. Parks often also include carousels, food stalls and restaurants. Some of them are equipped with discretely positioned loudspeakers from which soft, and sometimes loud, music is played. Such loudspeakers are encountered even in large nature parks and forests. One almost gets the impression that silence might make people feel uncomfortable. It is not without reason that the Chinese describe a good voice as *re nao*, hot and noisy.

Despite the energetic activity in the parks, there seems to be a level of control exercised over the way people behave. In the People's Park one sees men strolling around equipped with discretely hidden walkie-talkies who are obviously monitoring what is going on. Chinese parks seldom feature niches offering a degree of privacy or lawns that can be used. As Ryan Brooker explains, "When our office designed the plans for the new Xujiahui Park, the client (the city government) objected that we had included too many benches. At first we were dumbfounded, until we realized that the aim was to avoid gatherings of people. The park is not supposed to offer too many places where people can linger."

Western visitors are generally struck by the fact that regulations can be read and heard everywhere. Announcements in the subway direct people to take care when entering and exiting trains and not to forget anything. Banners encouraged citizens to look forward to Expo 2010 and to behave in a civilized manner, and signs ask passers-by to cross streets in a "civilized" way or to speak Standard Mandarin instead of dialect. Ling Dexiang, a professor of Chinese at Jiaotong University, says, "China's major cities are still in their infancy. The Chinese are traditionally a peasant people and now increasing numbers of them are moving to the cities." Adapting to life in the big cities, which includes learning how to behave in traffic, will probably take some time yet.

Scene in the old quarter of Shanghai

Plane trees brought to Shanghai by the French provide welcome shade during the hot and humid summer months.

Aerial photo of Shanghai with the Huangpu River, which flows into the Yangtze
Photo: Modis Web satellite image, NASA

Sunday morning in Fuxing Park. People come to play sport, sing and dance, and there is often a great deal of noise.

The Chinese Pavilion for the Expo 2010 under construction (March 2009). The building work has been done by migrant workers, who streamed into the city in large numbers.

Apartment buildings in the old town. Pedlars offer fruit, vegetables and everyday items for sale.

The People's Square in the center of Shanghai, an important traffic hub; the subway station alone is used by an estimated 400,000 people daily.

View of the city's two highest towers in the new district of Pudong. Only thirty years ago this area was a swampland.

Between 2000 and 2010, ten new subway lines were opened in Shanghai. A total of fourteen should be in operation by 2012. The Chinese Pavilion for Expo 2010 can be seen in the background.

Industrial areas near the city are being converted: dockyards once stood on the area being used for Expo 2010.

1800 Shanghai had approximately 200,000 inhabitants and was a relatively large city even then. By 1900 the population had grown to around one million, by 1972 to roughly ten million and by 2000 to around sixteen million.

Today, in 2010, around twenty million people live in Shanghai and it continues to draw immigrants from all parts of the country. Every day migrant workers from China's poorer rural communities flood into its urban area. Between six and seven million are estimated to be in Shanghai. Most migrant workers are young men who have left their families in rural regions to search for a job in the coastal cities in eastern China. The housing conditions are cramped, and it is not unusual for twenty people to share living space. Migrant workers often sign on for daily or weekly employment in construction, the hotel and restaurant industry, massage parlors, and other service industries at the lower end of the wage scale. The growing migration flows are due, not least, to the loosening of residence regulations. China has a system of household registration (the *hukou* system) that binds a person to his or her assigned place of residence. Due to the *hukou* regulations, people were usually unable in the past to move to and settle in other places. The system was introduced in the fifties and sixties after the founding of the People's Republic, and its goal was to prevent slum belts from forming around cities. But the *hukou* regulations have been gradually relaxed as part of the economic reforms over the last few decades.

## URBAN PLANNING CHALLENGES

Shanghai's greatest challenge is to gain permanent control of the population and the land. The administrative district of Shanghai covers a total of 6340 km2, which is slightly less than the area covered by the entire State of Delaware (6447 km2) in the United States. Of this total area, about one-third is built-up. The core zone inside the first ring road totals about six hundred square kilometers, of which nearly forty percent is built-up area. According to the urban planner Cai Zhen of the China Academy of Urban Planning and Design in Shanghai, this figure ideally should be no more than thirty percent. Toward the city center the population density increases dramatically, at a greater rate than in other Chinese cities. On average there are 2978 people per square kilometer of land, and in some districts in the center, this figure is even as high as 40,000. Cai Zhen believes that the shortage of space is a far greater challenge for Shanghai than for other comparable-sized cities. The metropolitan area of Beijing, for example, is twice as large as that of Shanghai, but at the same time has one-sixth fewer inhabitants. Furthermore, in contrast to Shanghai, other cities such as Beijing and Shenzhen created and implemented plans for green and sustainable urban development early on.

Another major problem is traffic. Traffic jams plague the city center, and five thousand to eight thousand new cars are added to Shanghai's streets every month. To remedy this problem, the government has introduced a higher tax for cars with greater emissions. Fees for license plates have been raised and may even cost more than the price of a small car. The auctioning of license plates provides the public authorities with additional income and limits the group of car owners to social groups with high-purchasing power. Free bike loans are also under discussion. In addition, the city is rapidly expanding its subway system. During the past decade, ten new lines have been added to Line 1, which was completed in 1995, and three others are in the planning. The subway currently transports around four million passengers a day in a network covering more than 250 kilometers.

Construction is going on everywhere in Shanghai and each year new high-rises are completed at a rapid rate. According to Cai Zhen, Shanghai has experienced a major increase in construction projects over the past few years. It almost seems as if the number of new buildings is out of synch with the population increase. Why are so many new buildings going up? Cai believes that they are mainly the result of the state's interest in tax revenue. Private land ownership is not permitted in China, but the state can award land usage rights to private individuals. It also levies asset taxes on real estate. The state wears the hat of both property owner and tax collector, and for the local governments the revenue gained from awarding land rights and collecting taxes is an important source of income.

This is why financial interests influence planning issues such as the decision to zone a given lot as building land. There does not seem to be any strict formal procedure for allowing land to be put to new uses and a "flexible" practice reigns. The de facto user of the property

can convert the use into whatever is most profitable, regardless of public interest or compatibility with the surrounding area. Zoning plans do not seem to give consideration to the long term. Furthermore, they are not public and even the architects involved in a construction project are usually only able to examine the lot affected. This results in buildings of entirely different styles standing side by side. According to Ryan Brooker, a Canadian architect who works in Shanghai, the authorities want to avoid situations in which the public learns in advance about planned changes such as decisions to tear down buildings. After all, the state pays compensation for demolished buildings, with the amount depending on factors such as the building's age and general condition. There have been cases in which people who knew about demolition plans in advance carried out all kinds of superficial, last-minute renovations in their buildings in order to get more compensation.

Modern urban planning is relatively new in China. In the fifties and sixties, urban planning was carried out in the fashion of the former Soviet Union with the goal of stimulating economic development. During the Cultural Revolution, between 1966 and 1976, urban planning came to a complete standstill. Only in the late eighties did practitioners begin to regard it as a means to check unwanted developments. However, they often lack expertise. Chinese urban planners are faced with new challenges and in many respects they continue to find themselves in a highly experimental phase. At times they take their cue from experiences in Western countries and adopt concepts such as greenbelts or "new towns."

## ONE CITY AND NINE SATELLITES

The Shanghai government issued the "One City and Nine Towns" directive in 2000 in order to ease the strain on the city center. The project provides for the construction of new towns in the peripheral areas around Shanghai, with projected populations of around 50,000 to 100,000 people per city. Some of these so-called new towns (there are now more than nine) have already been completed; others still are under construction.

Shifts to peripheral areas took place as early as the fifties, when parts of the neighboring province of Jiangsu were transferred to Shanghai. At that time thousands of factories were relocated to the outskirts of the city. Another reorganization took place in the nineties, when the administrative area of Shanghai was expanded to include several rural regions. Afterward 470,000 households were resettled to the peripheral areas.

The structure of the new satellite cities resembles that of the "new towns" in Hong Kong and recalls the "social city" developed by Ebenezer Howard, an English architect and urban planner. In 1898 Howard designed a system of interlinked garden cities that were grouped around a larger central city. Most of the new towns around Shanghai target a well-to-do Chinese clientele and foreign nationals; almost all mimic the style of a Western country, with the exception of two towns created in the traditional Chinese style. The towns were designed in cooperation with architecture firms from the respective countries. For example, Thames Town has been built in the English style with a pseudo-Gothic church, timber-framed buildings and a fish-and-chips restaurant. This English "set" in the midst of China has an artificial, surreal feel that reminds the architect Ryan Brooker of an English horror film. According to Brooker, you find yourself in a place devoid of people and have the feeling that something is not quite right. Other cities will be built in a German, Dutch, Scandinavian, Italian, Spanish and American style.

The expectations concerning these new towns have not been met. The nationals of Western countries usually prefer traditional or modern homes in the center of Shanghai, and the Chinese often use the mansions only as weekend homes. In many cases there is inadequate infrastructure: some of the new towns were designed exclusively as residential communities without consideration for factors such as traffic connections, shopping opportunities and educational centers. The result is empty cities. A true shift of the population to the peripheral areas has not taken place. It remains to be seen just how much the new towns can contribute to easing the strains on the city center.

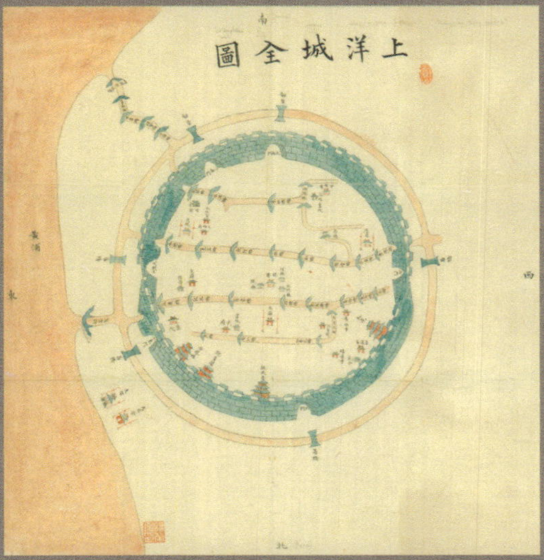


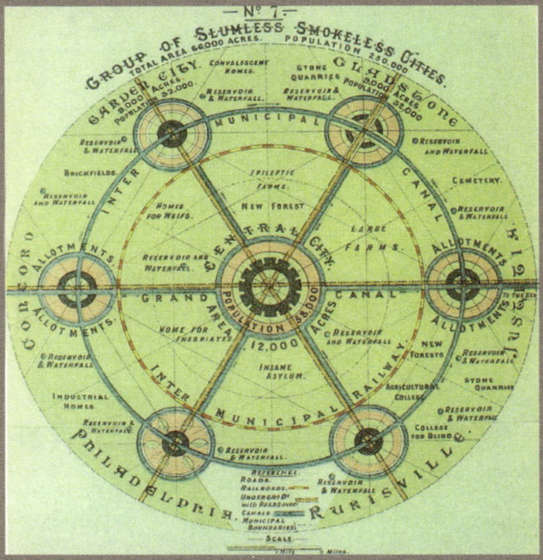

Old Shanghai
Illustration: virtualshanghai.net

Garden city concept by Ebenezer Howard, 1902: residential towns are arranged in an interconnected ring around a core city and linked to it by radial streets, railways and subway systems.
Illustration: de.academic.ru

In 2000 the Shanghai government issued the "One City and Nine Towns" directive.
The project involves the construction of new towns on the periphery of Shanghai in accordance with Ebenezer Howard's garden city concept.
Illustration: Shanghai Municipal Government

Ginkgos on the Expo 2010 site. By the beginning of 2010 some 14,000 trees had been planted on the site.

Shanghai is one of the world's biggest harbor cities. View of the Huangpu River, which divides the old western and new developed eastern part of the city.

The site of Expo 2010 in southern Shanghai. The total area measures 5.28 square kilometers.

Trees provide welcome shade in summer. Those who can, try to avoid the sun.

## GREEN CITY

Shanghai has ambitious urban greening plans, especially with an eye toward the World Expo. The government's declared goal is to green forty percent of city space by 2010. Moreover, every inhabitant is supposed to have access to a green area covering at least three thousand square meters within five hundred meters of their home. To achieve this aim, the government has specified a minimum green area of thirty percent for new construction projects, providing subsidies in return. But it has not always been easy to put these plans into action, and companies have been buying their way out of their obligations by paying to create green areas elsewhere.

According to the Shanghai Urban Planning Center, in 1990 green areas made up 12.4 percent of urban space. This figure increased to around twenty percent in 1999 and to approximately thirty-five percent in 2003—putting Shanghai ahead of other Asian cities such as Tokyo and Osaka.

However, the authorities apply a rather "creative" method to calculate green and forested areas. In order to work out the total amount of green area, they include, in addition to public parks, all kinds of green spaces such as traffic islands and the borders along canals and highways. Furthermore, the total green area is put in relation only to the built-up areas, i.e., roughly one-third of Shanghai, in order to reach a higher ratio. On the other hand, for the calculation of forested area, only the areas outside the city center are considered and any tree will be included in the calculations, including street trees or those standing in parks. Trees are totaled up by applying the rule of "two thousand trees equal one hectare of forest."

One large project centers on the forest belt that is currently being planted in a ring around Shanghai. A total of one hundred kilometers long, this woodland runs along the outer ring road and consists of inner and outer strips that are some one hundred and five hundred meters wide respectively. The project is particularly impressive given the fact that there were originally no woods on Shanghai's soil. Located at the mouth of the Yangtze, the city was built on swamp that was filled in with land, and eleven percent of its total area still consists of water today. Shanghai and the surrounding provinces are known as a water region, traditionally rich in rice, tea and silk, and that has produced generations of merchants. Its residents have far stronger ties to the sea than to trees and woods, and the forestation of vast areas is a relatively recent phenomenon. Whereas the planting of urban woodlands has a long tradition in Europe and the United States, it is still in its infancy in China. In view of the Shanghai's ecological resolutions for the upcoming decades, a permanent plant production site in the center of the city would be a refreshing, progressive vision.

Another interesting topic is the selection of plants. For a long time there was no great variety of trees in the city because urban planners previously hardly gave any consideration to this issue. Since Shanghai is located in a transitional area between semitropical and temperate climate zones, a large variety of conifers and deciduous species have the potential to flourish there. China itself is rich in plants since it was affected far less by the Pleistocene Ice Ages than the West. Many of the botanical species that became extinct at that time in Europe and North America have survived in China.

Trees that are found in large numbers in Shanghai include *Cinnamomum camphora* (camphor tree), *Magnolia grandiflora* (southern magnolia), *Osmanthus fragrans* (sweet osmanthus), *Ginkgo biloba* (gingko), *Cedrus deodara* (Himalayan cedar), *Metasequoia glyptostroboides* (dawn redwood), *Zelkova schneideriana* and *Platanus x. acerifolia* (London plane tree). Shanghai boasts many long boulevards lined mainly with London plane trees, which provide welcome shade during the hot summers. The London plane is a cross between the European and American variety. It was bred by the English in the seventeenth century and later introduced to Shanghai by the French colonialists. Xu Yilun, who owns a vintage bookstore and grew up in Shanghai, says that the French originally planted the plane trees along the edges of their concession in order to mark the border to the outside. They were motivated by the frequent disputes between the competing French and English, whose territories were located right next to each other.

Tree-nursery area in the neighboring province of Anhui. It is said that a third of all the trees required for Expo 2010 have come from this province alone.

In the rural areas around Shanghai farmers often run small private tree plantations (in this case on the island of Chongming, which is part of the Shanghai administrative zone).

"Near-Natural Forest" experimental plantation in the district of Pudong

**"NEAR-NATURAL FOREST" PROJECT**
People have recently begun to see greening and forestation as important measures to improve the natural environment. However, Professor Da Liangjun of East China Normal University believes that the population of indigenous trees in the city is still too small. Shanghai greening authorities still seem to give preference to planting foreign and nonnative species and do not pay sufficient attention to native trees. Such trees have no problem coping with local soil and climatic conditions. They are more robust and require much less care, which is of particular interest from an economic perspective. They also help enhance soil quality.

Professor Da's area of specialization is urban ecology. He completed part of his university education in Japan and returned to Shanghai in the late nineties. Inspired by Japanese projects and supported by a Japanese company, he began experimenting with plantings of local trees in Shanghai's eastern district of Pudong in 2000.

But which trees can be considered indigenous? This is a relevant question since not all the species that have adapted to local conditions can actually be found in the city. Searching for suitable seeds, Professor Da's team made important finds in Sheshan, a hilly area southwest of Shanghai, and on the islands of Sheshan and Da Jinshan. There is still forest on the islands, but it is a secondary forest, say the professor's assistants. The seeds were germinated for the experimental plantation and then grown in containers and planted. Because Shanghai has a high water table and its soil is very saline, earth was first brought in from other areas. A number of evergreen trees and shrubs were selected, including *Cyclobalanopsis glauca* (*Quercus glauca*), *Cyclobalanopsis myrsinaefolia*, *Castanopsis sclerophylla*, *Machilus thunbergii*, *Distylium racemosum* and *Ligustrum quihoui*. Additional indigenous varieties, spread by birds and the wind, joined them over time. They include *Ulmus parvifolia*, *Sapium sebiferum*, *Salix matsudana*, and *Broussonetia papyrifea*.

The trees require little care and they are left to grow naturally.

Today, around ten years later, the trees are several meters tall and form a canopy of leaves. After consultations with Professor Da, a section of the new forest belt around Shanghai was also planted with native trees. This shows that the municipal authorities are taking a growing interest in the subject.

In response to the question of why the tree nurseries around Shanghai cultivate so few indigenous trees, the professor's assistants explain that people are driven first and foremost by economic considerations, which leads to the selection of fast-growing plants. Trees that grow more slowly, including many native evergreen varieties, are not efficient enough from an economic viewpoint. In addition, issues such as the selection of native plants and biodiversity are not important for most people. They prefer aesthetically appealing plants, often buying shrubs and ornamental plants, or they favor trees that blossom or have leaves that change color in autumn.

**LOCAL AND REGIONAL PLANT PRODUCTION**
Most trees in Shanghai come from tree nurseries in other regions of China. The majority originate in the neighboring provinces of Anhui, Jiangsu, Jiangxi and Zhejiang, where there are more favorable soil and climatic conditions. Large tree nursery areas can also be found farther north in the province of Shandong, where the groundwater table is five to seven meters under the earth's surface and the annual amount of rainfall is about half that in Shanghai.

With its location near the sea, Shanghai has a slightly saline soil. The groundwater table is just seventy centimeters under the earth's surface, and the climate is very humid with around 1100 millimeters of rainfall per year. These are generally not ideal conditions for plant production. However, the economic developments and the related promotion of urban planning have created an increasing demand for green areas, and since the nineties a growing number of tree nurseries have been established in Shanghai's outlying districts. Seedlings are bought from neighboring provinces and then grown and acclimatized locally. For reasons of cost and space, most tree nurseries are rather small (with fewer than one hundred hectares). All told, the nurseries in Shanghai cover a total area of around 12,500 hectares and practically all are private enterprises. Under Mao Tse Tung there were only three tree nurseries in Shanghai, run by the state and founded in the fifties. They continued operations until the late eighties. One was transformed into the botanical garden and another was converted into a public park.

*Iuvenalis, Satura III, 232–261 Plu*
*set ipsum languorem peperit cib*
*stomacho. Nam quae meritoria s*

**Here full many a patient dies from want of sleep; but that exhaustion is produced by the undigested food that loads the fevered stomach. For what lodging-houses allow of sleep? None but the very wealthy can sleep at Rome. Hence is the source of the disease. The passing of wagons in the narrow curves of the streets, and the mutual revilings of the team drivers brought to a stand-still, would banish sleep even from Drusus and sea-calves. If duty calls him, the rich man will be borne through the yielding crowd, and pass rapidly over their heads on the shoulders of his tall Liburnian, and, as he goes, will read or write, or even sleep inside his litter, for his sedan with windows closed entices sleep. And still he will arrive before us. In front of us, as we hurry on, a tide of human beings stops the way; the mass that follows behind presses on our loins in dense concourse; one man pokes me with his elbow, another with a hard pole; one knocks a beam against my head, another a ten-gallon cask. My legs are coated thick with mud; then, anon, I am trampled upon by great heels all round me, and the hob-nail of the soldier's caliga remains imprinted on my toe. Do you not see with what a smoke the sportula is frequented? A hundred guests and each followed by his portable kitchen. Even Corbulo himself could scarcely carry such a number of huge vessels, so many things piled upon his head, which, without bending his neck, the wretched little slave supports; and keeps fanning his fire as he runs along. Tunics that have been patched together are torn asunder again. Presently, as the tug approaches, the long fir-tree quivers, other wagons are conveying pine-trees; they totter from their height, and threaten ruin to the crowd. For if that wain, that is transporting blocks of Ligustican stone, is upset, and pours its mountain-load upon the masses below, what is there left of their bodies? Who can find their limbs or bones?**

Iuvenalis, Satura III, 232–261
In: Evans, Lewis, *Juvenal, Sulpicia, Persius, Caius Lucilius*, Harper & Brothers Publishers, 1861, New York, pp. 24–25

*capiti quas recto vertice portat ser*
*Scinduntur tunicae sartae modo.*
*atque altera pinum plaustra vehu*
*Nam si procubuit qui saxa Ligu*
*super agmina montem, quid sup*
*quis ossa invenit? Obtritum vulg*

# JUVENAL: THE POET OF CONTRADICTION

Text selected by Renzo Petraglio

"Only the very rich can sleep in Rome." All night and day the traffic is chaotic and noisy. Only the rich can afford houses that are quiet and set apart; the ill die of insomnia. This overall picture takes an ironic look, but without the usual barbed sarcasm, at one of the most characteristic features of the Western metropolis, cities that have expanded unregulated and, above all, beyond their objective capacities. The problem of traffic is even more dramatic today and highlights one of the greatest contradictions of all times: to what extent is it justifiable to speak of progress in relation to a technique or an opulence that has grown beyond all human proportion?

Juvenal, the poet of contradictions. An Anthology taken from the Satirical Works, edited by Luca Canali

East London is one of the largest growth areas of urban development in Europe. In the course of deindustrialization, which is now nearly complete, sprawling industrial sites, storage areas and railroad yards became vacant. The former working-class neighborhoods bordering these districts have a financially weak social structure, a high proportion of inhabitants with an immigration background, and poor infrastructure. Traditionally, these areas have had a negative image among the decision-makers in British society.

The growth philosophy of the nineties and the early years of the twenty-first century, and the successful economic experience of restructuring the docklands, formed the backdrop to the urban-planning scenarios developed for East London. Investors and developers were to serve as the driving force. In a real estate market that knew only limitless growth, it was envisaged that the public authorities would then set the general direction and intervene to make adjustments.

Due to the successful application in 2005 for a major sports event, public authorities began intervening more extensively in the urban-planning process. But as the financial crisis of 2008 turned into an economic crisis affecting all of Great Britain, it put a brake on many of the most important drivers of urban renewal. Investors and developers grew much more reserved and the growth scenarios, sales forecasts and profit calculations were suddenly made invalid. The initial shock waves have receded and a much slower pace is expected for the period after 2013, after the major sports event will have taken place. Estimates concerning the amount of land needed and the targeted density have been revised downward. As a result, the proportion of undeveloped land has increased and the question of the temporary use of building areas has assumed new urgency. Urban redevelopment can no longer be completed within five to ten years. The timeframe is now twenty to fifty years. Urban-planning concepts designed to mend the gaps, tears and flaws in the fabric of the city are now confronted with the fact that the areas in question cannot be developed at all or can only be developed at a much later date, even in places that are crucial for urban planning. The current objective is to find a way of coping with the gaps in the cityscape that will exist for a long time. Furthermore, the large number of undeveloped, fenced-in areas may have a negative effect on the market value and image of the new city districts.

One of the many options for dealing with these areas is to use them temporarily as tree nurseries. As a counterpart to West London and an antithesis to what exists today in London's East End, the restructuring program calls for a high concentration of parks, green areas, avenues, promenades and urban squares, and it can therefore be assumed that there will be a large and steady demand for trees over the next decades. Temporary tree nurseries could partially meet this demand, put the vacant building land to a productive use and thus introduce an attractive intermediate solution.

Seedlings and young saplings would be planted as early as possible in these temporary tree nurseries. They would be cared for, lined out in nursery rows and then, based on demand and developments, planted in the emerging parks and along the streets. The tree nurseries could be run in a variety of ways for this purpose: as branches of existing tree nurseries, as temporary enterprises that draw on and promote the local labor market, or as operations of the development organizations that are responsible for the relevant projects. This system offers many advantages besides the sensible intermediate use of the old industrial wasteland: the quick availability of acclimatized plants, short transportation routes and continuity at a local level with respect to care and replanting. Options could be kept relatively open concerning species selection, amounts and sizes, or principal planting schemes could be done in advance on the basis of a master plan. After all, plant production and planning are flexible enough to allow for changes in upcoming years and decades. Since trees in a tree nursery must be transplanted regularly, it is unlikely that the temporary structures will become permanent and take on a life of their own.

Olympic village construction site (Olympia 2012)
in London Stratford, March 25, 2008
Photo: Getty Images / Jason Hawkes

# TEMPORARY TREE NURSERIES

**Many of our cities are old. Their names and locations—the "vessel"—have remained the same. Rome is even considered an eternal city. But the content of this vessel, the city itself, has changed again and again, sometimes gradually, sometimes by leaps and bounds. Renewal and reconstruction can progress at a fast pace or proceed quite calmly, such as after a real estate crisis. Trees, woods, parks and other landscape elements, on the other hand, have their own rhythm. Tree nurseries, with their contrasting features—long-living trees and regular replanting, natural growth and production processes managed by man—are an unexpected point of intersection in which the rhythm of the city and undeveloped areas converge. The integration of tree nurseries into urban planning processes can give rise to various types of temporary open areas in the modern city.**

Photo essay by Ralf Günter Voss

**STRATFORD DEVELOPMENT, LONDON**

One example of the use of temporary tree nurseries is the Stratford Development in London, which will be the location of many of the buildings for the city's aforementioned major sporting event. Today, the decelerating pace of basic urban development contrasts with the usual speed at which buildings go up for large events. This is also true of Stratford. The complex planning and decision-making processes result in tight execution schedules and reduce the elbowroom that exists in normal construction time frames. Construction managers are only able to tell a short time in advance when something can be built, planted or fitted out. The responsible parties demand flexibility and the immediate availability of building materials and plants, especially when many construction projects are running in parallel. In this context it is hardly possible to take into account time-proven implementation procedures such as planting periods that are influenced by nature: Only in special cases can the planting time be limited to the leaf-free period that is ideal for transplanting trees. The availability of plants at short notice and the independence from climatic processes lead to higher costs, less sustainability and a higher risk of failure. As a precaution, thousands of trees are prepared for summer planting in separate sections of tree nurseries. They are planted in containers or so-called air pots and then transported to temporary storage facilities, where automatic dripper systems provide a supply of water and nutrients, and the trees' health and growth are regularly monitored. With this system, plants can be retrieved and delivered to building sites in just a few days, even outside the usual planting periods, if required.

**GEDDES GARDENS**

Temporary use is normally discussed within the scope of large restructuring programs and multi-stage construction projects for new buildings. Patrick Geddes (1854–1932), a Scottish biologist, anthropologist and urban researcher who studied how the residents' use of a city influenced its form, introduced "Geddes gardens" in Scottish cities like Edinburgh and Glasgow. These gardens filled in the gaps between buildings that could be found everywhere in the quickly changing townscapes of the late nineteenth and early twentieth centuries. The Geddes gardens were used to produce plants and food, but they were also supposed to have an educational effect on residents and children. In contrast to Germany's personalized Schrebergärten (allotment gardens), they were communal facilities. The gardens were of a temporary nature in principle and disappeared when the open spaces were developed—only to pop up at another location. Representing an early form of "urban farming," they blended in with the city's rhythm and ongoing renewal.

**LENNÉS TEMPORARY TREE NURSERIES IN BERLIN**

Tree nurseries that are used temporarily in between the stages of a comprehensive urban development program are a phenomenon that has occurred primarily in times of rapid growth. It is only during the last decades that nearly unlimited amounts of plants and a great variety of sizes have become readily available. This is an achievement of the large tree nurseries that are active across Europe and in some cases beyond its borders. Before these tree nurseries were established, the creation of large green areas and parks, and the planting of extensive streets in new city districts, were dependent on the offerings of local nurseries. This is why one can still find many former tree nursery areas on the periphery of European cities. Some existed only for a few years or decades. When Berlin was transformed into a large European city in the 1840s, the Prussian landscape architect Peter Joseph Lenné (1789–1866) relied on temporary nurseries to provide trees for the new parks, green areas, streets and promenades. Without exception, these areas are now covered with buildings and have become part of the city.

**DAGENHAM DOCKS**

There are plans to convert the Dagenham Docks, an old industrial area situated directly on the Thames, into a sustainable industrial park. The objective is to create synergy effects by pooling expertise and bringing together companies with comparable focuses. The waste products, degraded materials, waste heat and residual energy from one company will serve as raw materials for neighboring companies.

Due to their rapid evolution, industrial areas place short-lived functional demands on the surrounding outside space. As a result, landscape concepts must offer flexibility and allow areas to be occupied and vacated at short notice. An analogy in the natural environment is the floodplain forest, which regularly changes its form (for example, after flooding), as new open areas emerge and other clearings are closed. The principle of a changing form within a fixed spatial and thematic framework was adopted in the design of the industrial park on the Thames. The entire area will be planted with trees. A clearing will only emerge and be developed when a concrete building is erected. The trees that are removed will be transplanted to another area or sold to one of the other development projects in the surrounding district. Once a site becomes vacant, it will be replanted with trees. In principle the whole park works like a tree nursery in which industrial production is assigned to the open areas. The trees can be planted at the launch of the restructuring program, sending a strong political message about industrial strategy. By combining industrial and plant production with the emotional significance of trees in the city and the flexible, temporary character of the entire complex, the planting concept, with its tree nursery parallels, will meet the new demands of urban development.

The former Tempelhof Airport in Berlin

Photo: Vogt Landscape Zurich

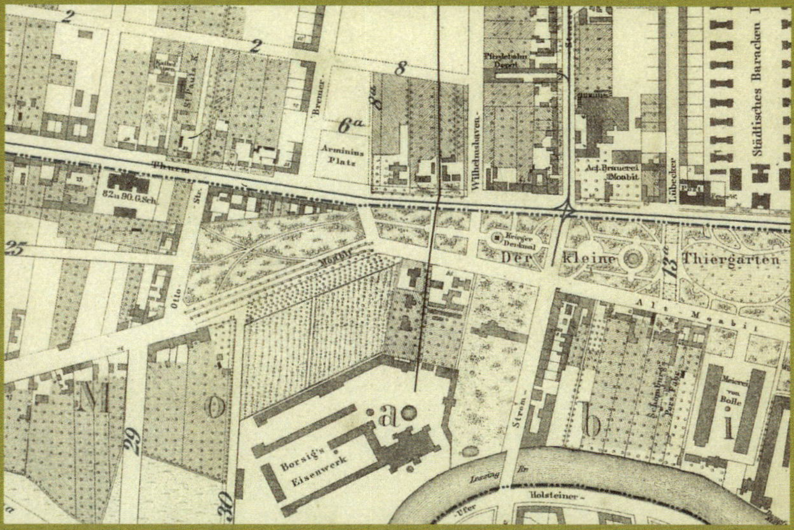

**TEMPELHOF**
The vast size of the former Tempelhof Airport in Berlin has made it necessary to design on a large scale. The proper balance between vacant land and densely planted areas is more important than the individual tree, bench or playground. The competition submission by VOGT provides for a forestlike park in the southern part of the Tempelhof site to counterbalance the openness of the central area. This wooded space has been conceived not only as a woodland in the park, but also as a tree nursery that will produce the street trees planned for the urban development areas in the northern section and the International Building Exhibition. Clearings of different sizes will be embedded in the tree nursery and can be used for various activities such as soccer games, barbecues and sunbathing. These activities are also offered in other parks in Berlin such as the Tiergarten, but at Tempelhof they are integrated into the different spaces and chambers of the park woodlands at the center of the tree nursery, transforming the path between the clearings into a journey of discovery. The local production of trees, harmonious proportions and diverse uses create a new type of open area that crosses a tree nursery with a city forest.

Section of the site plan of the capital city and residence of Berlin and the surrounding region, executed by Wilhelm Liebenow, 1888. Temporary tree nurseries planned by Peter Josef Lenné
Illustration: Landesarchiv Berlin, F Rep. 270, A 8162

Section of the official cartographical map of Berlin, district surveying offices, montage comprising four sheets from 1958–1960. The tree nurseries have been replaced by buildings.
Illustration: Landesarchiv Berlin, F Rep. 270, A 2000

### KAPLANKAYA

The large-scale project for upscale tourism on Turkey's Mediterranean coast features high-quality hotels, resorts, villas, marinas and the required infrastructure. It is situated in a beautiful yet remote natural landscape on a scraggy terrain with little vegetation and clay-rich rocky soil, dominated by the features of the local topography. In this area it is important not to bring in new elements from the outside, but to derive them from the existing landscape. The walls that will protect the site and allow it to be highly functional will be built from excavated rock. The finer material will be processed and used as compacted pavement for streets and paths. Trees, shrubs and low-growing plants will be cultivated from local material in a special nursery. This will create jobs and prepare local workers for their subsequent employment in garden maintenance and additional plant production. Plants grown locally are better adapted to the microclimate and are readily available thanks to short transport routes. In addition, they bring a low risk of failure. The project's tree nursery will thus provide the plant material that creates the site's unique character. Finally, the plants will fill the gardens and parks, and line the city squares, hotel grounds, streets and promenades. The existing landscape will be transformed into a redesigned environment.

### DUBAI

Dubai's astonishing growth over the past few years has taken numerous forms. One example is the yet-to-be-built design created under the direction of the Tokyo-based SANAA architecture firm for a luxurious shoppers' paradise with connected hotels and numerous service facilities. The project was part of an overarching master plan to transform a large section of the desert into urban fabric. The design concept for the gigantic shopping world envisaged the nearly complete coverage of the site by buildings without the use of high rises. Various inner courtyards were integrated like oases. The economic concept included a large share of retail space, and while this space could have been built quite quickly, it would not have been possible—despite the global focus—to sell or rent out the stores and fill them with life in the same timeframe. As a result, the question of intermediate use came up.

In order to reduce the required irrigation and optimize sustainable use, the concept required a large number of plants to be suitable for the location and adapted to the dry climate. However, not enough plants are cultivated locally today, which is why even public agencies have now started producing plants themselves. Since the project was divided into two sections, it lent itself well to the creation of a small local tree nursery that would temporarily use the undeveloped area. However, since only gray water could be used for reasons of sustainability, this type of plant production site could have worked only if there was surplus gray water generated in the area. The first construction section would have had to produce enough wastewater to facilitate the successful operation of the tree nursery in the second section.

Tree nursery on the site of the large-scale Kaplankaya project near Bodrum on the Aegean, Turkey
Photo: Capital Partners Turkey

Orient Irrigation Services tree nursery in Dhaid near Dubai, United Arab Emirates
Photo: Vogt Landscape Zurich

# GREEN BELT

**London has it. Frankfurt and Vienna have them. And many smaller cities in Europe use them to curb their ravenous appetite for building on the last patches of open land. Green belts are a kind of appetite suppressant for rapidly growing cities. Particularly in England, they have become an effective urban planning tool for preventing cities' uncontrolled growth into the surrounding countryside, creating recreational space for residents and providing for agriculture with production sites close to the urban market. In London, the process of deindustrialization has led to the emergence of a high amount of industrial wasteland along the boundary between the city and its green belt. Transformed and repurposed, this wasteland has been turned into sites for a variety of interesting projects at the interface between the cultural landscape and urban or suburban areas. These projects are bringing the tree nursery back to the city as a production site and design idea.**

Essay by Silke Schmeing
Photographs by Vogt Landscape Limited London

London Green Belt

The green belt encircling London is not a new phenomenon. Under discussion since the seventeenth century, it was finally established in 1955 and enshrined in law. At that time the city of London, with 8.6 million inhabitants, was bursting at the seams (today there are 7.4 million inhabitants in Greater London and twenty million in the entire metropolitan area). Moreover, living conditions for the working class had become increasingly precarious. Additional measures were taken, such as the new towns built around London after 1945, but these did little to improve living conditions. The green belt, by contrast, has caught on as an urban planning tool throughout England. As a fixed boundary around the city measuring several kilometers wide, it forces the urban area to grow denser rather than spread into its environs. The green belt reflects a change in the relationship between inside and outside in the history of the continental European city. Long after the Middles Ages had come to an end, the city and the surrounding countryside were clearly separated by a city wall that enabled the inhabitants to defend against attackers from the outside. But the two areas were more closely connected than they are today because food was produced for the city in its immediate environs. Today most of the city walls have been torn down and the areas they once covered are used for traffic infrastructure or parks. As a modern counterpart to the city wall, the green belt no longer offers protection against attacks from the outside, but protects the outside from being invaded by the city.

Initiatives have repeatedly been launched to intensify the agricultural use of green belts. Their vast open areas raise the question of why the thousands of trees that ensure a better climate in our cities are produced so far away and then transported to their urban destinations at great expense of money and energy. Shouldn't tree nurseries be given permanent space in the green belt close to the city?

In the case of London, one difficulty is that the economic (and agricultural) use of its green belt is subject to justifiably strict regulations, and tree nurseries would limit one of its most important features—open accessibility. However, the growing industrial wasteland on the edges of the London green belt offers ideal sites close to the city for producing plants for urban greening. Tree nurseries in this area could help to connect the city and the green belt, illustrate the origins of city vegetation and give a modern urban landscape a unique identity. Projects such as the temporary tree nursery in Stratford or the Dagenham Docks Sustainable Industries Park create new links between plant production and design interventions—links that mediate between the natural landscape, the cultural landscape and the traditions of European park culture.

After all, tree nurseries have never disappeared entirely from cities, at least as a formal reference. Their structures were present in many temporary urban tree nurseries, including the ones used by Peter Joseph Lenné in eighteenth-century Berlin, and they are visible today in the positions of trees in classical park design. The variety of forms ranges from grid plantings such as those in London's Stockley Park, to rows of trees and promenades in formally laid out parks, to ancient patterns such as the quincunx, which was taken up primarily in the tree arrangements of French baroque parks. As with many other classical arrangements, in this case the design patterns were derived from the processes and needs of everyday life—and they anticipated the oft-misunderstood modernist principle of "form follows function." From the formations of Roman legions and the dots on dice to the efficient use of space in tree nurseries, the quincunx has stood the test of time and is now a set feature of the repertoire of basic design forms, along with the double row, the triad and others.

In the eighteenth century, landscape architects began turning away from these strict design principles, creating landscape gardens, public parks and wildlife gardens. But projects today are once again finding ways to breathe contemporary life into classical forms.

TREE ARRANGEMENT
Grid, quincunx, clearing, filling, based on a study by Nicola Eiffler, Vogt Landscape Zurich

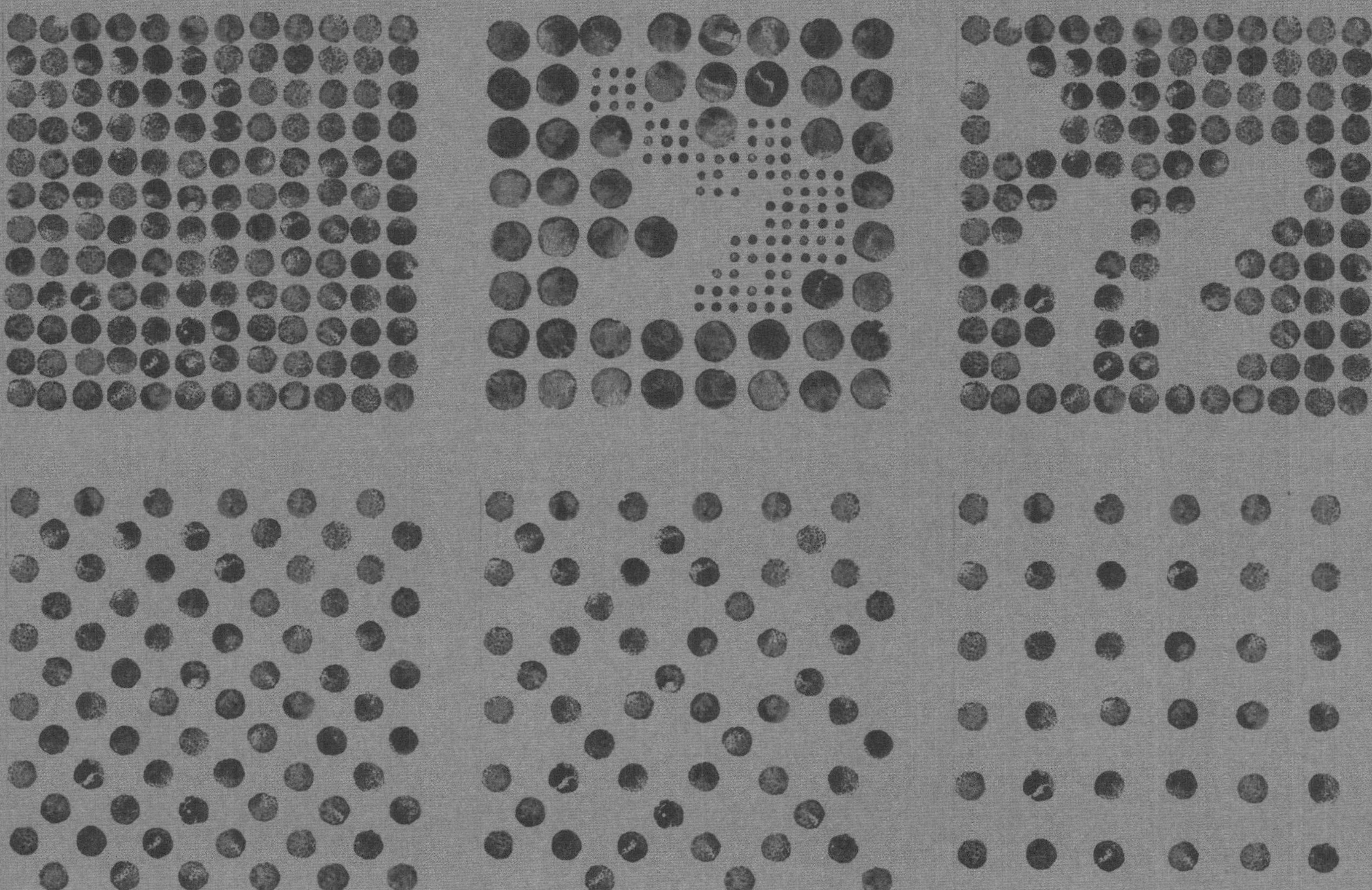

As a result, the tradition of European park design is being carried on in the present-day urban environment, which is shaped less by bourgeois parks and more by industrial wasteland like the Dagenham Docks site and by city development areas such as in Stratford. In the design of the exterior spaces, the strictly applied formal repertoire of earlier ages has been expanded and loosened. It is combined with the pragmatic approaches taken by tree nurseries and forms flexible design principles that are suited to the fast-paced, constantly changing modern city and can survive as a connective yet autonomous element between the green belt's regional character and the city's geometry.

Stockley Park, London

# DAGENHAM DOCKS

## TREE NURSERY AS PARK

**The realization of the premise of "sustainability" can be just as varied as the concept is broad. What sustainability means for buildings, green space or production depends on both the objectives and the specific location and its resources. What conserves resources in the ecological, economic or social climate of Shanghai might have a completely different, perhaps even negative, impact in Zurich. While sustainability is a global issue, its implementation is, to a high degree, local. In this respect, the Dagenham Docks Sustainable Industries Park is a paradox: It combines two elements of natural landscape and urban landscape that are as global as they are artificial—industrial zone and tree nursery—to create a local conglomerate of sustainable design.**

Essay by Silke Schmeing
A project by Vogt Landscape Limited London and Sergison Bates Architects LLP, London

Bird's-eye view of the Dagenham Docks project area, London
Photo: Thames Gateway Park, London

At the Dagenham Docks in East London, the natural environment of the Thames meets residential and industrial zones. With this meeting comes a clash of conflicting demands that are imposed on the exterior space. The goal of the development concept is therefore to embed the industrial park in a comprehensive exterior design that is sustainable on multiple levels. The core area is being planned to enable flexible industrial use that creates spatial and technical synergies. Waste products and waste heat from one company, for example, are to be made available for use by neighboring companies; the overall spatial and design configuration is to be designed such that building modifications and new facilities can be easily incorporated. Another component of the concept is the linking of the ensemble with the surrounding residential areas and the existing secondary ecosystems such that the area attains its own urban identity rooted in a local context. In terms of landscaping, existing conditions are as interesting as they are challenging, given that the area on the banks of the Thames is a secondary landscape that has been transformed by centuries of human activity. In the middle of the nineteenth century, the alluvial land that had been previously subject to regular flooding was shielded from the waters of the Thames by the construction of a wall, after which the land was drained, artificially elevated with landfill and finally settled. As a result of these changes, the original landscape and the natural course of the river have completely disappeared. The only remaining traces of a landscape once dominated by water are to be found in the form of drainage channels that lead into the canalized Thames.

Within these parameters, the exterior design seeks to connect to old and new landscape and urban elements, reinvigorating them at times; or it seeks to preserve valuable secondary biotopes, incorporating them into the new concept. The two main points of reference it falls back upon in this endeavor are the original alluvial landscape along the banks of the Thames, and the tree nursery, which not only supplies trees for the surroundings in a quick and sustainable manner, but also represents an overall design aspect. It is reinterpreted as a kind of "missing link" between the alluvial forest and the industrial zone, especially in light of how it provides analogies to both forms and offers many other practical aspects that address the complex requirements of the area. Much as the alluvial forest is in constant flux due to flooding, the disappearance of plants and the growth of new ones while at the very same time retaining its basic form, so too is the tree nursery constantly changing within the framework of its basic formal principles. And like industrial zones, tree nurseries are also artificial landscape elements which are governed by their own set of laws that are comparable all over the world. Functionalism is, in this case, not a frequently employed catchword or a design motto, but rather a simple necessity. The form which arises out of function is, in both cases, a geometrical grid with irregularities resulting from the day-to-day operations. Due to shifts in demand, changes in production technology, availability of labor or raw materials, for example, industrial buildings are remodeled, added on to, torn down or replaced at a much quicker pace than is the case for most other buildings. In the tree nursery, plants are constantly being transplanted or removed for sale; temporary clearings come about, as do new areas with young plants. The species composition is determined by factors such as demand, climate, soil type and condition; the density of plants is influenced by the plants' species, age and the desired growth form. In other words, the height, density, composition and age structure of the grid is constantly changing. The change within the overall form presents the most important constant.

The aesthetics and particular local character of the two artificial landscapes, with their irregular grids, open spaces and small ecosystems, only reveal themselves to the visitor upon second glance, particularly when seen from the pedestrian perspective. Especially in the Sustainable Industries Park, the unusual spatial effect and atmosphere is most impressive for those who experience it in person and on foot.

Another similarity between industrial zone and tree nursery can be found in the soil. In both areas, it has undergone substantial change through human activity. In industrial zones, it is frequently compacted by machines and contaminated by waste products; in tree nurseries, by contrast, it is processed and treated with pesticides, nutrients and other substances to yield a substratum that is

as productive as possible, thereby enabling rapid, undisturbed plant growth.

These parallels, as well as the practical prerequisites, gave rise to the idea of a uniform grid of trees covering the entire area of the Sustainable Industries Park. It is an expression of reverence for the "woodlands" as a typical English landscape, and at the same time an abstraction of the notion of the tree nursery: a highly adaptable new type of urban forest, in which clearings for industrial use can be created as needed. Where buildings are torn down or where unused areas become vacant, trees and plants that are taken from other areas of the tree nursery can fill the gaps in order to complete the grid of trees. In this way, the tree nursery as design principle not only secures the sustainable production of trees on site while avoiding excessive transportation, it also introduces the emotional value of the forest into the urban environment in an abstract form. What this amounts to is an urban landscape that vacillates between forest and tree nursery, between a pragmatic concept for using space and high quality habitat for residents, between old trees, full of character, and the young tree planted in the grid as a mass-produced industrial article.

Aerial photo of the flood plain next to the Thames showing the existing ditches and embankments
Photo: Google Earth 2008

Dagenham Docks industrial wasteland
Photo: Sergison Bates Architects LLP, London

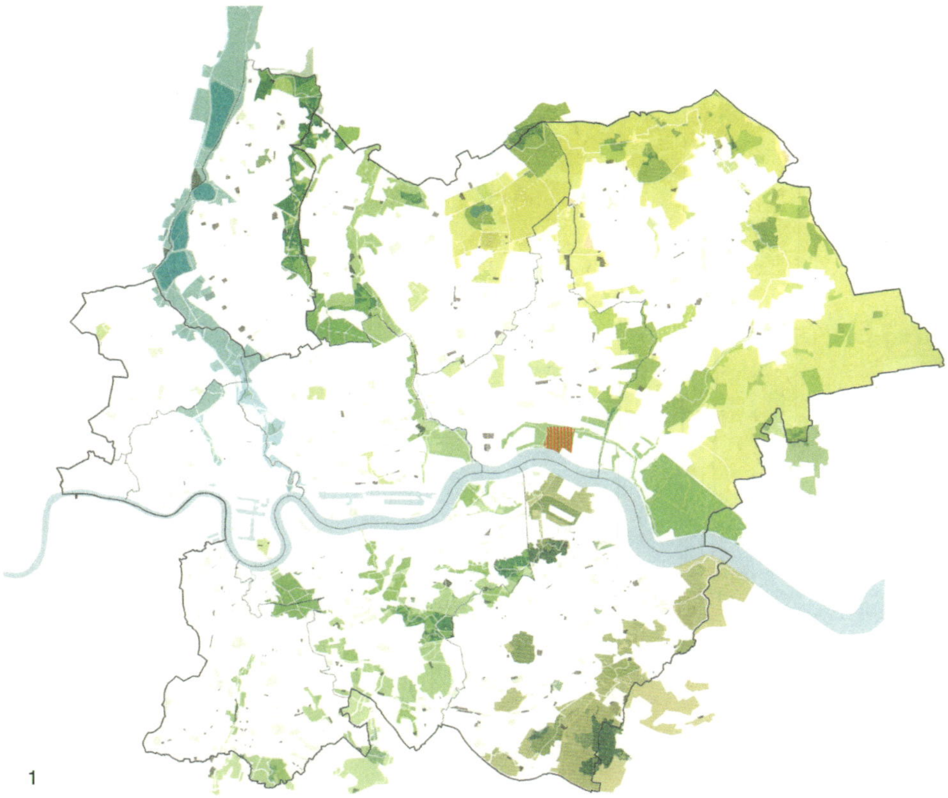

1

2

3

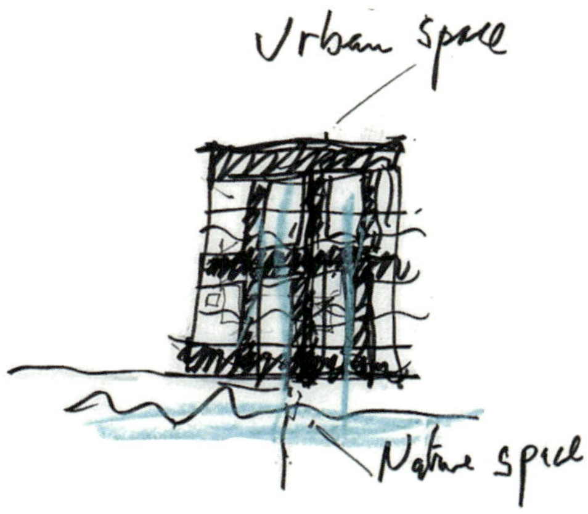


4

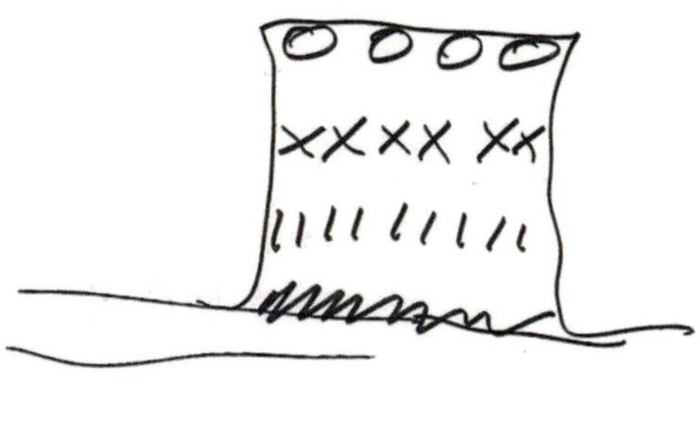

5

6

**WOODLANDS**

Based on the native English forest plant communities, the planting of trees in the Sustainable Industries Park is organized according to site-specific, differentiated types of forest. In areas close to the river, indigenous species of alluvial, moisture-loving trees such as willows, elms and poplars are planted in a more widely spaced grid. The different types of alluvial zones are also taken into consideration. Trees from dry forests are used for drier zones that are farther removed from the river. Here too, different kinds of forests can be recognized by their particular species composition. The density of the plant grid gradually increases as you move from the banks of the river into areas that are farther afield; this is a further reference to the natural growth of the forest plant communities. For the planting of trees along streets and paths, a specific species spectrum of classic street trees has been designated. Moreover, the street planting is the only fixed planting in the entire park. In contrast to all the other plants on the grounds, these trees are not subject to further transplanting.

This creates a staggered system of planting that cites various forest types and forest plant communities, with different scenarios and atmospheres produced through the trees' density, species composition and age structure; at the same time, the development of the grounds is made visible and comprehensible. Meanwhile, a stimulating contrast is created between the artificial view of pruned trees planted in rows and the more natural species composition.

Trees and forests are commonly associated with permanence. In the Sustainable Industries Park, however, regular transplantations and the tree nursery character of the entire ensemble puts them in the context of a temporary installation; the trees themselves become a mobile element, which calls the permanence and rootedness of the modern tree into question.

These contradictions are not only an expression of artistic intention; they also show that a sustainable concept with a local reference does not necessarily produce a naturalist or naturelike scenario; but it definitely creates a scenario which is site-specific.

DIAGRAMS
1 Native forest communities in the woodlands around London
2 Wetlands around London
Illustrations: Greater London Authority

DESIGN SKETCHES
3 Existing wetlands comprising ponds and ditches
4 Urban vs. natural structure
5 Tree species gradient: the tree species change from north to south along the water gradient
6 Vegetation gradient

VEGETATION
7 Greenwich Eco-park, London
8 Abbey Wood, London
9 Poplars and birches, London
Sketches and photos: Vogt Landscape Limited London

7

8

9

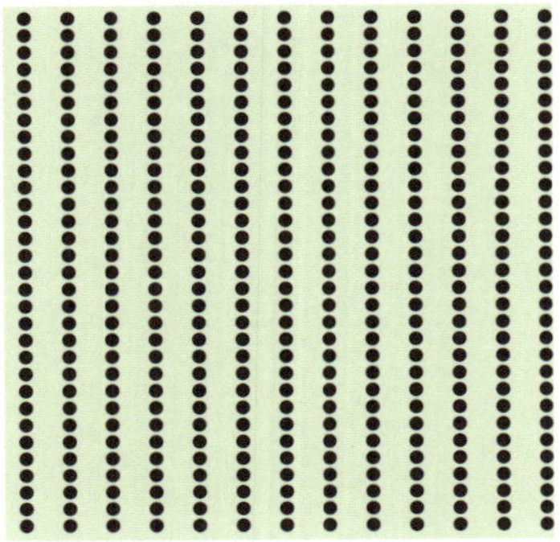

t = 0, 4000 young trees per hectare in a grid of 1 × 2.5 m

t = (years)

t = 5, 3340 young trees per hectare are transplanted

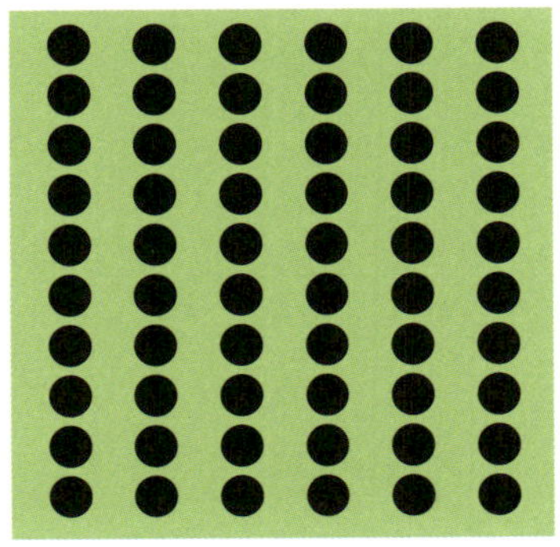

t = 10, 660 semi-adult trees per hectare in a grid of 3 × 5 m

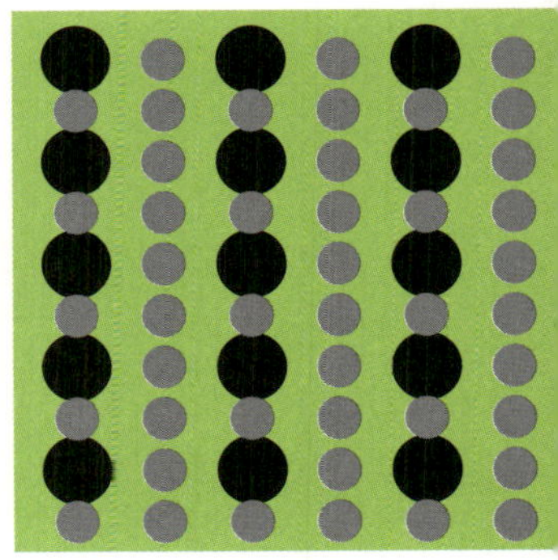

t = 15, 500 semi-adult trees per hectare are transplanted

2010

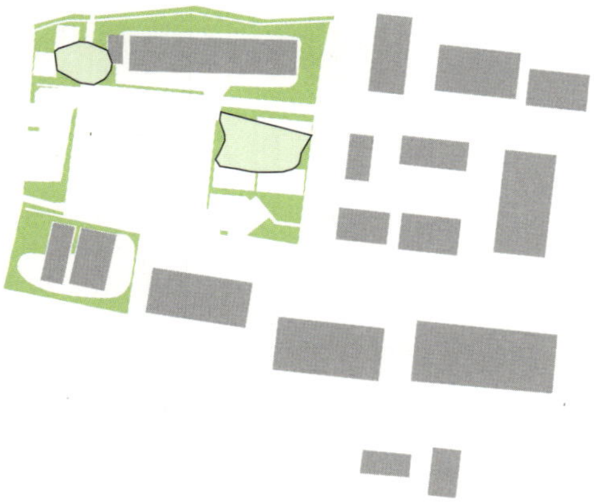

2015

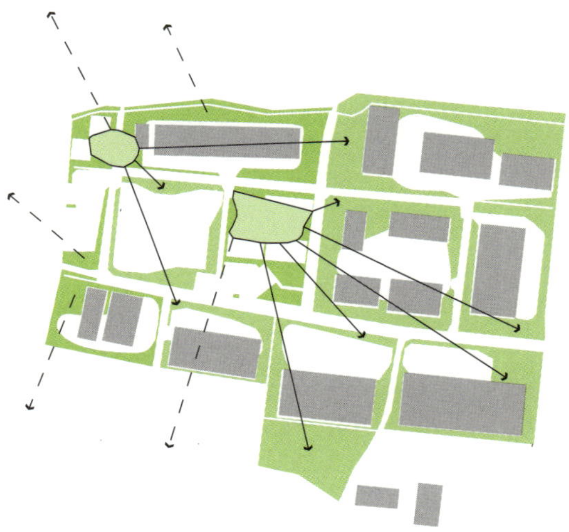

2020

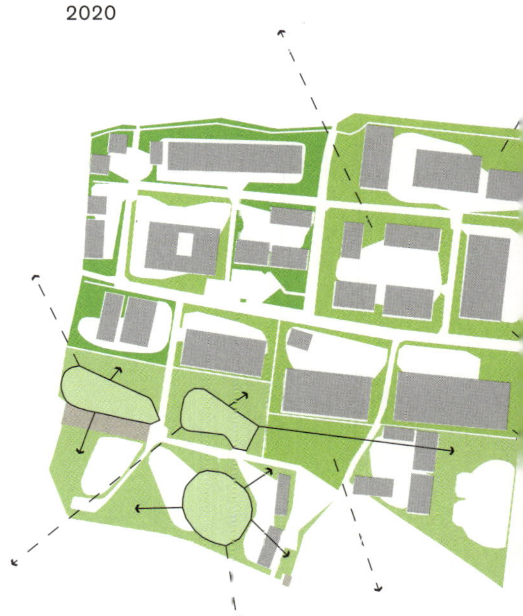

Projected building
Young trees in 1 × 2.5 m grid (t = 0)
Young trees are planted (t = 5)
Semi-adult trees in 3 × 5 m grid (t = 10)
Semi-adult trees are planted (t = 15)
Semi-adult trees in 6 × 10 m grid (t = 20)
Adult trees in 6 × 10 m grid (t = 40)
Tree transplantation within the area
Tree transplantation to the surroundings

Drainage canals

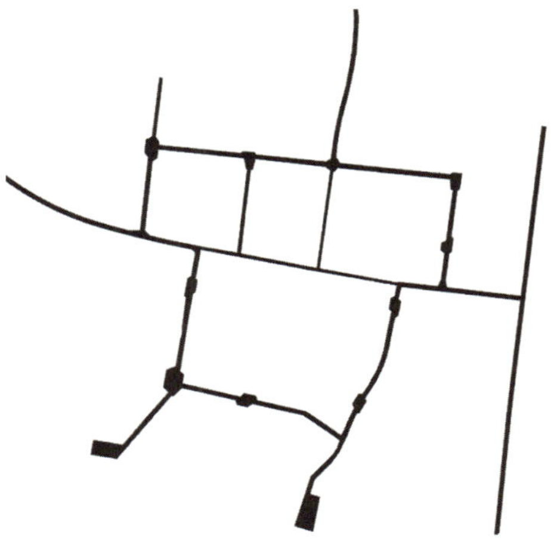

Street network

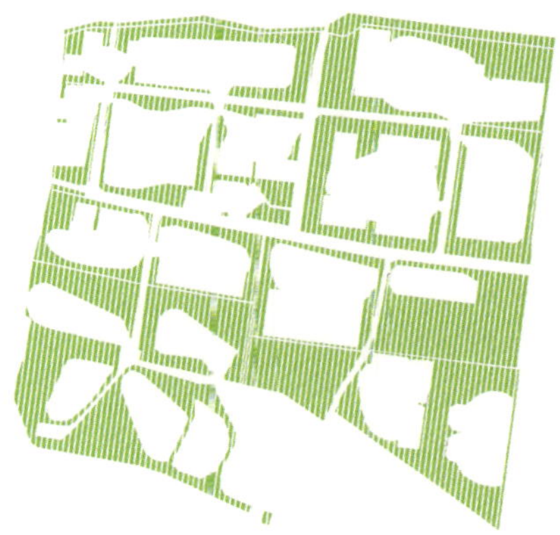

Woodland planted in rows

Diagrams: Vogt Landscape Limited London

t = 20, 160 semi-adult trees per hectare in a grid of 6 × 10 m

t = 40, 160 adult trees per hectare in a grid of 6 × 10 m

2040

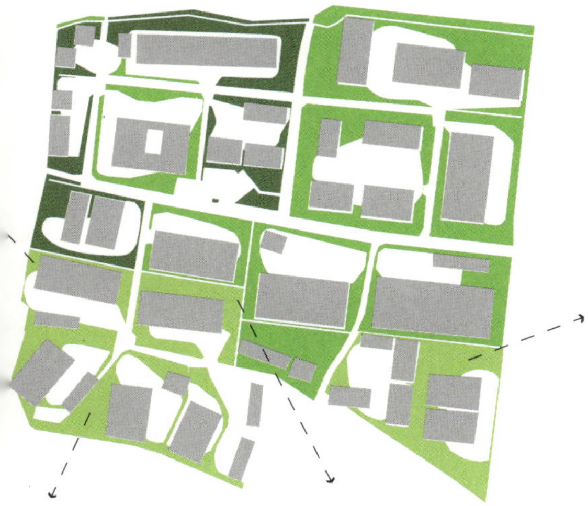

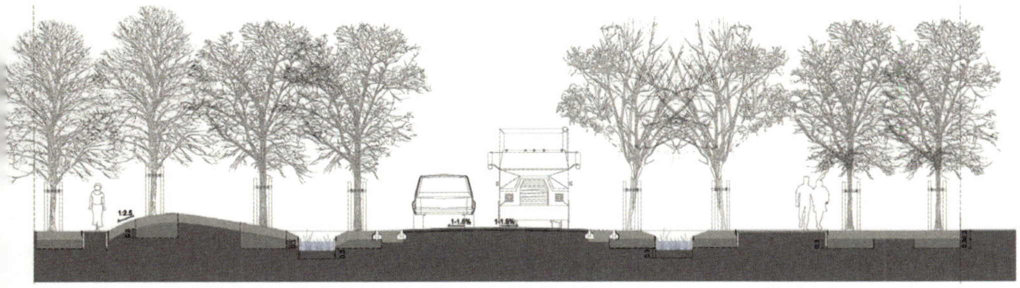

Cross-section: drainage canals and row plantings

**TREE NURSERY AS PARK**
It should be changeable and homogenous, easy to maintain and reasonable in cost; it should provide industry with space that is flexible in use and an infrastructure that is clearly laid out and suitable for heavy transport; and finally, it should offer residents a local identity, a high quality of life and security. These contradictory demands made on the Dagenham Docks Sustainable Industries Park have led to the creation of a new type of urban landscape, one which interprets the tree nursery not only as a local supplier of trees, but also as a spatial design element, and which takes industrial plant production out of the rural context and returns it to an urban industrial context.

Corresponding to the phase-by-phase development and evolution of the park, the tree production is made visible as a process and integrated into the overall composition. Initially then, intensively used tree nursery zones are concentrated on designated areas in the center of the industrial park—sites that are set aside for production only, from which the plants will gradually be removed and distributed until the entire grounds are supplied with trees; meanwhile, the tree nurseries will by then have been sufficiently thinned out so that they can be incorporated into the grid of trees.

If the need arises, it is possible to plan new tree nursery areas in the outer lying areas of the park; in the long run, it is difficult to foresee the progress of development and, as a result, the extent of the need for plants. In addition, the Sustainable Industries Park is a modular system without clearly marked boundaries—the park concept is an open design and can be expanded or reduced in any given direction at any time.

While in city parks the processual aspect of nature is often evident, the exterior space of the Sustainable Industries Park emphasizes the production process. More so than in most other ensembles, here a complex interplay of artificial, natural and human influences is evident. The exterior space wants neither to emulate nature nor an ideal of nature, as does the landscape park; at the same time it does not seek to express the order and aesthetics of a formal park. Essentially, it is not to be understood as a park in the conventional sense, for it does not offer the spaces, moods and conventions that are expected of such a park. Instead, it is obviously a man-made, urban form of nature. Here the tree is not employed as a scenic entity, but rather as part of a production series. Does that make it more beautiful or more ugly, does it increase or decrease its value, for people or for the city as ecosystem?

Paul Richens likes trees, bushes and plants in general, above all the sort that grows on roofs. He tramps up the stairs of the Maria Fidelis School, broad-backed and wearing a worn fleece jacket and a crown of unruly gray hair. Richens is not out of breath. He climbs stairs everyday up to London's platform roofs. He takes the stairs easily, all the while talking about how the pupils at the Maria Fidelis School carried all the soil up here to create the roof garden, two tons in a single day, as well as building materials, and how the entire school is altogether enthusiastic about the garden on their roof.

There he stands, on the roof, Paul Richens. He used to be a film producer, the manager of an international media business, a frequent flyer. Then he had his first heart attack. Then the second. Today he is a gardener.

In the Maria Fidelis School roof garden he explains the system he has invented for spreading two tons of earth on a large surface of thinly constructed London roof. Richens potters about, explaining how the pupils wove the gigantic baskets and nailed together the broad plinths He points out beds containing pumpkins, strawberries, leek stalks, sprouting onions and carrots, as well as a small tree surrounded by yellow-orange flowers. Richens, a gentle giant silhouetted against the setting sun, digs a herb out of his rucksack and plants it loosely between the cabbages and raspberry bushes—an "unbeatable organic fertilizer."

"Unbeatable?"

Richens continues to poke around in the soil, digging and loosening.

"Yes, unbeatable. It's very important to me to be an organic gardener because there will come a time when we will no longer be able to use petrochemical fertilizers for our farms and gardens—simply because we are going to run out of oil. The sooner we acquire the knowledge we need about organic gardening the better."

The city around us is a huge polluter. London, with its 7.5 million inhabitants, three international airports, its infrastructure for railways and cars, and its poorly insulated houses—if one adds air traffic to this mix Greater London annually produces sixty-seven million tons of $CO_2$, which amounts to eleven percent of the UK's total emissions. The city consumes enormous amounts of energy—electricity is generated by coal-fired power stations while valuable organic waste is buried in garbage dumps instead of being used to generate energy. Houses are poorly insulated and car emissions are unacceptably high. As the climate plan issued by the mayor of London makes clear, this is a city with an enormous potential for the reduction of greenhouse gases.

Sixty percent below 1990 levels by 2025—this is the goal formulated by the former mayor Ken Livingstone in his climate plan, in which he also made it clear that, while ambitious, this target could be achieved with existing technologies. Richens, hoe in hand, is convinced that his roof gardens can also help achieve this goal.

With the sudden onset of rain transforming the Maria Fidelis School into dripping dreariness, we hurry to the next location, an office building on the Gray's Inn Road. We climb some more stairs, with Richens striding easily ahead. He throws open a door leading to a maritime dune landscape, high up on the roof in the midst of pouring rain: a wide, sandy surface crisscrossed by raised wooden pathways and featuring all types of wild plants, shrubs growing in pots and young trees, here and there a bench and a garden table.

Richens walks ahead, taking long strides, pointing out rare plants sprouting between the flues and ventilation pipes, then leans against the guardrail.

"Look over there at the next roof," he says.

"It's a gray surface."

"That's just my point, you see. London has big problems with the so-called urban heat island effect. What this means it that when the sun shines the city warms up at an exponentially higher rate than its surroundings. It acts like a heat island that stores up heat and thereby contributes to global warming."

"So you see living roofs as a countermeasure?"

"Exactly."

With his roof gardens Richens is part of a trend that is finding widespread support not only in London but also elsewhere in the world. From New York and Chicago to Tokyo and Seoul, all major cities faced with the problem of urban heat islands are recommending the creation of green roofs.

While in office Ken Livingstone began encouraging the creation of green roofs and his successor, the Conservative Boris Johnson, has maintained this policy. The plan for the creation of living roofs in

# LIVING ROOFS

## GARDENS OVER LONDON

**They are growing, spouting and spreading: the green roofs of London. Vegetables, bushes, grasses and trees on platform roofs are all helping to promote biodiversity, improve the urban microclimate and open the eyes of the city's residents.**

Travelouge and photographs by Christoph Keller

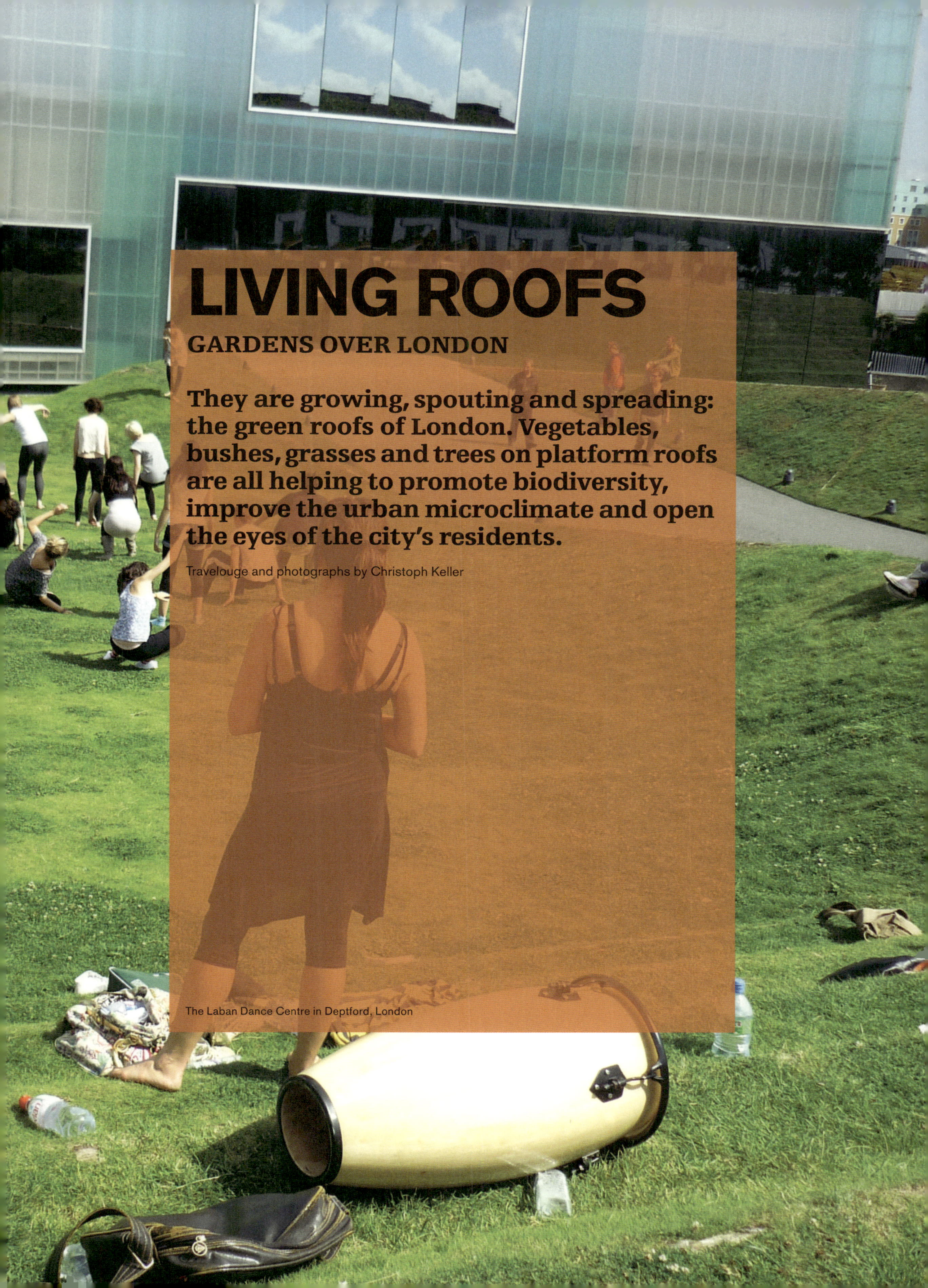

The Laban Dance Centre in Deptford, London

London describes them as benefiting London's residents by creating additional outside living spaces, increasing biodiversity, reducing flood risk by absorbing heavy rainfall, providing shade and improving the overall appearance of the city. Living roofs are now being integrated into large-scale construction projects from the outset, for example, in King's Cross, currently the site of one of Europe's most extensive construction projects, which I am led through by Jane Riddiford, the executive manager of Global Generation.

We make our way between construction machinery, surrounded by the din of jackhammers and dump trucks—a new district is being built here comprising 2000 office and residential units on sixty-seven hectares of wasteland. Plans for the area include public squares, a new harbor on Regent's Canal and new locations for a number of institutions, including London's University of the Arts. The consortium led by the property development giant Argent Group envisions King's Cross as setting an example for energy-efficient, sustainable construction, with excellent thermal insulation and buildings topped by living roofs. The open-faced Riddiford, looking somewhat disheveled, her blond hair tied back, stands on a small rise in the midst of the building din with cranes turning overhead and speaks about biodiversity.

"Biodiversity, yes. This whole twenty-hectare area of King's Cross used to be a freight terminal but then gradually became abandoned. The result was a wasteland, shabby and, as it were, unproductive, but also a place colonized by many rare wild plants."

"And that is now being lost."

"That is being lost. And that is why we have done our best to ensure that there will be living roofs on top of these massive new buildings, green roofs with vegetable gardens and, in one case, a small forest."

Riddiford, who comes from New Zealand and grew up surrounded by nature, has also made her campaign to establish green roofs into a social project. Global Generation's living roofs are being constructed as part of a neighborhood project involving young people with difficult social backgrounds from the King's Cross area. They have already shown what they can do when given shovels and seedlings—in the form of the mobile *Skip Garden* which is made up of series of dumpsters on the edge of the construction site. Richens was also involved in this project and supervised the young people during the planting of the seven large dumpsters made accessible by carefully built stairs. The seven dumpsters are a showpiece for how people like Riddiford and Richens would like to see the roofs of King's Cross, i.e., planted with rhubarb, zucchini, Swiss chard, onions, a range of berry bushes, and here and there a young tree to provide shade.

"What," I ask Riddiford, "does the Argent Group consortium have to say about you ideas?"

"Well, that was really quite astounding. It seems to me there's a real process of rethinking these issues taking place. We didn't encounter any resistance at all. For example, the supermarket chain Sainsbury's wants to create a two-thousand square meter vegetable garden on their new headquarters in King's Cross, including a small avenue of trees—that really sends out a strong signal. And the people from the Guardian, which is also having a new main office built here, personally helped out for a whole day when we were building the *Skip Garden* and now they also want a garden on the roof of their new building."

"Despite the financial crisis?"

"Interestingly enough, a lot of firms take their social responsibilities more seriously precisely when there is a recession, and naturally that is encouraging. On the other hand, one has to remain a little circumspect because as always there are many who do this merely to improve their reputation. They send their employees once a year to the gardener and that's it. We call that greenwashing, and it certainly has nothing to do with what we represent."

A city that offers spaces for close-to-nature experiences, that creates roof gardens and trees: Jane Riddiford and Paul Richens, Global Generation and Sainsbury's, King's Cross Development and the Mayor of London, the idea of living roofs—these are all part of a movement that is bringing together an increasing number of London's residents. The neighborhood group operating a compost facility in Coram's Fields, not far from the British Museum, is part of this movement as are the numerous organic shops found in every district. It also includes the small alternative cafés near London Fields overflowing with people on Saturdays and Sundays, London's highly active ornithologists and the increasing numbers of cyclists seen in the inner city (who include Mayor Boris Johnson).

London is becoming green, for example on the edge of the inner city in the former industrial belt that today forms a strip of often empty factories and warehouses. In Greenwich, on the bank of a dirty canal, near a building site at the end of a row of irregularly arranged sheds stands the Laban Dance Centre, an elegant, unobtrusive building designed by the architects Herzog & de Meuron. In front of it lies an artificial, hilly landscape that is very green and obviously carefully tended.

Standing here is Dusty Gedge, sporting a leather jacket, medium-length hair and a broad smile. He is the executive director of livingroofs.org, a national nongovernmental organization that campaigns for the creation of green roofs. In 2008 Dusty was selected as one of fifteen London Leaders, individuals chosen by the city's mayor to promote the transformation of London. He is also president of the European Federation of Green Roof Associations. But above all, Gedge is an inveterate campaigner for green roofs.

We take the lift to the top of the building, continue up ladders and stairs, and finally reach a green area recessed into the curved roof of the Laban Dance Centre. It is not really a green roof but more a kind of wasteland, generously strewn with stones and overgrown by all types of wild flowers.

It is a little disappointing, but that is exactly the point, says Gedge.

"This isn't a green, I mean *green* roof, but what was here previously, before the Laban Dance Centre was built? A wasteland, a bit barren and dry. But this is intentional. To put it simply, when a building is created where there used to be a forest, then there should be trees on the roof, and when a building is constructed in the desert, there should be sand on top."

"What's the idea behind that?"

"The idea is that the roof should be used to reproduce the biodiversity that was destroyed on the ground below. That's the main motivation behind almost half the living roofs in London: the goal of saving biodiversity. For example, this roof is supposed to provide an environment that offers a home for rare bees, endangered plants and above all the black redstart, a bird that has almost died out."

Gedge was one of the first people to recognize the potential dynamism of this type of development —and one of the first to exploit it. It all began around the year 2000, when the London municipal government gave its approval for the remodeling and partial redevelopment of the industrial belt and the inner city. At the same time it became clear that these industrial wastelands provided an important habitat for all kinds of creatures. One possible solution presented itself in the form of living roofs. Then came the hot summers of 2003, 2004 and 2005, putting climate change on the agenda—calculations were published as to the number of heat-related deaths that could be expected by 2020 if the climate continued to warm. Here too, living roofs seemed to provide an answer.

Gedge realized that something significant was happening and founded a firm that specialized in roof gardens. He needed to do quite some work convincing people and overcome numerous misgivings he confronted in the executive suites of a number of firms. However, Gedge at least had the advantage of being able to point to concrete examples in other countries, above all to Switzerland and the work of the geographer Stephan Brenneisen, who had used his research into biodiversity on green roofs to influence legislation in the city of Basel and other places. These developments provided Gedge with photographic documentation of the results of the compulsory greening of roofs in Basel, above all on newly built platform roofs. The breakthrough came when he was able to realize his living roofs vision for Canary Wharf, which is regarded today as a flagship project in the field.

Gedge sits on the roof of the Laban Dance Centre with his legs dangling, telephoning almost nonstop and already thinking about the next project.

"We have to understand that many firms take their obligation to green their roofs very seriously. For most of them it has to do with expressing an attitude, a philosophy that also has an effect in other areas. It's usually one person who takes up the idea, promotes it and brings it to fruition; that's the person we need to rely on."

"And how big is the potential for London as a whole?"

"I calculated that once. We could use London's roofs to construct a green area 24 times as big as Richmond Park, which is pretty big."

One firm that does more than greenwashing is the renowned advertizing company Wolff Olins, which has a staff of 140 working in London, New York and Abu Dhabi. Wolff Olins has worked for all the world's big firms and organizations, both commercial and non-commercial, from adidas to World Vision, and it designed the logo for the Olympic and Paralympic Games slated for 2012 in London. The firm's headquarters is located near King's Cross on Regent's Canal in a former dock building. When I arrive a whole delegation, from the art director to the building manager, is waiting to greet me in the airy, spacious lobby. And again there are stairs to climb.

When we arrive on the platform roof we stand in the midst of sprouting beds while Bethany Cowy, the Art Director at Wolff Olins, explains that this garden is an expression of her firm's philosophy, which has a lot to do with optimism combined with a good dose of the desire to experiment.

"So," I ask, "do you see a vegetable garden and trees on the roof as an expression of corporate social responsibility?"

"Yes. We are optimistic and confident that firms and the economy in general can achieve things that are good for the society. And it is our task to make our clients aware of what they can contribute to make the world we live in a better place. That is the attitude we also take vis-à-vis ourselves—we are constantly asking what effects our own activity is having on our surroundings and what we can improve."

"And what does the CEO say about the roof garden?"

Cowy laughs.

"He's an enthusiastic gardener and was the first to support the project."

Joanna Ham, the Senior Art Director with Wolff Olins, confirms that her firm believes in the project and wants to make practical use of it. Some people come up here during their lunch break to do a little gardening work, and others use the garden for consultations with clients—a place of relaxation. Stuart Robinson, the building manager, shows me the small but efficient composting facility and the rainwater collection tank. Then we climb down again via ladders and stairs and take a look around the canteen. Today's menu includes rhubarb and beans. Written underneath, and heavily underlined are the words "from our garden."

This article is based on a report the author did in 2009 for the Swiss radio broadcaster DRS 2.

*Skip Garden* in King's Cross, London, created by Global Generation and local young people

"How will we live in the year 2109?"– a shop window installation in Oxford Street

Dusty Gedge, managing director of livingroofs.org, a national nongovernmental organization that promotes green roofs, on the roof of the Laban Dance Centre in Deptford

The advertising agency Wolff Olins near King's Cross on the Regent Canal in a former dockyard building

## AUTHORS AND PROTAGONISTS

### FOREWORD

**Hans Ulrich Gantenbein** Photographer, otherwise known by the abbreviation H9, actively involved in the media industry. Since 1997 he has concentrated on press, reportage and landscape photography. His passion is panorama photography, which he has practiced since 1991.
Contribution: photos in A Tree Is a Tree Is a Tree, p. 4

**Sophia Carstensen** Gardener and landscape architect. Development of planting concept, tree selection and tree planting for the Novartis Campus Park in Basel, Project by Vogt Landscape Zurich.
Contribution: photo in Fastwood, p. 6

**Fritz H. Schweingruber** Shown here teaching amidst avalanche barriers above Davos, Switzerland. Studied biology in Bern, Zurich and Tucson, Arizona, 1966-1973. During the period 1972-2001, headed the Jahrring (annual growth ring) research group at the Swiss Institute for Forest, Snow and Landscape Research. Intensive collaboration with Russian research groups in Krasnoyarsk and Ekaterinburg, and the Climate Research Unit in Norwich, England. Created wood-anatomy atlases of Europe and, working with other research groups, the Sahara, Iran and Russia. Named associate professor at the University of Basel in 1976. Current research is focused on annual growth rings and the anatomy of the wood and bark of herbs and dwarf-shrubs among dicotyledonous plants of the northern hemisphere.
Contribution: Transplanted, p. 10

**Georges Lesnino** Shown here giving a lecture in France. After studying forestry he completed his doctorate in the field of wood science. As a research assistant at the Institute for Wood Science at the TU München, he studied such topics as wood anatomy, annual growth ring analysis and wood characteristics. Since 1996 he has managed a technical assessment office specializing in tree diagnosis (traffic safety, tree statics), annual growth ring analysis (age determination) and wood anatomy (wood type determination, root wood determination).
Contribution: Transplanted, p. 10

### FOREST CARTOGRAPHY

**Brigitta Ammann** Shown here sampling a short core in Alaska with Herber E. Wright. Studied biology in Bern, Bergen, Norway and Durham, North Carolina, with an emphasis on plant ecology and paleoecology. The main focus of her research is ecology with long time lines, i.e., the dynamics of populations and ecosystems that elude direct observation and experimentation, since they require more time than is available to a single research project or human lifetime. The key question is, How did ecosystems react to climate changes in the past?
Contribution: Tree Migrations, p. 20

**Britta Pollmann** Studied biology and archeology at the University of Bonn and the University of Tübingen. From 2004 to 2008, research assistant at the Institute of Prehistoric and Archeological Science at the University of Basel. Since 2008 she has been working on her dissertation as part of the project "Understanding Wetland Occupation in Later Prehistoric Europe" as well as studies of archeobotanical material at the prehistoric lakeshore dwellings at Lake Luokesas (Lithuania); working title: "Archaeobotanical Macroremains of the Late Bronze Age/Iron Age Lake-Dwelling on Lake Luokesas/Lithuania."
Contribution: Conserved Forest, p. 30

**Stefanie Jacomet Schibler** Shown here during a botanical excursion in Termen, Switzerland. Studied botany, prehistory and early history, zoology and geography at the University of Basel. Dissertation on plant remnants found in pile dwellings in Zurich's Seefeld district in 1979, followed by postdoc studies at the University of Basel and the establishment of a research group in archeobotany. She is particularly interested in the study of human influence on landscape since the introduction of agriculture and animal husbandry. Her research focuses in part on the advancement of the methodological principles of archeobotany as well as quantification principles, in particular for prehistoric grain discoveries. Since 1997 she has been the titular professor for archeobotany at the University of Basel, teaching and conducting research at the Institute of Prehistoric and Archeological Science (IPNA).
Contribution: Hemaphrodites, p. 36

**Christopher Smout** is retired from the chair of Scottish History at St. Andrews University, Scotland, and has become a woodland historian. He is Historiographer Royal in Scotland, a Fellow of the British Academy and of the Royal Society of Edinburgh.
He provided expert input for Hemaphrodites. (The Forests of the Scottish Highlands), p. 48

**Andreas Bürgi** DPhil, literary historian. Co-editor of *Sämtliche Schriften* (Collected Works) of Ulrich Bräker, research projects on the literary and cultural history of the eighteenth century. Most recent publication: *Relief der Urschweiz. Entstehung und Bedeutung des Landschaftsmodells von Franz Ludwig Pfyffer* (Relief of Central Switzerland. Creation and Significance of the Landscape Model by Franz Ludwig Pfyffer).
Contribution: Research in Forest Cartography, p. 50

### HUNTERS AND COLLECTORS

**Heinz Schneider** DPhil. studied biology at the University of Basel, completed his doctorate at the University of Zurich on "Sprossorganisation und Blattarchitektur bei Betulaceae und extratropischen Fagaceae" (The Organization of Shoots and Leaf Architecture Among Betulaceae and Extratropical Fagaceae). Since 1994, employed at the Botanical Institute of the University of Basel as curator of plant collections. His scientific interests include flora and landscape changes in Central Europe, functional morphology and systematics of seed plants as well as illustrations of plants in art and science.
Contribution: The Conquest of Floristic Realms, p. 64

**Christoph Keller** Journalist and author. Editor-in-chief of Society program that airs on the Swiss radio station DRS2. Author, regular contributor to *MAGAZIN* of the *Tages-Anzeiger* newspaper, as well as to the newspapers *Berner Zeitung* and *Basler Zeitung*. Lecturer at MAZ – Die Schweizer Journalistenschule (Swiss School of Journalism) in Lucerne and at the Zurich University of the Arts. Presenter at national and international events. His press work has earned him numerous awards, including, on two occasions, the Zurich Journalist Prize. Most recent publication, *Alamor drei Tage*, Limmat Verlag, Zurich, 2007.
Contributions: Darwin in Switzerland, p. 72;
Living Roofs, p. 232

**Koen van de Moortel** Shown here in the Wespelaar Arboretum in Belgium, beside its founder, **Philippe de Spoelberch** (on the right). A gardener, he lives in Tremelo, Belgium. For the last ten years, he has photographed rhododendrons in bloom in his country's most famous gardens and parks.
Contribution: Rhododendron Mania, p. 74

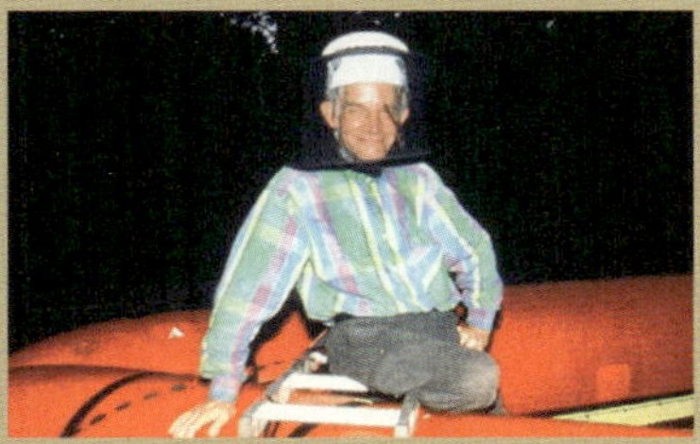

**Roman Kaiser** Shown here on his fragrance-collecting expedition to French Guiana, 1996. Studied chemistry at Winterthur Technical College; in 1968 he joined the Givaudan Research Center in Dubendorf, near Zurich, as a fragrance and flavor chemist. His work at Givaudan has focused on investigating and reconstituting essential oils, absolutes and similar natural products, as well as synthesizing natural scent components; since 1975 he has worked primarily on the investigation and reconstitution of all types of natural scents using "headspace" techniques that include complementary analytical methods. He is considered a pioneer of this method and many of these scent reconstitutions have been used for the creation of famous fragrances. His current research is mainly directed towards a future publication, a book entitled *The Scent of the Vanishing Flora*, compiling and discussing the scent composition of the most endangered species worldwide.
Contribution: Scent Seeker, p. 76

**TREE FACTORY**

**Olaf Unverzart** Photographer and artist. Studied art photography at the Academy of Visual Arts Leipzig. A number of exhibitions since 1997 and long-standing work for international publications. From 2006 to 2009, held a teaching position at the Academy of Fine Arts in Nuremberg. Most recent awards include the gold medal of the Deutscher Fotobuchpreis (German Photobook Prize) for *Leichtes Gepäck*, Verlag für moderne Kunst Nuremberg; and the gold medal of the LeadAward for his series *Deutsche Szenen* (German Scenes), published in *ZeitMagazin*, 2009. His fifth book, *Don't fade to grey*, will be published in 2010.
Contribution: Pistoia, p. 102

**Günther Vogt** Landscape architect. Professional training at the Oeschberg Horticulture School in Switzerland. Studied landscape architecture at the intercantonal Rapperswil Technikum University of Applied Science. Since 2000, owner of Vogt Landscape Zurich, with branch offices in Munich, Berlin and London. Since 2005, associate professor for Landscape Architecture at ETH Zurich. Since 2007, chairman of the network City and Landscape (NSL) at ETH Zurich.
Contribution: A Tree Is a Tree Is a Tree, p. 4; Tree Journeys, p. 90; Mass-producing Arcadia?, p. 104

**Karl Schmuki** Historian, since 1987 research assistant at the Abbey Library of Saint Gall. Expert on Systematics and Aesthetics:
A Chronicle (Cloister gardens: symbolism and structure), p. 119

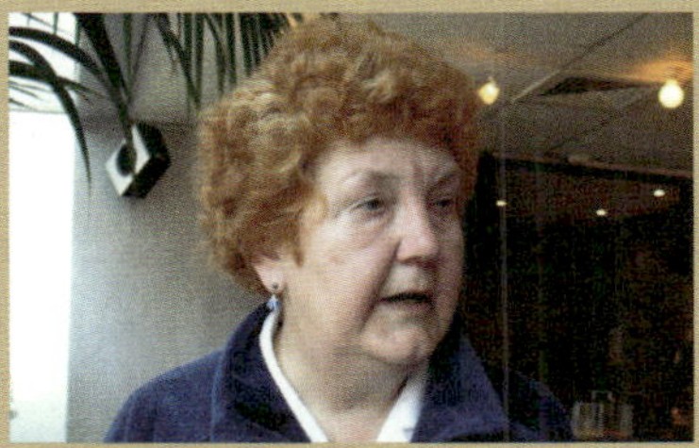

**Carla Teune** Former curator of the Hortus Botanicus Leiden and passionate plant collector.
Interview in Systematics and Aesthetics:
A Chronicle (The Hortus Botanicus Leiden), p. 120

**Rainer Lingnau** Sales employee at Bruns Pflanzen, tree nursery in Bad Zwischenahn, Germany.
Interview in Systematics and Aesthetics:
A Chronicle (Tree Nurseries: trade and production), p. 126

**Jan Coussement** Sales employee at Sylva, forestry nursery in Waarschoot, Belgium.
Interview in Systematics and Aesthetics:
A Chronicle (Sylva and Sylma), p. 128

**Christof van de Hülle** Executive director at Sylma, forestry and ornamental greenhouse-based tree nursery in Lovendegem, Belgium.
Interview in Systematics and Aesthetics:
A Chronicle (Sylva and Sylma), p. 128

**Jim Hillier** Employee in the family-owned company Hillier Nurseries, a wholesale nursery near Romsey, England.
Interview in Systematics and Aesthetics:
A Chronicle (Hillier Nurseries) p. 130

**Antonio Ceccarelli** Sales employee at Vannucci Piante, a wholesale plant nursery in Pistoia, Italy.
Interview in Systematics and Aesthetics:
A Chronicle (The Pistoia tree nursery center and Vannucci Piante), p. 132

**Jan Breedijk** Employee at Nieuwkoop Europe, a nursery for tropical plants near Aalsmeer, the Netherlands.
Interview in The History of *Phalaenopsis* sp. (Origins of the worldwide trade in plants), p. 138

**Peter Bak** Executive director, together with his sister Alli Bak, of Corn. Bak, a company specializing in the production of bromeliads, located in Assendelft, the Netherlands.
Interview in The History of the *Phalaenopsis* sp. (Origins of the worldwide trade in plants), p. 138

**René Schoone** Executive director, together with his brother Kees Schoone, of Floricultura, a company specializing in the production of orchids in the laboratory in Assendelft, the Netherlands.
Interview in The History of *Phalaenopsis* sp. (Propagation) p. 138

**Jacques van der Weijden** Former owner of Green Balanz, a company specializing in the production of orchids in Aalsmeer, the Netherlands.
Interview in The History of the *Phalaenopsis* sp. (Cultivation and preparation for sale), p. 144

**Sander Kroll** Managing director of Ki Plant, a company specializing in plants and plant images in Aalsmeer, the Netherlands.
Interview in The History of the *Phalaenopsis* sp. (Auctioning), p. 144

**Wim Hoogendoorn** Former tree nursery specialist in Boskoop, the Netherlands.
Interview in Boskoop (Boskoop's rich tradition of tree production), p. 148

**Hildi van Gelderen-Esveld** Daughter of the late C. J. Esveld. For many years, she and her husband, Dick van Gelderen, ran the famous plant nursery of her deceased father, the PlantenTuin Esveld in Boskoop, the Netherlands.
See Boskoop: an ode to plant production in modern times (Boskoop today), p. 154

**SAHEL VERT**

**Souleymane Bassoum** Agronomist and acclaimed expert on sustainable agriculture in West Africa. Since 1987, has been supporting and coordinating the Senegalese project partners of Fastenopfer, an aid agency that focuses on issues of food and nutrition security and debt relief. He also coordinates Agrécol Afrique, an NGO that promotes sustainable and biological agriculture and fair trade in Senegal and West Africa. He works together with organizations involved in biological farming and fair trade in Latin America and Europe. Since 2010 he has been project coordinator of the Swiss-Senegalese revitalization project "Sahel Vert" (www.sahel-vert.org).
Contribution: Barça ou Barsakh, p. 170

**Dominique Ghiggi** In the arboretum of Charles Hadad, Sindia, Senegal. Studied biology at the University of Basel and completed her master's degree in landscape architecture at ETH Zurich. From 2002 to 2007, employee at Vogt Landscape Zurich. Since 2008, self-employed landscape architect and research assistant at the chair of Günther Vogt at the ETH Zurich, Department of Architecture. Owns and operates a firm in Zurich, together with Carola Antón (antón & ghiggi landschaft architektur).
Contributions: Fastwood, p. 6; Hermaphrodites, p. 36; Traditional British, p. 68; Scent Seeker, p. 76; Systematics and Aesthetics: A Chronicle, p. 116; The History of *Phalaenopsis* sp., p. 136; Boskoop, p. 148; Sénou: A Botanical Refugium in Senegal, p. 178

**Jörg Müller** Shown here on the *Falaise* above the village of Teli in Dogonland, Mali. Carpentry apprenticeship in Stuttgart and Markgröningen, architecture studies in Dresden, Glasgow and Zurich. Since 2004, self-employed architect in Zurich.
Contributions: Sénou: A Botanical Refugium in Senegal, p. 178; photos in Barça ou Barsakh, p. 170

**Jacqueline Moesch Mampuya** Dance educator and, in 2002, founder of the Centre Mampuya, an ecological center for the revitalization of natural resources in Senegal.
See Sénou: A Botanical Refugium in Senegal, p.178

**Urban Fraefel** Professor at the University of Applied Sciences of Northwestern Switzerland and President of the association Centre Mampuya in Senegal.
See Sénou: A Botanical Refugium in Senegal, p.178

**Christoph Seidler** Shown here during his stay on Spitsbergen. Studied international relations in Dresden, Lausanne, Berlin and Oslo. After working for the United Nations in Geneva, he now writes as a science journalist about developments in the Arctic for SPIEGEL ONLINE and other publications. In 2007 he received the Friedrich Vogel Award for economic journalism. In 2009 his book *Arctic Monopoly. The Battle for Natural Resources in the Polar Region*, a SPIEGEL book, was published by the Deutsche Verlags-Anstalt Munich.
Contribution: The Svalbard Global Seed Vault, p. 188

**Cary Fowler** Head of the Global Crop Diversity Trust, an international organization that supports the operation, management and coordination of the Svalbard Global Seed Vault.
See The Svalbard Global Seed Vault, p. 188

**Tomas Caspary** Since 1992, architect in Tanzania. Working in the low-cost sector, he builds churches, schools, clinics and living quarters for workers and single mothers, lays water pipes, installs photovoltaic systems and conducts further training for craftsmen in the informal sector. From 1989 to 1990 he studied traditional construction methods and spatial concepts in southern Ethiopia among the Gurage and Konso tribes. Living on the outskirts of Arusha, he is attempting, on a few acres of land, to renaturalize a canyon whose slopes have been overgrazed.
Contribution: Arusha: Urban Agriculture, p. 194

**BETTER CITY**

**Christine Zimmerli** Studied law in Basel, visited China during studies (1997 and 2000). From 2005 to 2008, worked in Shanghai as Country Manager China for a Swiss language services company. In 2009 she worked as reporter for the book project *Tree Nurseries* at the chair of Günther Vogt, ETH Zurich. During this period, she collaborated with the Swiss musician Natascha Stohler for a video project entitled *Shanghai in Motion*.
Contributions: Ancient Giants, p. 110; Better City, Better Life, p. 202

**Liu Chunjiang** Professor at the Institute of Landscape Architecture and Engineering, Jiaotong University, Shanghai. Shown here during an excursion to Anhui.
Interview in Better City, Better Life ("Near-Natural Forest" project), p. 211

**Liu Gang** Executive director of Shanghai Maple Horticulture Co. Ltd., a tree nursery in Songjiang district, approximately thirty kilometers to the southwest of the Shanghai city center.
Interview in Better City, Better Life (Local and regional plant production), p. 211

**Renzo Petraglio** Shown here in the Centre Jeunes Kamenge of Bujumbura, Burundi. Studied theology and classical philology. Wrote his dissertation on the connections between the Hebrew, Greek and Latin Bibles (1973), and another on Latin (1975). Worked for many years on the translation of the Bible at the theological faculty in Fribourg and taught Greek, Latin and history of religion at the Liceo Cantonale di Locarno, Switzerland. Since 1993 he has spent every summer teaching at the Centre Jeunes Kamenge of Bujumbura, Burundi.
Contribution: Selection of Latin texts, Vergilius, Georgica IV, 116–148, p. 14; Iuvenalis, Satura III, 232–261, p. 212

**Ralf Günter Voss** Landscape architect, Dipl.-Ing. Studied landscape architecture at the University of Hanover and University of Edinburgh. Has worked as a landscape architect since 1996. Since 2003, employee at Vogt Landscape Zurich.
Contribution: Temporary Tree Nurseries, p. 214

**Silke Schmeing** Landscape architect at Federal Technical College of Engineering. Studied landscape architecture at the intercantonal Rapperswil Technikum University of Applied Science. Seven years of work experience as copywriter and conceptual designer in advertising and communication. Since 2007, employed with Vogt Landscape Zurich.
Contributions: Green Belt, p. 220; Dagenham Docks, p. 224

**Paul Ritchens** Former film producer and manager in the international media business; today he is an organic gardener and is active in the fight against London's urban heat-island effect. **Jane Riddiford** Executive director of Global Generations, is an advocate in King's Cross for "living roofs," green roofs with vegetable gardens or small forests.
Interview in Living Roofs, p. 232

**ACKNOWLEDGMENTS**
**I want to especially thank Günther Vogt for his trust and the authors and protagonists in the book for their cooperation as well as Maurice and Michael Van Dyck for their generous support.**

**Many thanks also go to a long list of family, friends and colleagues:**
**Susanne Ghiggi, Carol Ghiggi, Giovanni Ghiggi, Anne-Gaëlle Feger, Lala Feger, Sebastiano Brandolini, Jürg Walter, Antonio von Schirnding, Thomas Kissling, Hans Hortig, Franziska Bark, Alice Foxley, Carola Antón, Anette Freytag, Jasper Hugtenburg, Tom Griffiths, Remy Turquin, Irène Djao-Rakitine, Hansruedi Bär, Christian Häberling, Oliver Rackham, Ahmet Balkan, Christoph Heiermann, Petra Zibulski, Gé Vaartjes, Jeff Hawkins, Jana Niederöst, Peter Kamber, Peter von Ballmoos, Andreas Burri, Birgit Verstoep, Andreas Matschenz, Patrick Hogan, Paul Przyborski, Lars Müller, Katharina Kulke, Sandra Leitte, Joe O'Donnell, John O'Toole, Ellen Mey, Linda Malzacher, Esther Butterworth, Martina Mullis, Nadine Unterharrer and Kareen Klein**

**TREE NURSERIES**
**CULTIVATING THE URBAN JUNGLE**

Edited by Chair of Günther Vogt, Department of Architecture,
ETH Zurich, Dominique Ghiggi

Design: Integral Lars Müller / Lars Müller, Esther Butterworth, Martina Mullis
Translations: Joe O'Donnell, Adam Blauhut, Peter Rigney, Lucinda Byatt
Copyediting and proofreading: John O'Toole
Lithography: Ast & Fischer, Wabern, Switzerland
Paper: Munken Lynx 150 g/m$^2$
Printing and Binding: Kösel, Altusried-Krugzell, Germany



Lars Müller Publishers
Baden, Switzerland
www.lars-muller-publishers.com

ISBN 978-3-03778-218-7
ISBN 978-3-03778-217-0 (German edition)

Printed in Germany

9 8 7 6 5 4 3 2 1

Published with the generous support of Arbor nv

Front cover photo:
Shanghai, Wanping Lu
Photo: Jürgen Krusche

Back cover photo:
Olivastro millenario. An olive tree between three and four thousand years old in Luras (Sassari Province), Sardinia/Italy
Photo: Dominique Ghiggi